ACCOUNTING FOR RAPE

Accounting for Rape presents an original perspective on the subject of rape and sexual violence. The authors scrutinise existing social psychological experimental research on rape, in particular rape-perception research, which, they argue, fails to analyse the subtlety and political significance of rape-supportive reasoning and the forms that it takes, thus also underestimating the extent of rape-supportive reasoning. The authors provide a critical interrogation of dominant theories and methodologies, and thought-provoking analyses of conversational data, exploring everyday accounting practices in relation to reports of both female and male rape. They synthesise discursive psychology and a feminist standpoint to explore precisely how rape and rape victimhood are defined in ways that reflect the social, political and cultural conditions of society.

They show how the gender and sexual orientation of alleged victims and perpetrators is crucial to social participants when making sense of a rape report and in apportioning blame and sympathy. They also examine how arguments that are critical of alleged victims are built in ways that are 'face saving' for the participants in the conversations, and how victim-blaming arguments are presented as 'common sense'. Crucial to this is the way in which rape-supportive talk is underpinned by a range of deeply ingrained cultural sense-making resources that construct and legitimate hegemonic forms of heterosexual identities and gender relations and neo-liberal notions of ideal citizenship. Finally, the authors demonstrate the potential of the application for their approach in both professional and academic contexts to promote attitude change.

The book will be of great interest to those studying social and clinical psychology, cultural studies, sociology, women's studies and communication studies.

Irina Anderson is a principal lecturer in Psychology at the University of East London.

Kathy Doherty is a principal lecturer in Communication Studies at Sheffield Hallam University.

WOMEN AND PSYCHOLOGY
Series Editor: Jane Ussher
School of Psychology, University of Western Sydney

This series brings together current theory and research on women and psychology. Drawing on scholarship from a number of different areas of psychology, it bridges the gap between abstract research and the reality of women's lives by integrating theory and practice, research and policy.

Each book addresses a 'cutting edge' issue of research, covering such topics as postnatal depression, eating disorders, theories and methodologies.

The series provides accessible and concise accounts of key issues in the study of women and psychology, and clearly demonstrates the centrality of psychology to debates within women's studies or feminism.

The Series Editor would be pleased to discuss proposals for new books in the series.

Other titles in this series:

THE THIN WOMAN
Helen Malson

THE MENSTRUAL CYCLE
Anne E. Walker

POST-NATAL DEPRESSION
Paula Nicolson

RE-THINKING ABORTION
Mary Boyle

WOMEN AND AGING
Linda R. Gannon

BEING MARRIED. DOING GENDER
Caroline Dryden

UNDERSTANDING DEPRESSION
Janet M. Stoppard

FEMININITY AND THE PHYSICALLY ACTIVE WOMAN
Precilla Y.L. Choi

GENDER, LANGUAGE AND DISCOURSE
Anne Weatherall

THE SCIENCE/FICTION OF SEX
Annie Potts

THE PSYCHOLOGICAL DEVELOPMENT OF GIRLS AND WOMEN
Sheila Greene

JUST SEX?
Nicola Gavey

WOMAN'S RELATIONSHIP WITH HERSELF
Helen O'Grady

GENDER TALK
Susan A. Speer

BEAUTY AND MISOGYNY
Sheila Jeffreys

BODY WORK
Sylvia K. Blood

MANAGING THE MONSTROUS FEMININE
Jane M. Ussher

THE CAPACITY TO CARE
Wendy Hollway

SANCTIONING PREGNANCY
Harriet Gross and Helen Pattison

ACCOUNTING FOR RAPE

Psychology, Feminism and Discourse
Analysis in the Study of Sexual Violence

Irina Anderson & Kathy Doherty

Routledge
Taylor & Francis Group

LONDON AND NEW YORK

First published 2008 by Routledge
27 Church Road, Hove, East Sussex BN3 2FA

Simultaneously published in the USA and Canada
by Routledge
270 Madison Avenue, New York, NY 10016

Routledge is an imprint of the Taylor & Francis Group, an Informa business

Typeset in Times by Garfield Morgan, Swansea, West Glamorgan
Printed and bound in Great Britain by TJ International Ltd, Padstow, Cornwall
Paperback cover design by Terry Foley

This publication has been produced with paper manufactured to strict environmental
standards and with pulp derived from sustainable forests.

British Library Cataloguing in Publication Data
A catalogue record for this book is available from the British Library

Library of Congress Cataloging in Publication Data
Anderson, Irina, 1968–
Accounting for rape : psychology, feminism, and discourse analysis in the study of sexual
violence / Irina Anderson & Kathy Doherty.
p. cm.
Includes bibliographical references (p. 136).
ISBN-13: 978-0-415-21173-4 (hardback)
ISBN-13: 978-0-415-21174-1 (pbk.)
1. Rape–Research. 2. Rape–Psychological aspects. I. Doherty, Kathy. II. Title.
HV6558.A53 2008
362.883–dc22

2007025842

ISBN 978-0-415-21173-4 (hbk)
ISBN 978-0-415-21174-1 (pbk)

For my wonderful children and Jim, for my great mum and
for my grandmother, Olga and Lara (IA)

For Helen (my amazing mother) and the wonderful men in
my life, Stephen, Barney and Eric (KD)

CONTENTS

ACKNOWLEDGEMENTS

Irina would like to thank the staff and students at the School of Psychology, University of East London, for their support during this project, and especially David Rose and Pippa Dell, for their continued interest in this book.

Kathy would like to acknowledge the support of the C3RI at Sheffield Hallam University in financing several periods of study leave to concentrate on writing this book and would also like to thank her colleagues and students in Communication Studies for all those insightful and lively discussions on the topics of discourse, gender and sexual violence, and for keeping the faith.

1

RAPE-SUPPORTIVE CULTURE AND THE RAPE VICTIM

Extract 1

I keep wondering maybe if I had done something different when I first saw him that it wouldn't have happened – neither he nor I would be in trouble. Maybe it was my fault. See, that's where I get when I think about it. My father always said whatever a man did to a woman, she provoked it.

(Rape victim, cited in Holmstrom and Burgess, 1978)

Extract 2

You may recall that Mr. Diggle and the woman in question danced and drank the night away at the Grosvenor House Hotel and returned to a friend's flat, whereupon the lady lawyer undressed in front of Mr. Diggle, who then made what turned out to be an unwelcome advance. Mr. Diggle, given the circumstances, behaved as you would imagine any half-drunk, virile man would. If any damage has been done to the reputation of the legal profession, it is by the stupid, unnamed woman, who apparently continues to earn her living as a lawyer yet clearly possesses not an ounce of common sense.

(Anne Robinson, *Daily Mirror*, 15/2/1995)

Extract 3

Despite the climate of the times I regard her invitation to come to her bedroom when she was scantily clad (she was wearing a calf-length dressing gown), as opposed to asking you to wait until she was more suitably dressed, as an amber light.

(Judge Bell, *Daily Mirror*, 28/1/1995)

Extract 4

These allegations are, 'at the lowest end of the scale . . . at the borderline between touching and being excessively effusive'.
(Judge Medawar, *Evening Standard*, 28/2/2005)

Extract 5

If you take out uncovered meat and place it outside . . . without cover, and the cats come to eat it . . . whose fault is it, the cats' or the uncovered meat's? The uncovered meat is the problem. If she was in her room, in her home, in her hijab [the headdress worn by some Muslim women], no problem would have occurred.
(Sheik Taj Din al-Hilali, Australia's most senior Muslim cleric, *Guardian*, 26/10/2006)

Social reasoning about rape

This book examines social explanations for rape (see Appendix). Our focus is on explanations as 'accounts' which are meant to excuse, justify or exonerate the socially sanctionable behaviour of self or others (Scott and Lyman, 1968; Antaki, 1994), where issues such as what happened, why and who is at fault or to blame are discussed and debated. Nobody chooses to be raped. And yet, as each of the examples above show, in talk about alleged incidents of rape, rapists are often exonerated while it is the victim who is found culpable. This pattern of attribution represents a common cultural reaction to reports of sexual violence. Each of the women in the above examples brought a charge of rape against an alleged perpetrator. Each one, in some sense, is seeking support and retribution for an act identified by them as rape. However, in each case the victims are not believed but instead derogated both in terms of character (e.g. 'the stupid, unnamed woman') or behaviour (e.g. 'her invitation to come to her bedroom when she was scantily clad').

In the first example, the victim blames herself for the rape and has clearly internalised her father's views on women's role in 'provoking' violence and 'causing' male behaviour in general. In the second example, extracted from the remarks of British journalist Anne Robinson, it is the alleged *perpetrator* who is defined as the innocent victim of a feckless 'sexually provocative' woman. His behaviour is normalised, exonerating him from responsibility for the act, and the victim's behaviour is positioned as deviant and thus blameworthy. In the third extract, once again, the victim is positioned as provocateur. She is positioned as responsible, via her choice of clothing, for both the sexual arousal of her attacker and for implying consent to intercourse. In this account, agency and responsibility are removed from the alleged rapist by casting the victim as the rightful guardian and regulator of his behaviour. In all cases these accounts function to minimise the severity of an experience that has been reported as a violent assault, and in extracts 2 and 3 this is accomplished by reframing the incident as 'normal' heterosexual behaviour. Extracts 4 and 5 illustrate the continued resilience of such judgements. Far from being a thing of the past, victim-blaming continues to be a feature of society. The Amnesty International Survey (2005) into blame judgements in rape produced disturbing results, showing that of the 1095 adults interviewed, 22% of the respondents thought that the woman is at least partially or totally responsible for the rape if she were alone in a deserted spot at the time of the attack. The same number of respondents thought that she is partially or totally responsible if she has had many sexual partners. Thirty per cent of respondents thought that the woman is partially or totally responsible if she was drunk at the time of the rape, 37% thought the same if she failed to say 'no' clearly enough and 26% thought that she is partially or totally responsible if she was wearing revealing clothing at the time of the rape.

Extract 4 refers to Judge Medawar's summing up of a child sexual abuse case. He rejected the case without putting it to a jury, prompting Scotland Yard officers to consider the unusual step of mounting a challenge to the judge's ruling. Extract 5 refers to the recent furore caused by Australia's mufti Sheik Taj Din al-Hilali's remarks relating to several gang rapes in Australia. Although this example is clearly intersected by religious and racial issues, it nevertheless illustrates the global nature and resilience of these judgements, so much so that several social commentators have perceived a recent change, for the worse, in attitudes towards rape. For example, Julie Bindel (*The Guardian*, 25/10/2006) wrote that:

> While in the 1980s and 1990s police and public attitudes towards rape victims seemed to be improving, they more recently appear to be ricocheting backwards. So much so, that a couple of years ago I made a pact with myself, which I vowed never to reveal publicly. At this juncture I feel I must, though: if I was raped now, I do not think I would report it to the police.

The author also says that, 'Those who report their attackers and see their cases either discontinued or the defendant acquitted – as happens with almost 95% of reported rapes – are now faced with the risk of being identified, vilified and even criminalised', and describes recent cases where, for example, 'Various footballers accused of "roasting" women have been exonerated, while the women who accused them of rape are vilified as "prostitutes" and "gold-diggers".'

Such negative, judgmental attributions are disturbingly common (a quick browse through most newspapers will reveal this to be the case) and (as will be discussed below) are likely to be extremely damaging to victims of rape. Over the last 30 years, the examination of social reasoning about rape from a variety of perspectives has produced a substantial research literature devoted to cultural understandings of rape and the experience of rape victims in both everyday social settings and institutional contexts. A pattern of derogatory judgements about rape victims has been documented at every level of society, prompting researchers to analyse how and consider why people respond to rape victims so negatively in comparison to victims of other criminal offences (Krahé, 1991). Although most people would recognise in the abstract that rape is a morally unjustifiable act, it seems that rape victims are nevertheless particularly likely to be monitored for their 'innocence' and the degree of that innocence in the incident itself (Lee, 1984). Public declarations of rape are scrutinised and debated in the media and in everyday interaction.

In this book, we adopt a feminist perspective to argue that rape is both socially produced and socially legitimated, as a mechanism that ultimately maintains patriarchal gender power relations. We start by reviewing classic feminist scholarship on the social definition of rape and the consequences of a 'rape-supportive culture' for the victims of rape. We then turn to mainstream, positivistic rape-perception research in psychology. Here we argue that the individualistic, highly cognitive perspective of humans as nothing more than elaborate information processors is deeply problematic for research that purports to examine how social judgements about rape are derived and perpetuated. If we are to explore meaningfully the social definition of rape and the impact of these practices on maintaining gender power relations, we must dispense with experimentalism and turn to a research framework informed by social constructionist epistemology and feminist practice. Here, the significance and practical consequences of the social construction of meaning in cultural and political context is placed centre stage. We further argue that participation in rape-perception research can be a disempowering experience for research subjects who have no forum to challenge or transform the standard victim-blaming views that they are presented with and invited to reproduce. We present three chapters of qualitative, discourse analysis research that examines social reasoning in response to reports of both female and male stranger rape, attending to the intricacies of the accounts presented and outlining the resources and argumentative strategies used by the participants when dealing with issues of accountability for the reported rape and to manage their own identities in the process. We will show that reasoning about rape is influenced by gender and heterosexuality norms and that the gender and sexuality of a victim become crucial issues for the participants in terms of the apportionment of blame and sympathy. These accounts are also saturated with neo-liberal discourse, which constructs good citizens as individually responsible for 'hazard/risk' management in relation to heterosexual encounters and sexual violence and therefore to blame for rape victim-hood. This argument neatly obscures the accountability of alleged perpetrators and the context of rape-supportive culture. We also examine how the metaphorical frames in play in the accounts for male and female rape construct the character and motivation of the alleged victim and rapist and the actual rape experience in different ways with differing implications for the management of accountability and apportionment of blame and sympathy. In the final chapter we discuss implications for the experience of rape victims and strategies for intervention and change.

Feminist scholarship on the social definition of rape

In a landmark paper on the social definition of rape, feminist scholars Burt and Estep (1981) highlighted the difficulties that claimants to the 'sexual assault victim' role routinely encounter in being granted 'genuine' victim status and thus in gaining access to the advantages that the 'victim' label would usually afford, e.g. sympathy, resources, temporary relief from responsibilities and legal recourse. They note that 'victims themselves, their significant others, and the social control agencies to which (rape victims) sometimes turn for help all need to be convinced that the claim to rape victim status is legitimate' (Burt and Estep, 1981: 15). As Williams similarly argues:

> For some crimes, robbery for example, the victim's responsibility is rarely questioned, but for rape the victim's responsibility is mostly always questioned.
>
> (Williams, 1984: 67)

These early discussions on the social definition of rape and the experience of rape victims were highly significant in establishing an important insight that is fundamental to the analysis of accounting practices for rape that are presented in this book. A key point communicated in this work is that victim-hood is a social creation. Definitions of what counts as 'rape' and who is to be treated as a 'genuine' victim – innocent rather than accountable – are constructed in discourse and practices that reflect the social, political and cultural conditions of society.

Burt and Estep (1981) identify several potential arguments that social participants might offer to challenge a sexual assault claim and suggest alternative identity categorisations that can be imposed on a claimant of rape victim status, demonstrating in principle how a range of cultural assumptions about gender and sexuality could underpin denials of rape. First, they note that arguments may be put forward that 'what happened'

5

was consensual as opposed to coerced intercourse – that is, that the encounter was 'just sex'. In these types of argument, a victim's perception of the situation is positioned as problematic by re-defining a violent and coercive experience as consensual and/or even pleasurable. In this case a victim role claimant may be re-categorised as too naïve or stupid to appreciate that normative heterosexual encounters are 'adversarial'. This model of sexuality is legitimated in the sexology literature and in sex manuals where female resistance behaviour is represented as part and parcel of the (hetero)sexual 'game' of courtship and mating, functioning to increase male arousal (Jackson, 1987; Nicolson, 1994). The male sexual impulse is constructed as active, aggressive and straightforward and as central to what it means to be masculine – 'real men' are always on the lookout for sex and would never refuse an opportunity for sex should it be presented. Once sexually aroused, men are understood as having tenuous self-control over their actions until they are sexually satisfied – specifically via penetration of the vagina by the penis. Jackson (1987) points out that in Havelock Ellis's writings a close association between male sexuality, power and violence was constructed as a biological necessity and therefore as inevitable, as was the connection between female sexual pleasure and pain. This version of sexuality and sexual practice is romanticised in a variety of forms of popular culture (Ussher, 1997; Lees, 1997) where the sexual role of the heterosexual male is represented as one of pursuit and conquest where the female must be (and will expect to be) 'coaxed' into submission, by force if necessary. Jackson (1987) argues that the phallocentric model of heterosexuality and sexual practice promoted in the classic writings of Ellis, Kinsey (see Weinberg, 1976) and Masters and Johnson (1966) – and in the sex manuals that followed – defines and institutionalises male domination and female submission as natural and essential. Nicola Gavey (2005) cogently argues that heterosexual norms are thus highly problematic, as a model for sexual relationships and operating as a cultural 'scaffold' for rape. Feminine sexuality is constructed as passive and acquiescent, but at the same time potentially dangerous and provocative, shackled by socially required femininity. In relation to this version of gender identity, sexually forceful men can be (and are) constructed as romantic heroes. Women's consent is always up for question when heterosexuality is scripted in this way because it allows for too much ambiguity around what is rape and what is 'just sex'. Normative heterosexuality is imbued with a dominance–submission dynamic leaving little room for notions of women's active desire, pleasure or consent and little or no imperative for men to check that women are actively consenting to sex and/or finding the experience pleasurable. Victim discrediting strategies, working to normalise the violence of rape, often pivot on the issue of consent. In 1996 for example, in a New Zealand case, a judge commented that 'if every man stopped the first time a woman said "No", the world would be a much less exciting place to live' (cited in Gavey, 2005).

Heterosexual norms therefore provide the discursive building blocks from which to construct a denial of rape victim status. A rape victim role claimant may be told that her experience was perfectly 'normal' and nothing out of the ordinary. The alleged perpetrator's behaviour, it may be concluded, was unproblematic – he was merely treating the woman's resistance as part of 'natural' courtship behaviour, and as such he has nothing to account for. The problem, she will be told, is therefore with her – with her perception of the events or with her inability to communicate clearly enough that her resistance was real and not 'feigned' (Crawford, 1995). Alternatively, drawing on the cultural stereotype of femininity that constructs women as manipulative or vindictive, a rape victim claimant may be accused of lying about the rape, of denying consent after the event, perhaps to exact revenge on an erstwhile 'lover'. As will be examined in the empirical chapters that follow, the issue of what counts as 'sex' or what counts as 'rape' is routinely treated as a matter for dispute in everyday, academic and institutional discourses about sexuality and sexual violence. Because rape is an act of violence perpetrated on the sexual body, rape is too often written off as 'just sex' or as an act primarily motivated by sexual desire. However it is clear, as many feminist scholars have argued (e.g. Griffin, 1971; Brownmiller, 1975; Scully, 1990; Ussher, 1997; Scarce, 1997; Doherty and Anderson, 2004; Gavey, 2005) that these kinds of arguments systematically downplay the often life-threatening and profoundly humiliating nature of the experience reported by victims of rape and sexual assault.

The second broad type of argument which challenges a claim to 'genuine' rape victim status, noted by Burt and Estep, is to concede that coerced intercourse probably did occur but to minimise the significance of this event by arguing that no damage was done either because the victim wasn't particularly injured or because the victim is somehow unimportant and not worthy of sympathy. A possible categorisation for an alleged victim in the first case is that s/he is a 'sexual masochist' who allegedly enjoys violent sex. It may be acknowledged that the event in question was coercive, but then further argued that coercion is a normal and pleasurable feature of sexual experience for the particular individual concerned. Once again, such accusations miss the basic point that rape is experienced as a non-consensual act of *aggression*, far removed from the power play that may or may not operate in *consensual* sexual contexts. The negative impact of a rape experience can also be minimised by categorising those claiming the victim role as insignificant and thus not worthy of too much sympathy. Burt and Estep highlight how some individuals are considered by society to be 'open territory' victims, devalued, and who get marked as 'fair game', often because they can be seen to have transgressed from the normative expectations of their gender role, e.g. sex workers, the poor, lesbians, gay men, single women or 'fallen' women.

Finally: 'When all other competing definitions fail, ideology still facilitates retreat to blaming the victim' (Burt and Estep, 1981: 23). Even if it is accepted that forced intercourse occurred, and even if it's difficult to sustain a categorisation of the victim as 'fair game', Burt and Estep argue that there is still a cultural tendency to find victim role claimants accountable and render the assailant's agency in the alleged attack invisible. This may be accomplished by insisting that an alleged victim either provoked the attack or was somehow reckless in his/her behaviour and is thus blameworthy in failing to prevent the attack. Burt and Estep point out that the 'irresistible sexual impulse' model of male sexuality promotes the view that men have little conscious control over their sexuality. Since they are at the mercy of a primal biological sex drive they can't possibly be held accountable either for becoming sexually aroused or for their actions when aroused. This discourse instead casts women as the 'gatekeepers' of the male sexual impulse. An alleged victim may thus be blamed for a rape perpetrated against her by arguing that, in order to have been raped, she *must* have somehow failed in her 'duty' to control the assailant's behaviour (Burt, 1980; Burt and Estep, 1981). Or, she may be accused of 'inviting' the advances of an unsuspecting male, sometimes by her mere presence. Constructions of the victim as either provocative in appearance or reckless in behaviour are at the centrepiece of such arguments. In categorising rape victim claimants as provocative or reckless, they are made accountable by the implication that the cause of the rape was primarily their own 'risk-taking' behaviour. Women in particular may be accused of being 'wilfully reckless' with their moral reputation by being 'out of place', literally a bad girl, unaccompanied in the masculine sphere of public life, *making herself* vulnerable to the 'attentions' of men.

In chapter 4 we will examine in detail how in conversations about female rape, the victims are constructed as 'reckless' for failing to prevent rape. This analysis is informed by postmodern analyses of hazard/risk which stress that hazards are social fabrications, the 'reifications of moral judgements about the riskiness of choices made by human beings' (Fox, 1999: 209). We will show how notions of what is hazardous or risky is socially constructed and differentiated according to gender stereotypes. As Fox argues,

Hazards are constructed from contingent and partial descriptions of the world and the attribution of riskiness is grounded not in objective estimation but entirely upon what Foucault calls power/knowledge; the 'knowledgeability' which both discursively constructs objects and confirms the authority of the person claiming the knowledge.

(Fox, 1999: 210)

The point here is that there are a number of ways in which people could construct and experience their knowledge of the future as one that imposes different types of 'hazardous uncertainty' in their lives (Wilkinson, 2001); it is the selective interpretation by professionals, politicians and individuals that influences exactly which 'risks' are deemed worthy of attention. The construction of hazard/risk in relation to sexual violence takes place in the context of patriarchal society and as such, we contend that arguments about what is 'risky' for women and men can be seen to function to maintain gender power relations and gendered norms of behaviour in this context. Accusations of irresponsible risk-taking take on a moral dimension where raped individuals are blamed (rather than the perpetrators of rape) on the grounds that they failed in their responsibility to avoid what has been deemed by society as 'hazardous' for 'good', i.e. 'feminine', women.

Several feminist scholars use the term 'rape myth' to refer to the culturally located attitudes and beliefs about rape discussed above, and this concept has also been widely adopted in the social psychology of rape perception (see chapter 2). In an early paper Burt defined rape myths as 'prejudicial, stereotyped or false beliefs about rape, rape victims and rapists' (Burt, 1980), which emerge from and reinforce stereotypical assumptions about femininity, masculinity and normative heterosexuality. Rape myths are identified as arguments that tend to attribute responsibility to the victims, exonerate the perpetrators of rape and trivialise the severity of a rape experience, but which are not supported by empirical evidence (see Doherty and Anderson, 1998), e.g. victims precipitate rape by their behaviour or appearance; rape is not damaging because after all, it is only sex; real rape victims have signs of injury to prove it because you can't be raped against your will; women often lie about rape because they are malicious and deceitful; real rapists are psychopathic individuals (Brownmiller, 1975; Burt, 1980; Ward, 1995). Burt and Estep speculated that for many people these rape myths provide a 'common sense' resource for making sense of rape incidents. In the empirical chapters that follow we examine whether and precisely how the rape-supportive arguments highlighted by Burt and Estep enter into conversations about incidents of rape.

Secondary victimisation and rape-supportive culture

Studies of rape victim experience have increased our understanding of how survival in the aftermath of rape can be seriously impaired by negative reactions – of either disbelief, blame or a general lack of sympathy and support – in a process termed by Williams in her landmark paper as 'secondary victimisation' (Williams, 1984). An individual becomes a victim in the primary experience of the rape act but can be further victimised by negative and judgemental reactions following the rape incident, which may prompt feelings of guilt or shame *on the part of victims* about their conduct in relation to the crime perpetrated against them. At its most extreme, this can take on the form of 'blatant and illogical victim-blaming' (Williams, 1984: 67) where the focus of discussion becomes the 'contribution' of victims to their own victimhood.

Williams' paper emphasises the need to undertake a critical examination of the social context of rape and the social environment that victims must confront in the aftermath of an attack. It establishes an important principle which strongly influences the analysis of accounting practices for rape discussed in this book. Her point is that, by engaging in victim-blaming and generally unsupportive practices, 'Society and community also become offenders' (Williams, 1984: 79). Russell (1982) argues that victim-blaming in cases of rape is so widely and uncritically practised in Western cultures that they could accurately be characterised as 'rape-supportive' or tolerant of rape (Rozee and Koss, 2001). The notion of a 'rape-supportive culture' usefully captures the hostile nature of the social environment that many rape survivors experience in the aftermath of rape. The concept of rape-supportive culture is at the heart of much feminist scholarship on rape and society, and importantly, it challenges us to recognise and deal with our own expectations and values regarding issues of gender, sexuality and sexual violence and the impact that they may have on rape victims. As Renner *et al.* concur, 'Rape is not just the victim's problem, it is also the problem of those that secondarily victimise her' (1988: 171). A clear supportive and positive response to rape victims could make all the difference to their self image, the way they view their experience (Lees, 1993) and the way in which society deals with the issue of rape.

As will be discussed in the remainder of this chapter, there is some evidence to suggest that socio-cultural supports for rape are structurally integrated at all levels of society (Rozee and Koss, 2001). Rape victims suffer secondary victimisation intrapersonally (self-blame) and interpersonally in both 'mundane' and institutional settings such as the police station, emergency rooms and in the rape trial court. We will see how negative reactions contribute to significant post-rape distress, play an important role in the underreporting of rape to the police and close friends and relatives (Renner *et al.*, 1988; Koss and Harvey, 1991) and are an important factor in the shockingly low conviction rates for rape in Great Britain.

Post-traumatic stress in the aftermath of rape

Initially described in terms of a 'crisis', then as 'Rape Trauma Syndrome', the psychological effects of being raped, as derived from clinical data, have been found to be devastating. The effects of rape, as recognised by the diagnostic category 'Rape Trauma Syndrome' (Burgess and Holmstrom, 1974) were originally thought to constitute a uniquely different reaction from that caused by other traumatic events. More recently, however, researchers have preferred to describe the psychological effects of rape as subsumed under the general diagnostic definition of 'Post-Traumatic Stress Disorder' (PTSD), where the elements that define rape – terror, fear, humiliation and an imminent risk of death and injury – are recognised as features commonly associated with other traumatic stressors. PTSD has now been noted in relation to male as well as female rape cases. Male rape survivors describe the experience of rape as life threatening, de-humanising and humiliating, as do female rape survivors (e.g. Groth and Burgess, 1980; Kaufman *et al.*, 1980; Goyer and Eddleman, 1984; Myers, 1989; Garnets *et al.*, 1990) and the clinical literature indicates that male rape survivors experience long-lasting and severe physical and psychological reactions (Isely and Gehrenbeck-Shim, 1997; Rogers, 1997; Turner, 2000).

Studies generally report a high incidence of acute and chronic PTSD following rape. For example, in the case of female rape, several studies have shown that as many as 57–80% of their samples of raped individuals meet the criteria for lifetime PTSD (Kilpatrick *et al.*, 1987; Bownes *et al.*, 1991, respectively; cited in Davis and Breslau, 1994). In their discussion of PTSD, Davis and Breslau (1994) clearly argue that the initial trauma of rape is compounded by the social processes of secondary victimisation, which they argue are directly implicated in the onset of severe and chronic post-traumatic distress (Davis and Breslau, 1994; Ullman, 1996). This distress is manifested as sleep disturbance, depression, persistent re-visualisation of the rape event, obsessive washing, fear of going out, and so on. The clinical literature thus indicates that the road to rape survival will be severely blocked if rape victims are treated with suspicion and met with derogatory comments – forced to continually re-visit the rape incident, to examine their own character and pick over the details of their own behaviour rather than see the alleged rapist held to account for his actions.

Secondary victimisation and the under-reporting of rape

There are several different sources of information on rape incidence available for consultation. The Home Office (the government department responsible for the police service and the justice system in England and Wales, national security and immigration) statistics department records the number of rapes reported to the police in any given year. In 1992 sexual offences (including rape) represented 10% of all violent crimes against the person recorded by the police in England and Wales. In 1994 there were 5,000 recorded rape offences. However, as the Home Office point out, these figures represent only the *reported* rapes. In other words, they do not necessarily encompass the *actual* number of rapes that occur, rapes that for a variety of reasons are not reported and are subsequently not officially recorded.

The British Crime Survey offers a more realistic estimate of rape inci-dence, in this respect. Here, anonymous, computerised self-completion questionnaires are administered to a population sample in order to provide data on the extent and nature of sexual victimisation in England and Wales. The 2000 British Crime Survey shows that around 1 in 20 women (4.9%) said they had been raped since age 16, an estimated 754,000 victims. About one in ten women (9.7%) said they had experienced some form of sexual victimisation (including rape) since age 16. According to the BCS self-completion survey in 2004/05, just under a quarter of women (23%) and 3% of men reported having experienced sexual assault since the age of 16, and in the year prior to interview nearly 3% of women and 1% of men had experienced sexual assault (Finney, 2006). The British Crime Survey data clearly indicates that the actual incidence of rape is far higher than official Home Office Statistics would suggest. In fact, only 18% of the sexual victimisation incidents recorded in the 2001 British Crime Survey had been reported to the police.

Comparison of official statistics with survey data in the United States reveals a similar picture. The evidence suggests that although rape figures are large – in one survey, 17.6% of women in the United States have survived a completed or attempted rape (Full Report of the Prevalence, Incidence, and Consequences of Violence Against Women: Findings from the National Violence Against Women Survey, November, 2000) – many rape victims choose not to report the incident to the authorities. For example, one early study based on 10,000 American households found that the rape rate was almost four times higher than the official rate (Ennis, *Criminal Victimisation in the United States: A Report of a National Survey* (1967), cited in Ngaire, 1992). Prosecution and conviction rates for rape are provided by Regan and Kelly (2003) for the Rape Crisis Network-Europe, whose database included questionnaires sent to the Justice Ministries of the European Union member states, aspirant states, Switzerland and Norway, seeking information on the numbers of rape cases recorded, prosecuted and resulting in conviction for the period 1998–2001, and all recent research containing either national prevalence data, including unreported rapes and analysis of the attrition process. For England and Wales, since 1985, although reporting of rape has increased, prosecution rates have fallen, so that whereas around 40% of cases were prosecuted up to 1993, prosecution rates fell to just under a quarter in the period 1998–2001. Similarly, whereas conviction rates for rape were 24% in 1985, they fell to an all time low in 2001 – to just 6%.

Finally there are a number of rape incidence estimates which are based on smaller scale, self-report studies conducted with random community and university campus samples. In the United Kingdom, a London-based self-report study revealed an alarmingly high incidence rate of rape. Two thousand women were approached in a variety of places such as bus queues, colleges and high streets. Of the 1236 women who responded, nearly 20% reported that they had been raped (cited in Ngaire, 1992), a figure twice as high as the British Crime Survey statistic.

We can therefore conclude, and it is generally acknowledged to be the case, that official statistics do underestimate the incidence of rape in society. In other words, large numbers of women and men actively choose not to report a rape to the official authorities. Why? What might prevent or discourage a victim from speaking out about being subjected to sexual violence?

Report defence factors

The concept of 'report defence' elements, developed by McMullen in his discussion of male rape (McMullen, 1990), is useful in understanding the reasons why rape victims may be reluctant to make their experience public. McMullen argues that there are several powerful factors that prohibit the reporting of rape, most of which have to do with anticipated or actual negative societal responses experienced by rape victims in the aftermath of rape. These include factors such as the initial shock of the rape and fear of retaliation by the rapist but also embarrassment and the fear of being blamed or stigmatised by an unsympathetic, 'rape-supportive' social response. As members of a rape-supportive culture, rape survivors may also blame themselves (e.g. Wood and Rennie, 1994; Ward, 1995; Scarce, 1997; Lees, 1997; Ussher, 1997; West, 2000).

A decision to report a rape incident may thus ultimately rest on whether the victim believes that they conform to the culturally defined 'ideal' or 'genuine' victim type. Before a rape can be reported, it needs to be defined as such by the individual, and the individual then needs to be supported in that definition by others. As Burt and Estep (1981) point out, the criteria for definition of self and others as a 'legitimate' claimant to rape victim status mirror societal norms and standards of conduct relating to gender and sexuality. Victims are expected to establish their credibility in terms of both character and behaviour in relation to these norms. To have confidence in reporting rape, victims must therefore see themselves (and believe that they will be seen) as socially valued and socially respected and as conforming to stereotypical behaviour appropriate for the gender role. It is typical for women who may be viewed as 'drunk' or 'high' at the time of their rape not to report the incident, especially not to official agencies such as the police, for fear of reprisal and blame (Schwartz and DeKeseredy, 1997). Rape victims may speculate that people will think, or they themselves may think that 'I shouldn't have been wearing that dress'; 'I shouldn't have been out alone' or 'I'm a man, I should have been able to fight him off'. And, as discussed above, rape victim role claimants are more than likely to face generalised scepticism in a culture where rape is so often confused with consensual, pleasurable sexual encounters and relationships. If rape victims are to convince others that they are 'genuine' victims, then they must be judged to be 'respectable', to have 'done everything right' in terms of conforming to gendered norms of behaviour and to not have had any prior knowledge of their attacker.

Ngaire argues that 'rape is believed to be a crime with an unusually large dark figure' (Ngaire, 1992). Research has shown that an unwanted sexual experience is more likely to be reported and believed if it corresponds to the 'classic stranger rape' situation (Williams, 1984; Ward, 1995), where signs of force and injury, a struggle between two strangers and presence of a weapon are the characteristics (among others) frequently used by the police, the legal system, laypeople and rape victims themselves to define the occurrence of rape. Williams suggests that 'the classic rape' provides the victim with the evidence that she needs to convince herself and others that she was indeed a 'true rape victim', which may subsequently affect the decision to report the incident.

Woman-centred research has attempted to paint a fuller picture of the kinds of definitions that victimised individuals themselves may use to define their own experiences. Kelly (1987) targeted women who had not contacted official agencies such as the police, the courts and the social services and through interviewing these women found ten categories of sexual violence which were meaningful to the respondents, only one of which matched specifically to rape as defined legally where 'rape . . . consists of a male having sexual intercourse with an adult female without her consent' (*Blackstone's Criminal Practice*, 1992). Categories of unwanted sexual experiences defined by the women themselves included 'pressure' to have sex (covering experiences where women felt pressured by a man's behaviour or expectations but they chose not to say no); sexual abuse (covering all forms of sexual violence women experienced before the age of 16) and 'coercive' sex (referring to women's experiences as being 'like rape' where their consent was coerced or participation forced). The following extracts examined in Kelly's research, taken from two women's retrospective accounts, illustrate how cultural understandings of what counts as 'real rape' influence women's understandings of their experience and subsequent decisions to report the event or not:

> No, not rape not in the [sighs] . . . not actually physically forced to have sex, only . . . coerced I think, yes.
>
> (Kelly, 1987: 57)

> I remember an occasion where he wouldn't let me get up, and he was very strong. He pulled my arms above my head, I didn't put up much of a struggle. I mean I wouldn't have seen that as rape because I associated rape with strangers, dark, night and struggle. I

didn't put up much of a struggle, but I didn't want to, so in a sense that was rape, yes.

(Kelly, 1987: 57)

There are therefore several report defence elements that may cause victims to delay reporting or to remain silent about the rapes perpetrated against them. However, if a rape is reported to official agencies, there is evidence to suggest that rape victims may well be justified in their expectation that there will be a struggle to gain access to help, support and justice.

The agency response to rape victims

In a major early study of the agency response to rape victims, Holstrom and Burgess (1978) followed a total of 146 cases of rape, beginning with the police and the hospitals who may initially be notified and ending with the legal court trial (if that stage is reached at all), as well as the friends and family surrounding the victim long after the official process of victim 'support' has ended. By following each case in great detail, ranging from observations of hospital admissions to recordings of police interviews, the authors found negative responses to be a feature of rape victim experience, although among the police these were in the minority (Holmstrom and Burgess, 1978); indeed, these results can also be found in more recent studies (Ullman, 1996). However, the authors caution against 'glossing over the fact that these [negative responses] do exist' (Ullman, 1996: 39).

Ward (1995) notes that the police have been widely criticised for their unsympathetic treatment of rape victims. Comparative studies have generally shown that the police hold more negative perceptions of victims than other professionals (e.g. Feild, 1978a; Feldman-Summers and Palmer, 1980; Lee and Cheung, 1991), although some recent studies suggest that other professionals such as counsellors also hold negative rape-victim directed attitudes (Kassing and Prieto, 2003). For example, in an early survey study designed to compare the attitudes towards rape held by citizens, police officers, counsellors and sex offenders, Feild (1978a) found that police officers were more similar to rapists in their attitudes than they were to any of the other groups surveyed in the study. In particular they agreed with sexual offenders about sexual motivation for rape, the abnormality of rapists and the reduced desirability of women following rape. Feldman-Summers and Palmer (1980) similarly found that the police, prosecutors and judges were more likely than rape crisis counsellors to argue that rape is contingent on women's behaviour. LeDoux and Hazelwood (1985) reported that American police officers in their survey did not trivialise rape but did, however, once again, point to victims in their understanding of rape causality, agreeing with the view that women provoke rape by their behaviour or appearance. Similarly, Muram et al. (1995) document a high prevalence of negative attitudes towards rape victims among police officers in their study located at the Memphis Police Academy.

In a more recent study, Campbell and Johnson (1997) asked a sample of police officers to give definitions of rape in their own words. They found that the officers' perception of rape was not uniform, and three typologies of definition emerged. Over 50% of the sample offered definitions that were a mixture of old and reformed legal definitions of rape combined with 'rape myths' (inaccurate views about rape grounded in cultural understandings of gender and sexuality). Most of these officers did not include notions of force or coercion in their definitions of rape, missed key legal elements of rape and ascribed stereotypical ideas, e.g. 'sometimes a guy can't stop himself; 'he gets egged on by the girl').

Police policy on the treatment of rape victims in Britain has changed radically since the early 1990s, and some effort has been made to offer a more 'user-friendly' service to both female and male rape victims (Gregory and Lees, 1999). Initiatives include special training courses for officers who deal with sexual assault victims, the provision of specially equipped rape suites for medical examinations and most recently, the introduction of a chaperone system. Chaperones are specially trained police officers, appointed by the detective inspector, who have the responsibility of ensuring that a victim is treated with respect, that the best possible evidence to support the case is obtained and that the victim is kept informed of progress with the prosecution.

Gregory and Lees (1999) discuss the results of a handful of studies on rape victim experiences conducted since the introduction of the initiatives outlined above. The evidence reviewed offers some encouraging signs of improvement in the treatment of rape victims, and the authors highlight one or two examples of outstanding multi-agency projects (e.g. the REACH project in Northumbria). Around three-quarters of women interviewed in a study carried out within the London Metropolitan Police area (Gregory and Lees, 1999) reported that they were broadly satisfied with the way they were treated by female police officers. However, just under half of the sample of rape or attempted rape victims said that they were dissatisfied with the delayed, inappropriate or inefficient response from the male police officers who had dealt with their cases, some reporting that the rape complaint had not been taken seriously (even in one case, where the victim had given an account of a classic 'stranger rape'). Some victims, reporting mixed views of the police, objected to inappropriate questions, such as enquiries about what they were wearing at the time of the attack. A third of the complainants interviewed by Temkin (1999) were wholly, mainly or partly negative about their experience of reporting rape. Their dissatisfaction was related to being treated with disbelief and to harsh or unsympathetic lines of questioning. Temkin concludes that stereotypical attitudes towards gender, sexuality and sexual violence still exist in the police force.

Half of the officers she interviewed for example considered that a quarter of all rapes reported to the police are false.

The evidence therefore suggests that although increasing numbers of victims are receiving better treatment, significant numbers of victims continue to experience negative, unsympathetic or unhelpful responses in their dealings with the police. Much of the evidence points to the particular failure of male police officers in this regard (see also Brown and King, 1998[1]). It would seem that it is somewhat of a lottery as to what kind of service a rape victim will in practice receive (DI Sue Hill, cited in Gregory and Lees, 1999) and many are kept in the dark about the progress and outcome of investigations (Gregory and Lees, 1999). In spite of the improvements in rape suite facilities, the overwhelming majority of victims still find the process of medical examination in the aftermath of rape inhumane and traumatising, particularly when carried out by male surgeons. Gregory and Lees (1999) and Temkin (1996) note that many of the victims in their surveys experienced unsympathetic, 'business-like' treatment from the doctors they saw. There is some evidence that police doctors are ill informed about the likely behaviour of victims suffering from post-traumatic stress, allowing the stoicism of victims in the context of the medical examination to be interpreted by defence counsel as lack of victim distress, to be admitted as evidence in favour of the alleged perpetrator. It would seem that a significant number of police officers and an even greater number of medical examiners believe that rape is a sexually motivated crime, that rapists are merely following 'irresistible impulses' and that rape victims cause rape by provoking an attack or failing to prevent it.

Sue Lees (Lees, 1997; Gregory and Lees, 1999) carried out two major surveys on male rape during 1995, one completed by male victims of rape and another that involved an analysis of police records. Together, they offer some indication of the front-line police response to male victims of sexual assault and the experience of men in the aftermath of rape. In the early 1990s the London Metropolitan Police introduced the services offered to female rape victims to male rape victims. However, around 15% of the research participants felt that the police had not taken their complaint at all seriously. A common complaint was that even if action was taken, the police reacted with embarrassment, making it difficult for the complainant to offer a full account of the incident or to continue with the case (Lees, 1997). Some victims reported hearing sniggering behind their backs, and some police officers interviewed admitted that male rape is still a subject of black humour in the canteen culture of police stations. Finally, victim feedback suggested that gay men were treated less sympathetically than heterosexual men. The detailed analysis of cultural understandings of male rape, which follows in chapter 5 of this book, provides support for this finding and offers some insight into the discursive resources and practices available in our culture that produce and sustain this reaction.

Police officers interviewed for the Channel 4 documentary *Still Getting Away With Rape* (focusing on rape against women) first screened in April 2001 acknowledged that false allegations of rape are few and far between. However, it seems that the police, perhaps frustrated by the failure of the Crown Prosecution Service (CPS) to sustain convictions for rape, actively discourage many women from pursuing an allegation of rape. Front-line services provided by the police for some rape victims are certainly improving. However, the police do hold considerable power in determining whether a reported rape will be taken seriously and investigated and brought to the attention of the CPS. It would seem that the police, albeit with a realistic eye on conviction rates and the treatment that a rape victim is likely to receive in court, in practice reinforce the rape-supportive message that unless all the criteria for 'credible rape victim' can be met (as discussed above), a victim's account is unlikely to be believed and it is unlikely that the attacker will be convicted. The appalling level of secondary victimisation experienced by rape victims in court is the topic for discussion in the next section.

Judicial rape

Lees (1993, 1997) argues that in cases of rape it is the victim, not the perpetrator, who is on trial and that the experience of secondary victimisation is so profound in this context to be tantamount to 'judicial rape', 'a spectacle of degradation visited upon the victim rather than the offender' (1997: 73). Similarly, Raitt and Zeedyk (2000) conclude that the treatment of rape victims in the criminal justice system is so notorious that 'many women describe the judicial response to rape as worse than the rape itself' (Raitt and Zeedyk, 2000: 88).

The shockingly low conviction rates for rape cases brought to court in England and Wales highlight the fact that rape is a 'low risk, high reward crime' for the perpetrator. Raitt and Zeedyk point out that while in recent years there has been an increase in the numbers of recorded rapes in many countries, corresponding proportions of those prosecuted have often decreased. For example, in Scotland, while the numbers of recorded rapes between 1986 and 1995 rose by 61.7%, in 1995, only 12.1% of these rapes were prosecuted, and only 7.9% these prosecutions resulted in conviction. Home Office statistics in England and Wales (1995) reveal that despite an almost threefold increase in the number of cases recorded by the police between 1985 and 1995, the percentage of convictions for rape have fallen by more than 50%: from 24.4% of all recorded rapes in 1985 to 11.7% of all recorded rapes in 1995. In 2000, the conviction rate for recorded rapes in Great Britain was just 7%.

The defence tactics used by those in the criminal justice system have been cited as a major reason for the decrease in prosecutions and convictions of recorded rapes. Most often, these include the derogation of character and behaviour of the victim in the witness stand. Although laws such as 'rape shield laws' (Raitt and Zeedyk, 2000) have been introduced in order to circumvent negative character assassinations of the victim, these have been less than effective because they are very rarely applied in practice. For example, defence barristers still routinely imply that a female rape victim is promiscuous. They need permission from the judge to ask questions about a victim's sexual experience (making an argument that it is relevant to the allegation of rape), yet barristers will admit that they routinely apply for this permission with the express aim of discrediting the victim as a slut (*Dispatches*, April, 2001).

Researchers for Channel 4's *Dispatches* (in consultation with Sue Lees) monitored 30 rape cases in early 2001 over a period of two weeks. This evidence provides insight into the shameful treatment received by many rape victims in the courts. Even in cases where it could be established that the victim probably did not consent to intercourse, in practice the victim was still confronted with a routine defence strategy which was, on the one hand, to discredit the victim ('they blackened my character and that was like being raped all over again[2]) and, on the other hand, to establish the 'good character' of the perpetrator. The issue for the jury was presented as not so much, 'did he rape her' but, 'is she rape-able' and thus 'do we want to convict this man of rape?' In a move identified by Burt and Estep (1981) discussed above, defence barristers will try to suggest that even if the woman insists she didn't consent, at the end of the day it will be argued that she is still to blame, she is a naïve, silly or 'damaged' girl who brought it all on herself. Her credibility as a rational, respectable woman and her status as a reliable witness are systematically destroyed. Discrediting victims by positioning them as 'open territory victims' on the grounds of 'mental instability', as a 'drinker', or as in search of 'deviant sex' was commonplace in this sample of trials.

In 2002, the then Home Secretary David Blunkett presented a command paper, *Protecting the Public* (HMSO, November, 2002), to parliament, outlining an overhaul of the laws on sexual offences. Accused rapists now have to prove their innocence if the prosecution can show that the victim was subject to threats or force, unconscious, unlawfully detained, unable to communicate because of a disability, or had agreement to sex provided on their behalf by a third party. In these cases, the onus will fall on the defendant to prove that consent was given. Blunkett argues that the new 'consent list' is 'Designed to send a clear signal to the public about the circumstances in which sexual activity is likely to be wrong' (*Protecting the Public*, HMSO, p. 16) and as such is a welcome move. However, the need for such a law speaks volumes about the struggle that rape victims have experienced and continue to experience in bringing a rape case to court and securing the conviction of their rapist. It may in practice make little difference to the justice secured for rape victims. The *Dispatches* research showed that rape victims are still likely to have their case tried by an often inexperienced and allegedly underpaid prosecution barrister and will still face defence lawyers hell bent on destroying their credibility, even when it is established that consent to intercourse was not given.

The social production and social legitimation of rape

Rape is a form of mass terrorism, for the victims of rape are chosen indiscriminately, but the propagandists for male supremacy broadcast that it is women who cause rape by being unchaste or in the wrong place at the wrong time – in essence by behaving as if they were free.

(Griffin, 1971: 35)

'Second-wave' feminist scholars position sexual violence as central to the analysis of patriarchy. For the first time, rape was identified as an act of domination denying the victim self-determination, as an act of extreme violence, which always carries the threat of death (e.g. Brownmiller, 1975). In her eloquent and groundbreaking discussion of rape, Susan Griffin highlighted the way that 'Rape and the fear of rape are a daily part of every woman's consciousness' (Griffin, 1971: 27). The generalised threat and fear associated with rape and the actual use of force both function to limit freedom by confining victims to their traditional gender roles. Writing in relation to female rape, Griffin links the social construction of female sexuality to the regulation of female passivity in every facet of everyday life:

Each girl as she grows into womankind is taught fear . . . Since, biologically speaking, women have the same if not greater potential for sexual expression as do men, the woman who is taught that she must behave differently from a man is also taught to distrust her own carnality. She must deny her own feelings and learn not to act from them. She fears herself. This is the essence of passivity, and of course, a woman's passivity is not simply sexual but functions to cripple her from self-expression in every area of her life.

(Griffin, 1971: 33)

Feminist analysis thus established rape as a political rather than a sexual act, an act of power and intimidation, described in Griffin's account (see above) as a form of mass terrorism. Subsequent work has emphasised that rape is part of a 'continuum of sexual violence' (Kelly, 1987) and that sexual violence is part of a general pattern of domination alongside other forms of economic and social control (Walby, 1990). The notion of continuum suggests that sexual violence is at some level a unitary phenomenon.

Kelly argues that all forms of sexual violation, from verbal abuse to rape and murder, have a common character in that they can all function to humiliate and induce fear, constraining the activities and choices of victims and reassuring perpetrators of their potency. The impact or 'seriousness' of any particular incident will depend on the subjective experience of the victim.

A key theme emerged from 'second-wave' feminist analyses of rape, that rape is both a socially produced and a socially legitimated phenomenon (Edwards, 1987). In most feminist writings on rape, a close connection is made between normative constructions of heterosexuality and sexual practice (see discussion above), the normalisation of aggression in hegemonic forms of masculinity and the maintenance of patriarchal gender power relations. Brownmiller (1975) for example argues that acts of rape are fuelled by cultural values that are perpetuated at every level of society, captured in the term 'machismo'. Griffin agues that rape is encouraged in a culture which rewards excessive displays of male aggression and domineering behaviour and where notions of female resistance, male dominance and sexual pleasure are meshed and often romanticised: 'Erotic pleasure cannot be separated from culture, and in our culture male eroticism is wedded to power' (Griffin, 1971: 29). Causal explanations of rape in feminist theory stress the significance of normative cultural constructions of what it is to be a man, the fantasies and fears about 'woman' and the dread of homosexuality that underpins misogyny in our culture, rather than pointing to the individual psychology of 'deviant perverts' as is usual in more liberal theorising (Walby, 1990; Ussher, 1997).

Feminist scholarship also emphasises that socially constructed, hegemonic, understandings of gender and heterosexuality (our everyday 'sexual scripts' – Gagnon and Simon, 1973) provide a framework of cultural norms for gendered behaviour, to which we are accountable. Normative understandings of gender and heterosexuality can also be employed to offer a range of socially acceptable excuses and justifications, a 'vocabulary of motive' (sometimes referred to as 'rape myths') that can be mobilised to legitimate an act of rape or to neutralise rape claims. Behaviour categorised as 'rape' by a rape victim may thus be rendered 'acceptable' by re-defining it as within the boundaries of normative heterosexual gender relations and behaviour. In practice, as Gavey (2005) argues, normative understandings of heterosexuality and gender relations allow too much scope for rape claims to be reformulated as 'just sex', setting the preconditions for rape and also providing the perfect cover story for rape. The existence of a vocabulary of motive, or 'techniques of neutralisation' (Sykes and Matza, 1957) for sexual violence offers society a means of exonerating acts of rape (using sense-making resources that are consistent with and which renew the gendered moral order) and, crucially, also a means of maintaining the patriarchal status quo and keeping women in their place. Rapists themselves can also mobilise societally condoned excuses and justifications for rape in advance of committing rape to absolve guilt and be morally free to act (Jackson, 1987). As Sykes and Matza argue, 'justifications . . . precede behaviour and make deviant behaviour possible' (1957: 666; cited in Antaki, 1994). The analyses presented in this book are inspired by the view of explanation-giving as a form of social regulation, a theme that was present in both early feminist accounts of rape and society and early sociological writing on accounts. Our aim is to explore cultural vocabularies of motive – the sense-making resources that allow perpetrators to act, their actions to be explained away and the testimony and subjective experience of victims to be dismissed or denied. We also examine the potential points of discursive resistance to rape supportive discourse.

Conclusion

Although there has been some erosion of public support for rape myths, due to increased media discussions of rape, e.g. as evidenced in a recent headline, 'Date rape is the new student fear' (*Times Higher Education Supplement*, 24/9/2004), and there has been some focus on the cultural disbanding of rape myths in newspapers and women's magazines (Verberg *et al.*, 2000), we have argued in this chapter that, in practice, rape claims are seldom met with a clear, supportive and positive response. We presented evidence that a cultural climate of secondary victimisation in the aftermath of rape is a reality for many victims and can be detrimental to psychological health, impact on decisions to report an incident of rape, to investigate a rape allegation and to convict an alleged rapist if a case comes to trial. Claimants to 'genuine sexual assault victim' status routinely encounter a range of social and institutional barriers and struggle to receive sympathy, adequate resources or justice. Feminist theory on rape stresses that rape is both socially produced and socially legitimated, and established the social definition of rape and rape victim-hood as central to understanding and improving the experience and treatment of rape victims. Hegemonic under-standings of gender and heterosexuality underpin causal reasoning about rape in a variety of contexts, providing the building blocks for the social construction of risk in relation to sexual violence, a vocabulary of motives and excuses for rape perpetrators and, ultimately, the maintenance of patriarchy. In the next chapter we examine social psychology's contribution to our understanding of reasoning about rape. We will see how in this literature explanation is individualised, treated as an internal, cognitive-perceptual process that can be meaningfully studied from an objectivist standpoint using experimental research and survey methodologies. We discuss and critically interrogate the theoretical underpinnings of experi-mental research on the social perception of rape, which aims to examine attributions of cause, fault and responsibility in depicted rapes, and we explore and evaluate some of the main research techniques and findings in this literature. In so doing, we question the extent to which there is or can be a comfortable (Ward, 1995) or 'symbiotic' relationship between feminist scholarship and the social psychology of rape perception. We conclude that the rape-perception paradigm has substantial drawbacks for researchers interested in exploring the social definition of rape. This is because there is a lack of fit between the precepts of liberal, psychological attribution theory and associated experimental methods and the research programme suggested by early feminist scholarship on the social definition of rape, where the significance of the social construction of meaning in cultural and political context was placed centre stage.

Appendix

Legal definitions of rape and other related acts are reproduced here (although, we are of course more interested in how lay definitions of these acts are constructed and reconstructed in ordinary talk about rape). According to the Sexual Offences Act, 2003 (a parliamentary Act passed by the UK), rape, assault by penetration and sexual assault are defined as follows:

1 Rape
(1) A person (A) commits an offence if –
    (a) he intentionally penetrates the vagina, anus or mouth of another person (B) with his penis,
    (b) B does not consent to the penetration, and
    (c) A does not reasonably believe that B consents.
(2) Whether a belief is reasonable is to be determined having regard to all the circumstances, including any steps A has taken to ascertain whether B consents.
(3) Sections 75 and 76 apply to an offence under this section.
(4) A person guilty of an offence under this section is liable, on conviction on indictment, to imprisonment for life.

2 Assault by penetration
(1) A person (A) commits an offence if –
    (a) he intentionally penetrates the vagina or anus of another person (B) with a part of his body or anything else,
    (b) the penetration is sexual,
    (c) B does not consent to the penetration, and
    (d) A does not reasonably believe that B consents.
(2) Whether a belief is reasonable is to be determined having regard to all the circumstances, including any steps A has taken to ascertain whether B consents.

(3) Sections 75 and 76 apply to an offence under this section.

(4) A person guilty of an offence under this section is liable, on conviction on indictment, to imprisonment for life.

3   Sexual assault

(1) A person (A) commits an offence if –
   (a) he intentionally touches another person (B),
   (b) the touching is sexual,
   (c) B does not consent to the touching, and
   (d) A does not reasonably believe that B consents.

(2) Whether a belief is reasonable is to be determined having regard to all the circumstances, including any steps A has taken to ascertain whether B consents.

(3) Sections 75 and 76 apply to an offence under this section.

(4) A person guilty of an offence under this section is liable –
   (a) on summary conviction, to imprisonment for a term not exceeding 6 months or a fine not exceeding the statutory maximum or both;
   (b) on conviction on indictment, to imprisonment for a term not exceeding 10 years.

Notes

1. Brown and King (1998) showed that male police officers still adhere more strongly to rape myths than female police officers do.
2. Testimony of a rape victim interviewed by *Dispatches* (2001).

2

THE SOCIAL PSYCHOLOGY OF RAPE PERCEPTION

The emergence of the social psychology of rape perception

'Second-wave' feminist analyses of sexual violence and society highlighted that sexual violence (in some form) is a commonplace experience and is a key site for the maintenance of patriarchy (Walby, 1990). As we discussed in chapter 1, feminist scholars have argued that rape is fuelled and legitimated by cultural constructions of hegemonic gender and hetero-sexuality and by 'rape-supportive' practices in institutional and mundane settings. We saw how feminist researchers explicitly topicalise the social definition of rape as a key factor in understanding and improving the treatment and experience of rape victims.

In this chapter we examine one of the most active and well-developed rape-related areas of research in academic psychology: the rape-perception programme (Ward, 1995; Pollard, 1992; Krahé, 1991). Rape-perception research examines causal reasoning about rape, attributions of fault, blame and responsibility and the beliefs and attitudinal characteristics of social observers. 'Second-wave' feminist activism and scholarship put the issue of sexual violence squarely on the agenda for the social sciences, and the emergence of a distinctly social psychological study of rape perception is at least partly attributable to the raised profile in general of sexual violence issues at the start of the 1970s. However, the great excitement surrounding the emergence of the theoretical framework of attribution theory in social psychology at around the same time also contributed significantly to the emergence of the study of rape perception as, primarily, a process of social cognition (Krahé, 1991).

It has been suggested that the social psychology of rape perception and feminist scholarship exist in a symbiotic relationship, each tradition learning from the other in its pursuit of knowledge about rape incidents and societal responses to rape (Ward, 1995). However, we are going to argue that this relationship may be more problematic than is currently thought. In this and the next chapter we critically reflect on the theoretical resource of attribution theory as utilised in the social psychology of rape perception and on the epistemological assumptions and research methods used. We argue that the adoption of attribution theory for the examination of social reasoning about rape was fundamentally flawed and inspired a programme of research with severe limitations both for the examination of accounts for rape in social interaction and for social critique.

Attribution theory in social psychology

As every student of psychology knows, attribution theory is one of the mainstays of social psychology. Its main interest lies in examining how individuals come to 'cognise' the social environment (Heider, 1958). Attribution may be viewed as the process of 'ascribing some phenomenon to its origin' (Hilton, 1990). Attribution theory, rather than being one monolithic theory, refers to a number of theoretical formulations which have attempted to standardise Heider's original proposals as conceptual models of the process of social attributional judgement and the consequences of those judgements (Jones and Davis, 1965; Jones et al., 1972; Kelley, 1967, 1973; Kelley and Michela, 1980). These 'mini-theories' (Antaki, 1984) all share a number of core concepts which form the enterprise of attribution theory. The attribution theory framework has been employed in the examination of social cognition in relation to a range of social and clinical issues, for example, attributional processes with respect to the development and maintenance of physical and mental disorders such as depression (Abramson and Martin, 1981; Brewin, 1985; Brewin and Antaki, 1987), people's explanations and causal beliefs for coronary heart disease (Devalle and Norman, 1992) or attributions for relationship difficulties (Fincham and Bradbury, 1987; Andrews and Brewin, 1990). The framework has similarly been used to examine success and failure in achievement settings (Weiner et al., 1972) and attributional style and well-being among the elderly (Houston et al., 2000).

The rape-perception paradigm grew out of this explosion in attribution theory studies. Conducted within a framework of objectivist epistemology and positivist methods, it offered the promise of a systematic, experimentally rigorous and productive approach to study social cognition about rape. In this chapter however, we critically explore the roots of attribution theory and its adoption in the study of social reasoning about rape.

Attribution theory deals with two major points in interpersonal relations: factors influencing the social perceiver's judgements about the behaviour of self and others, and the cognitive mechanisms whereby the cause of behaviour is located within people themselves or in environmental/situational conditions. These two points are at the heart of Heider's (known as the 'father of attribution theory') writings on the nature of interpersonal social relations in everyday life (Heider, 1958), from which modern attribution theory stems.

There are three crucial tenets of attribution theory. The first specifies that we gain an understanding of the social world by a process of rational *causal analysis* where the observed relationships between people, the various situations and the behaviour are perceived as causal in nature. Out of the milieu of social interaction, situation and environments, our basic motivational task is to gain an understanding of which people, objects, situations and the observed behaviours form stable and consistent conjunctive relationships and which do not. In this sense, attribution theory is concerned with the study of 'naïve epistemology' where what is of interest is the way in which individuals come to causally understand the social world and relations within it.

The second crucial tenet of attribution theory is that the function of this causal analysis is to narrow the range of possible causes to internal or external loci – in other words, to factors within the person or to situational/ environmental factors. For example, as pointed out by a journalist in relation to the historic move by nurses who voted to remove the 'no strike' contractual clause, it is important for both the societal perception of health care professionals and ultimately, the success of this action, to try to establish whether the causal locus is to be attributed to the nurses' internal characteristics where 'they are just a bunch of greedy, grasping bitches who don't give a damn about their patients' (internal attribution) or to environmental causes where they are 'people who realise that they are unable to live on their meagre pay and in addition, cope with the crumbling and inadequate resources of the Health Service' (external attribution) (Carol Sarler, *The People*, 26/3/1995). Thus, to make an internal or external attribution is to locate the causal origin of the observed effect or the condition that caused the behaviour to occur, internally or externally. Generally, the attributional framework is concerned with explicating the processes involved in the search for explanations for social behaviour where we endeavour to answer *why* a particular observed action or behaviour occurred.

The third, and perhaps most important tenet of the conceptual framework of attribution theory as envisaged by Heider, is his model of humans as rational and logical problem solvers, using a naive, scientific methodology to derive causality about social relations. According to Heider, the causal analysis of everyday life proceeds along similar, albeit 'naïve' lines as the formal scientific search for cause–effect relationships. Within this framework the individual is construed as essentially rational and logical, following normative inductivist procedures to observe and manipulate the various behaviours and actions and their presence or absence with the proposed causes, according to a 'naïve factor analysis'. The covariation principle, for example, theorises that people make attributional judgements by assessing the logical association or the degree of *covariation* between two variables, the cause and the effect.[1] This so-called 'covariation principle' (Strong, 1970; Mill, 1973; Heider, 1958; Kelley, 1967, 1973; Hilton, 1990) is said to derive from the natural sciences and represents an important method of formal scientific inquiry, first identified by the philosopher John Stuart Mill (1973; Hilton, 1990). The covariation principle is a strategy that a formal scientist engages in when searching for experimental causality. This principle of inquiry has been appropriated by attribution theorists such as Harold Kelley in his covariation model of attribution (1968, 1973) to explain how a layperson, albeit 'naïvely', searches for causal explanations for social behaviour in everyday life. In relation to social attributional reasoning, the covariation principle states that a behaviour is attributed to that condition which is present when the reaction is present and absent when the reaction is absent. In other words, the *cause* and *effect* for a behaviour are observed to *covary*. In the analysis of social action, covariation of condition and reaction is tested most frequently over time and over persons (Strong, 1970). Consistency over time establishes a relationship between condition and reaction, while consistency over persons establishes whether the person-actor or the environment causes the reaction or behaviour in question. In summary, 'the effect an environmental change has on the average person is attributed to the environmental occurrence as a property, the non average or idiosyncratic effect being attributed to the person' or 'the cause of a difference resides within the variant condition rather than in the conditions common to the diverse instances' (Heider, 1958: 168–169). Thus, attribution theory has been dominated by a 'man as scientist' (*sic*) analogy with a view of the layperson as a rational information processor, making logical conclusions about causal relations based on the 'evidence' available in the social world. Cognitive psychologists understand themselves to be engaged in the project of uncovering the basic building blocks of the human mind – the structures (e.g. personality traits, attitudes) and processes (e.g. attributional reasoning) that are assumed to reside within information-processing individuals, directing their behaviour (Fiske and Taylor, 1991).

Rape-perception research: the vignette method

Much rape-perception research has focused on identifying the factors involved in the formation of causal attributions as well as judgements of blame, fault and responsibility ascribed to victims and to perpetrators of rape. The majority of studies documented in this chapter utilise a standard methodological technique to examine the various factors influencing attributional judgements. The rapes that observers are asked to comment on are usually depicted rapes: the occurrence of the rape is presented to subjects in the form of a written short story called a 'vignette'. Some researchers have however argued that observations of real rapes would, in theory, be preferable. For example, Check and Malamuth (1983) write that

> Although the ideal criterion variable in rape research would involve actual observations of rapes, such research is not feasible. Consequently, rape researchers must rely on indirect measures. Three such measures that have received attention in the literature are sexual arousal to rape depictions, perceptions of rape victims and men's self-reported likelihood of raping.
>
> (Check and Malamuth, 1983: 345)

It is interesting that direct observation of real rape is rejected on grounds of 'feasibility' only by these researchers, and we will return to this and similar issues in chapter 3 as part of an extended critical evaluation of the methodological practices in rape-perception research.

The majority of rape-perception research has favoured the vignette method, and research has focused almost exclusively on factors relating to the victim. Vignettes typically provide relatively short descriptions of the circumstances surrounding the rape and the victim's response immediately following the rape. For example, the vignette will generally describe how the victim happened to be where she was at the time of the occurrence of the rape. A number of the vignettes feature 'student' victims, who may be described as attacked while walking home following a late session at the library, for example (Anderson and Beattie, 2001). A vignette will usually conclude with a description of how the victim responded to the rape – for example, whether she called the police – and may include detail about the existence of witnesses and their reaction to events. The rape itself tends to be dealt with very briefly, this description usually being confined to a single sentence. The typical task for the subjects is to read the vignette and then provide an explanation for the event described by offering a judgement of cause, blame, fault and responsibility, and opinions about guilt and sanctions.

Before turning to a discussion of some of the findings and conclusions in the rape-perception literature, there is an important point to be made about the dependent measures used in studies of rape perception. Researchers working in this field have employed a variety of dependent measures to evaluate observers' attributional reasoning about depicted rape incidents. Although causal attributions (following attribution theory – to internal or external loci) have been a frequently utilised measure, the same conceptual status is often afforded to the dependent measures of blame, fault and responsibility, and in practice, these terms get used interchangeably. However, these measures are not conceptually identical (Cameron and Stritzke, 2003; Försterling, 2001; Shaver, 1970, 1981, 1985; Shaver and Drown, 1980). Indeed, one early rape-perception study showed that the *responsibility* assigned to the victim of rape by observers was significantly higher than either fault or blame (Krulewitz and Nash, 1979), suggesting that the participants in the study afforded different conceptual meanings to these measures. It seems likely that attributions of responsibility are most clearly linked to issues of causality (though it may not imply intention) and that attributions of fault and blame function as moral evaluations. A bid was made for greater conceptual clarification rather than interchangeable use of such terms in sex and violence research (Shaver and Drown, 1980; Kanekar and Kolsawalla, 1980), but subsequent research has continued to subsume the conclusions drawn from these different measures under the general heading of 'causal attribution'. The problem with attribution theory's bi-polar conceptualisation of explanation is that the distinction is so broad that any nuances within each category may be conceptually subsumed by the broader attributional definition of either internal or external cause. As a result, although causality, blame, fault and responsibility are usually meas-ured on separate scales in rape-attribution research, few if any theoretical advances have been made regarding the conceptual status of these measures *as related specifically to rape perception* and the meaning that each term has as a feature of internal (or external) rape-victim attribution.

Experimental methods in the rape-perception paradigm therefore do not allow participants to display their sense-making practices in relation to rape beyond making a mark on a scale using categories predefined by the researcher. Neither do they allow us to examine the emergence and resolu-tion of disputes about the nature of 'what happened' – to examine sense making that might validate a victim's testimony or neutralise a rape claim – as the description of the incident is static and depicted in categories pro-vided by the *researcher*. We will return to these two central methodological issues in more detail in chapter 3 as we discuss the limitations of the rape-perception paradigm for the examination of accounting practices for rape in social interaction.

The impact of victim and perpetrator characteristics on the observer's judgements of depicted rapes

Social psychologists have uncovered a number of factors that have been found to impact on the level of victim blame and other negative attributions to victims in judgements about depicted rapes. These are often referred to as 'extraneous' factors, because they do not have any direct relationship to the incident itself. Instead, they often detail aspects thought likely to trigger rape myths, such as characteristics of the people involved (e.g. age, marital status, race, gender, attractiveness etc.) or other information such as the time the incident occurred or the location of the incident (Pollard, 1992). Several excellent reviews of rape-perception studies and their findings are available (e.g. Pollard, 1992; Ward, 1995), which we have drawn on here to offer a selective review of empirical research in this tradition. Some of the most reliable results in this paradigm relate to aspects of victim characteristics and pre-attack behaviours (Pollard, 1992) – dimensions that also feature in the analysis of talk about rape in the empirical chapters that follow. We therefore focus on studies manipulating these factors in our discussion of rape-perception findings here, which will provide a spring-board for our evaluation of the contribution of rape-perception research to our understanding of accounting practices for rape and the experience of rape victims.

Findings from rape-perception studies have revealed that people's rape-related judgements are affected by a number of victim characteristics and pre-attack behaviours such as victim's degree of resistance (Van Wie and Gross, 1995; Yescavage, 1999), 'respectability' (Luginbuhl and Mullin, 1981), physical appearance (Deitz *et al.*, 1984; Tieger, 1981), prior sexual experience (Borgida and White, 1978; Cann *et al.*, 1979; L'Armand and Pepitone, 1982; Tyson, 2003), intoxication (Richardson and Campbell, 1982; Stormo *et al.*, 1997) and dress at the time of the rape (Edmonds and Cahoon, 1986; Workman and Freeburg, 1999). Attributions about rape have also been examined in relation to various attitudinal characteristics of the observer, and research has shown that some interrelations exist between rape-related attributions and attitudes. It is worth noting that the rape-perception field continues to examine these factors in relation to rape; the findings from these newer studies tend to mirror the older studies' results (Tyson, 2003; Viki and Abrams, 2002; Wakelin and Long, 2003), perhaps because beliefs and stereotypes about rape, steeped in patriarchy, are resistant to change (see the recent Amnesty International survey, mentioned in the previous chapter, and its findings showing the persistence of tradi-tional stereotypes about women and rape among the general population).

Perhaps the first study to examine attributions concerning victims of rape manipulated the 'respectability' of the victim (Jones and Aronson, 1973). In this study 'respectability' was conceptualised as 'marital status' and was varied according to the victim being described as a virgin, a married woman or divorcee. They found that the divorced woman was attributed the least fault, and this finding was in line with their predicted attribution in relation to the 'just-world' hypothesis (Lerner and Matthews, 1967). In order to maintain the belief that the world is a basically just and fair place (a world where people deserve what they get and get what they deserve), the rape of a 'virginal' girl, who has not done anything 'wrong', has to be explained by attributing fault to her as an individual (this is the explanation advanced by the authors of the paper. Indeed, later studies which have manipulated 'respectability' in terms of the number of sexual partners, for example, have found the opposite effect, such as Pugh, 1983). Thus, this appears to be an isolated finding. In fact Luginbuhl and Mullin (1981) argued that marital status is not a particularly adequate measure of a victim's perceived respectability, and they subsequently attempted to manipulate this dimen-sion using occupational and marital status, comparing a nun or a student versus a topless dancer (intended to be perceived as a less respectable victim) and a married social worker versus a divorced topless dancer on bail for a heroin charge. We will comment on the problems associated with the unreflective use of such stereotypical identity categories in more detail in chapter 3. For the purposes of the present review of studies, however, we will simply report the findings that rape was presumed to be less damaging for the sexually experienced and 'unrespectable' victims. This finding is consistent with the rape myth identified by feminist scholars that rape is all too often understood by social participants as essentially 'just sex' – and thus can be treated as a trivial matter for victims assumed to be sexually experienced or sexually available. The findings show that socially 'respectable' victims are attributed less character blame (i.e. the type of person she is) and more attributions to chance factors of the attack. Male subjects also recommended much lower sentences for the rapists of less 'respectable' victims (17.6 vs. 53.7 years), a finding consistent with Burt and Estep's argument discussed in chapter 1, that some victims are perceived (or constructed) as more 'rape-worthy' than others, and the rapists of such victims are likely to be treated more leniently.

The effect of physical attractiveness of the victim on attributions made to that victim has typically been studied by presenting participants with photographs of what are judged (by a consensus opinion) to be attractive and less attractive individuals. This factor has also been manipulated verbally by inserting a sentence describing the victim's physical attractiveness within the vignette description. Tieger (1981) and Seligman et al. (1977) found that the perception of victim provocation was higher for 'unattractive' than 'attractive' victims. Thornton and Ryckman (1983) found more fault as well as higher characterological and behavioural blame was attributed to the 'unattractive' victim. Some authors argue that 'unattractive' victims are perceived as more provocative than the 'attractive' victim; observers appear to believe that 'unattractive' women are unlikely targets because they would only attract the 'sexual' attention of men if they actively procure it. A consistent, but more reliable, finding is that attackers of 'attractive' victims are treated more harshly in terms of ratings of blame, responsibility and recommended sentence length (Ferguson et al., 1987; Kanekar and Nazareth, 1988; Thornton, 1977; Calhoun et al., 1978; Deitz et al., 1984; Jacobson, 1981; Jacobson and Popovich, 1983).

A victim having a history of rape has also been found to be an influential factor on negative victim attributions, for example, in Tyson (2003), and McCaul et al. (1990) where the victim who has had a previous experience with rape has generally been found to be perceived more negatively than the victim who has not been raped previously. This finding was replicated by Schultz and Schneider (1991) who also found that social observers attribute more blame to the multiple-incident rape victim than to the first-incident victim.

In his review of studies on pre-attack behaviour, Pollard (1992) concludes that 'more fault is attributed to the victim if her behaviour is seen as increasing risk' (Pollard, 1992: 315). A number of factors have been found to increase negative victim perceptions on this dimension, including failure to take precautions by varying the route home (Pallak and Davies, 1982), being out late at night (Kanekar et al., 1985; Damrosch et al., 1987), degree of 'carelessness' (e.g. leaving the car unlocked to 'let' an assailant in) (Damrosch, 1985) and dressing 'sexily' (Cahoon and Edmonds, 1989; Edmonds and Cahoon, 1986). In general, the fewer precautions taken, the more 'careless' and the later the time when the rape took place (as assessed in dimensions specified by the researchers), the more likely it is that the victim will be negatively judged and that the attacker will be treated more leniently. Male subjects in particular tend to recommend less punishment for attackers of 'sexy' victims. Specific constructions of 'risk-taking' behaviour, e.g. victim intoxication, have been examined, with an intoxicated victim tending to be held more responsible than a sober victim (Richardson and Campbell, 1982). Significantly, Critchlow (1983, 1985) found that attributions to an intoxicated rape victim tend to be less favourable than those made about a comparably drunk attacker. They argue that inebriation seems to operate as a cultural excuse for a variety of serious crimes, including rape, with drunkenness appearing to be more acceptable for men as assailants than for women as victims.

Pollard (1992) notes that outside of the rape literature there is reasonable evidence of a general relationship between attribution of responsibility and perceived outcome probability, making it understandable that attribution of responsibility may be increased in situations that appear to increase the probability of victimisation. However, he further notes that arguing this position could only ever be socially acceptable if the attribution of behavioural responsibility does not have 'moral overtones' and if judgements about attacker responsibility and penalty are not affected, i.e. the victim's behaviour should not be seen as an *excuse* for rape (Pollard, 1992: 317). The evidence suggests that in the case of rape perception, however, the assignment of fault to the victim does tend to be related to a reduction in fault assignment to the attacker and a reduction in recommended sentence length. Male subjects in particular routinely ascribe more characterological and behavioual fault to female victims, especially when experimental manipulations encourage them to read the victim as potentially 'seductive' (Ward, 1995). However socially unacceptable in the abstract then, it would seem that female rape victims do get morally blamed. As we discussed in chapter 1, feminists would argue that this is because accounts for rape reproduce and preserve hegemonic, stereotypical understandings of gender relations and heterosexuality. In this context, behaviour deemed to be 'risky' or imprudent for women is also likely to be just the kind of behaviour that diverges from the feminine gender role norms of passivity and dependence. And, as Pollard, citing Brownmiller (1975), also concludes, to accept a special burden of self-protection, to be held responsible for one's own victimisation, is also to reinforce the concept that women must live in fear and cannot expect to achieve the personal freedom of men.

Although findings from the rape-perception literature give us a sense of the link between perceptions of risk-taking and explanations for rape, the treatment of hazard/risk in these studies as objectively definable doesn't however give us much of an insight into the social construction and defence of what counts as risky and associated attributions of cause and the negotiation of blame, fault and responsibility in social interaction, where social participants actively make sense of rape claims. We will argue that a detailed examination of this sense-making is crucial if we are to understand how victim-blaming arguments are routinely built and sustained in social life.

Operating within the social cognition paradigm then, rape-perception researchers have examined how social information about depicted rapes is processed, exploring the influence of transient situational factors on individual perceptions of cause, blame, fault and responsibility and judgements about punishment and retribution. Pollard (1992) notes that, in general, rape-perception studies actually report *fairly low* mean scores on scales measuring negative attributions to the victim, and typically attribute more responsibility to the rapist. Most rape-perception research findings are therefore reported in terms of the circumstances in which *the level of victim blame* is likely to be increased or decreased and often focus on *between subject* comparisons in this respect on dimensions such as gender, age or occupational status. It is perhaps not surprising then, and consistent with the tradition of liberal theorising in mainstream academic psychology, that most of the theory development in rape-perception work is concerned with explaining any observed extraneous factor effects in terms of *individual differences between observers*, assumed to emerge from differences in attitudes or other dispositional features (reviewed in the next section) as opposed to situating explanations for rape in cultural or societal conditions and processes. We shall return to the issue of low mean scores on dependent measures in rape-perception research at the conclusion of this chapter, to argue that rape-perception research thus risks misrepresenting the level and subtelty of victim-blaming in social interaction.

Motivational characteristics of observers: just-world theory and defensive attribution

The just-world theory (Lerner and Matthews, 1967) suggests that people have a motivational need to believe that the world is a fair and just place, that people get what they deserve and deserve what they get, and that we are motivated to believe in deserved outcomes to maintain a sense of control and efficacy over the environment. To believe that bad things happen to people without any apparent reason would make the world a chaotic place and subsequently would threaten our sense of control. Thus, people may blame victims because to believe that the victim's experience was undeserved would be to entertain the possibility that bad things occur without any rules or order and that the incident could happen to anybody – even the observer. Thus, to perceive a victim's ordeal as deserved helps to restore balance to a world generally perceived as ordered.

Some support for the just-world hypothesis has been found in judgements about rape where, for example, Kleinke and Meyer (1990) showed that men with a high belief in a just world were more punitive towards the victim of rape than men with a low belief in a just world. As discussed above, the just-world notion of exaggerated blame was also supported by Jones and Aronson (1973), where the most fault in their study was attributed to the victim described as a 'virgin'. However, although this research found that victim blame increased with more respectable victims (as predicted by the just-world framework), subsequent studies have failed to confirm this finding (Luginbuhl and Mullin, 1981; Paulsen, 1979; Kerr and Kurtz, 1977; Muller et al., 1994; Kristiansen and Giulietti, 1990). In general, and consistent with Burt and Estep's concept of the 'open territory victim' discussed in chapter 1, the findings have been in the opposite direction, where it tends to be the least, not the most, 'respectable' victims who are attributed more blame (Feldman-Summers and Lindner, 1976; Smith et al., 1976).

The just-world theory also predicts victim blame in some specific instances of victimisation. Walster (1966) suggests that as the observer's feelings of being vulnerable to the victim's situation increase, so will the blame attributed to that victim. Thus, victim–observer similarity will enhance victim blame as the control-maintenance mechanism swings into action. This theory predicts that female observers may blame female victims more than male observers. Although this finding has been supported in some studies (Jones and Aronson, 1973), in general, it has been found that in the majority of studies, female observers in fact make more pro-victim judgements than do male observers (Kleinke and Meyer, 1990).

The defensive-attribution hypothesis (Shaver, 1985) has also been employed to explain observed patterns in attributional reasoning about depicted rapes. This framework also suggests that victim-blaming occurs for self-protective reasons and predicts that victim blame will decrease as the similarity of the observer to the victim increases. This is conceptualised in this theory as a defence mechanism to protect the observer from being blamed themselves if a similar fate should befall him or her in the future. Thus, the hypothesis would predict that female observers would blame the rape victim less (on grounds of similarity as women), while male observers should blame female rape victims more. A large number of studies have supported the defensive-attribution hypothesis (Cann et al., 1979; Feild,

1978b; Kanekar and Vaz, 1988; Muller *et al.*, 1994), but negative attributions to female victims by female observers (and by male observers to male victims – Burt and DeMello, 2002) have also been reported. How can these findings be explained?

Perhaps the answer lies in the tendency of researchers to identify the broad category 'gender' (Gerber *et al.*, 2004; Rempala and Bernieri, 2005) as the most relevant dimension of perceived similarity between observers and depicted victims. Where observers are allowed some freedom to discuss an alleged rape and to express and justify their opinions about rape victims and perpetrators, findings show that female observers can and do make negative judgements about female victims – but in relation to much more *specific* dimensions of perceived similarity or difference, e.g. based on arguments about whether the rape was 'predictable' or not and thus whether the victim should be negatively compared to the observer, e.g. as a 'risk-taker' (Anderson, 1996). Thus if a female observer argues that a victim is 'not like me' on specific grounds, e.g. 'I wouldn't walk home alone at that time of night', and it is further argued that this behaviour is 'inappropriate', then it is possible to see how just-world beliefs *and* defensive attribution may be operating for some observers, to produce negative judgements about a victim along the lines of 'she's not like me and she got what she deserved'. As we will continue to argue, part of the problem with the tradition of lab-based paper-and-pencil research in the rape-perception paradigm is that it constrains the responses of participants far too much, making it impossible to see the complexities of sense-making about alleged rapes in social interaction in terms of both content and rhetoric, limiting our understanding of accounting practices for rape and the development of theory.

Attitudinal characteristics of observers: gender-role stereotyping and belief in rape myths

Within attitude theory, research has centred on two dimensions of attitudes related to rape perception – gender-role stereotyping and belief in rape myths. Gender-role stereotyping refers to those attitudes which are expressive of the endorsement of traditionally demarcated gender roles and gender stereotyped behaviours (Spence *et al.*, 1973; Feild, 1978a; Ong and Ward, 1999; Yamawaki and Tschanz, 2005). Usually, these are measured through questionnaires: high gender-role stereotyping would be measured by level of agreement with such statements as 'telling dirty jokes should be a masculine prerogative', 'it is acceptable for a woman to have a career but marriage and family should come first', 'it looks worse for a woman to be drunk than for a man to be drunk' and 'a man should fight when the woman he's with is insulted by another man'. Various subscales have been added, since the 1980s, to the gender-role stereotyping research, for example, sexual conservatism, adversarial sexual beliefs and acceptance of interpersonal violence (Burt, 1980). Sexual conservatism refers to restrictions on the appropriateness of sexual partners, sexual acts and circumstances under which sex should occur, for example: 'a woman who initiates a sexual encounter would probably have sex with anybody', 'men have a biologically stronger sexual drive than women' and 'I would have no respect for a woman who engages in sexual relationships without any emotional involvement'. Adversarial sexual beliefs refer to the expectation that sexual relationships are fundamentally exploitative, that each party to them is manipulative, sly, cheating, opaque to the other's understanding and not to be trusted, which would be represented by agreement with the following items: 'a woman will only respect a man who will lay down the law to her', 'women are usually sweet until they've caught a man, but then they let their true selves show' and 'men are out for only one thing'. And finally, acceptance of interpersonal violence refers to the belief that force and coercion are legitimate ways to gain compliance and that these are legitimate in intimate and sexual relationships. Such beliefs would be represented by agreement with such items as: 'being roughed up is sexually stimulating for many women', 'many times a woman will pretend she doesn't want to have intercourse because she doesn't want to seem loose, but she's really hoping a man will force her' and 'sometimes the only way a man can get a cold women turned on is to use force'.

In addition, gender-role stereotyping discussed above has been closely related to specifically rape-supportive attitudes such as 'rape myths'. Negative rape-victim perception has been shown to be predictably greater for those people who subscribe to 'rape myths', which were first defined by Burt (1980) as ' prejudicial, stereotyped or false beliefs about rape, rape victims and rapists', and which have since been defined further as 'attitudes and beliefs that are generally false but are widely and persistently held, and that serve to deny and justify male sexual aggression against women' (Frese et al., 2004; Lonsway and Fitzgerald, 1994; Mason et al., 2004). These myths include beliefs that 'women routinely lie about being raped', 'a women who says no really means yes', 'when women go round braless or wearing short skirts and tight tops, they are just asking for trouble', 'in the majority of rapes the victim is promiscuous or has a bad reputation' and 'if a girl engages in necking or petting and she lets things get out of hand, it is her own fault if her partner forces sex on her'.

Evidence suggests that the two observer attitude measures – the sex-role orientation of the observer and acceptance of rape myths – are positively correlated (e.g. Burt, 1980; Feild, 1978a; Jenkins and Dambrot, 1987; Saunders and Size, 1986). Similarly, Costin and Schwarz (1987) and Costin (1985) showed that acceptance of rape myths was significantly correlated with restrictive beliefs about women's social roles, a finding true of not only the United States but also England, Israel and West Germany. Other researchers have also found that traditional sex-role attitudes and rape myth acceptance are related (Check and Malamuth, 1983, 1985; Mayerson and Taylor, 1987; Schwarz and Brand, 1983).

Observer acceptance of adversarial beliefs about women's social roles and the extent to which observers hold acceptance with rape myths have been studied in conjunction with observer rape-victim perception. Studies have shown that subjects holding more traditional sex-role attitudes evaluate the rape victim in a specific case of rape more negatively than those who do not hold such adversarial beliefs (Acock and Ireland, 1983; Coller and Resick, 1987; Deitz et al., 1982; Mayerson and Taylor, 1987; Shotland and Goodstein, 1983). In addition, rape myth acceptance has also been found to have an impact on the attributions ascribed to a victim in a specific case scenario (Check and Malamuth, 1983; Krahé, 1988).

It is worth noting that both attitudinal and attributional studies have made a specific case of investigating the impact of the gender of the observer in their studies. It is now generally accepted in this literature that, overall, male observers tend to blame and attribute more responsibility to the rape victim than do females, and a large number of studies have reported this gender difference in relation to rape-victim evaluation (Calhoun et al., 1976; Cann et al., 1979; Brekke and Borgida, 1988; Deitz et al., 1984; Edmonds and Cahoon, 1986; Gerdes et al., 1988; Gilmartin-Zena, 1983; Johnson and Jackson, 1988; Johnson et al., 1989; Kanekar and Kolsawalla, 1977, 1980; Kanekar and Nazareth, 1988; Kleinke and Meyer, 1990; Luginbuhl and Mullin, 1981; Selby et al., 1977) and continue to do so (Anderson and Lyons, 2005; Davies and McCartney, 2003), although, as discussed above, there are exceptions to this general pattern (e.g. Acock and Ireland, 1983; Calhoun et al., 1981; Check and Malamuth, 1984; Feldman et al., 1998; Krahé, 1988). However, in general, there is strong evidence that female observers hold more pro-victim judgements while males tend to be more punitive towards rape victims. The effect of gender on rape-victim perception is thought to derive its impact from the different motivational (as discussed above) and attitudinal characteristics of men and women, e.g. females may be less accepting of rape myths than males (Costin, 1985; Giacopassi and Dull, 1986; Meulenhard and Linton, 1987; Ward, 1988), but there may be a number of other factors that exert a differential impact on female and male 'observers', e.g. empathy with the victim (Deitz et al., 1984; Deitz et al., 1982) or some other as yet unknown influence.

Some problems with attribution theory in rape-perception research

We noted at the start of this chapter that psychologists working within the social cognition tradition turned to attribution theory as a 'ready made' explanatory framework to examine rape perception. As feminist researchers, we embrace critical reflection to stress and explore the intricate interrelationship between empirical research, social experience and the researcher's engagement (or not) with social concerns (Wilkinson, 1988; Bhavnani, 1993; Harding, 1991; Parker, 1994). In this section we want to critically reflect on the disciplinary context of rape-perception research and in particular the theoretical grounding of knowledge production in rape-perception research in classic attribution theory.

As noted above, the enterprise of attribution theory derives its theoretical roots from Heider's suggestion that the layperson uses a procedure akin to Mill's experimental methods in analysing causality (Hilton, 1988). As such, the attributional process is conceived as essentially rational, logical and systematic. It is somewhat paradoxical for researchers to select a theory which documents and celebrates rationality, logic and 'naïve' experimentation to examine judgements that had already been described by feminist scholars as *biased* and *irrational* cognitive processes – those involved in blaming rape victims (Brewer, 1977; Anderson *et al.*, 2001). This anomaly is particularly well illustrated in Calhoun, Selby and Warring's 1976 study, which utilised principles from classic attribution theory to examine judgements about rape. Although the authors do not state directly that rape-victim blame is 'logical', this conclusion can be inferred from the theoretical foundations of their study.

Calhoun *et al.* postulated that individuals use the covariation principle (discussed above) to make attributions about the cause of an event, and to do this, they often seek information regarding the number of times the event has occurred and in how many different environments. Lay attributional reasoning is thus conceptualised as rigorous, 'rational' and 'systematic'. In their study, Calhoun *et al.* manipulated the covariation information of consistency over time and persons and examined their effects on attributional judgements about a victim of rape. Consistency over time was represented by information referring to whether the victim had been raped prior to the present incident, while consistency over persons, or 'typicalness', was presented to participants as a description of whether the victim's present rape was the only one in the area (atypical) or whether it was one of several (typical). These two pieces of information were systematically varied, and each participant read one of the variations of the covariation information embedded in a case history report giving personal details of the victim as well as a description of the rape incident on the night in question. After reading the case description, subjects rated the victim on the following scales: (a) 'degree to which the rape was caused by her personality traits'; (b) 'degree to which the rape was caused by her behaviour on the night of the rape'; (c) 'degree to which she was the kind of person who gets herself into such situations'; (d) 'degree to which the rape was her fault'; (e) 'degree to which the rape was due to the "bad luck" of the victim'.

Calhoun *et al.*'s findings revealed that for men in particular, the highest ratings to the victim's behaviour on the night as having 'caused' the rape and the highest attribution of 'fault' to the victim occurred when the raped individual was described as having been raped before and when there had been no other rapes in the area. It would be possible to conclude from these findings that men's explanations for rape are more often rooted in an easy acceptance of the victim-blaming assumptions in rape-supportive culture – and this conclusion would be consistent with the bulk of findings in the attitudes towards rape literature (e.g. see Ward, 1995). However, Calhoun *et al.* alternatively suggest that '*the men appear to adopt the interpretation of the rape episode more congruent with attribution theory*' (our italics; Calhoun *et al.*, 1976: 524). Given that attribution theory relies upon the principle that human reasoning is logical (i.e. rational and systematic), what Calhoun *et al.* seem to infer is that the *logical* conclusion given the information in the vignette is that the victim was to blame for the rape more than any other factor such as, for example, the rapist – and that men appear to come to this conclusion more easily than do women (i.e. are more 'logical' in these matters). The contention that victim-blaming can be a logical conclusion, a 'correct' judgement based on rational manipulation of 'the facts', implies that there is nothing inherently 'wrong' or inordinate about it, it is merely an artefact of systematic information-processing conducted by normal, rational thinkers. It is possible to see how conclusions such as this emerge from and are supported by the basic theoretical tenets of attribution theory, but they are deeply problematic terms of the more culturally and politically grounded feminist scholarship on rape discussed in chapter 1.

The other two tenets of attribution theory discussed above can be similarly problematised. The fact that attributional processes theorise the ascription of causality for events has an important bearing on rape-perception studies. Theorising rape judgements within a causal structure implies that at the outset of a rape allegation it is legitimate to place a question mark over who or what will be found to be the 'cause' of the incident. In attribution theory, all events are conceived as 'neutral' in terms of causal loci prior to attributional analysis – internal or external loci have an equal chance of being selected, *depending on the particular pieces of 'information' that the participants work with*. However, it is certainly not *politically* neutral to argue that a rape incident can, even should, theoretically, be seen to be 'neutral' in an attributional sense. In chapter 1, we drew attention to evidence that false claims of rape are extremely rare and to the many damaging consequences of invalidating a victim's testimony that they have experienced rape or, if it is accepted that rape did occur, suggesting that the victim is blameworthy. Furthermore, (as we discussed in chapter 1) many scholars have suggested that stereotypical constructions of gender and heterosexuality guide explanations for rape (Ussher, 1997; Gavey, 2005). Thus when cultural members engage in attributional analysis of a particular rape incident they are not reasoning with objective 'facts'; their sense-making is always already saturated with beliefs, preconceptions and ideologies about gender and sexual violence. The 'extraneous' factors deemed relevant will be constructed and debated according to societal norms and expectations about gender, sexuality and violence. The 'events are neutral prior to attributional analysis' assumption of attribution theory effectively implies that attributional reasoning about rape (or anything for that matter) takes place in a cultural vacuum – and that social participants are objective, dispassionate manipulators of social information (as discussed above). As such, this introduces a fundamentally flawed understating of the social processes involved in the generation, gathering and debating of knowledge considered by social participants to be relevant when making sense of rape. A related issue can be raised with respect to attribution theory's theoretical distinction between internal and external causes. To open up a rape judgement to the theoretically equal possibility of an internal or external outcome is to imply not only that the cause of the incident is up for debate, but also that the victim should be seen to have at least an equal chance of being selected as the cause – in other words that victims should routinely be treated as *just as likely* to be the cause of the rape as the rapist.

The widespread adoption of a 'people as information processors' metaphor amongst cognitivists is therefore problematic in that it promotes an overly mechanistic, simplistic view of human social life and discourages us from attempting to grasp how social participants are in the business of actively and publicly *constructing* a sense of reality, not just silently processing a world assumed to be objectively knowable (Antaki, 1994; Dryden, 1999). Bowers (1990) argues that the acceptance of the 'humans as information processors' metaphor can be traced back to the widespread acceptance of the criteria that Turing selected as important when deciding whether minds are similar to machines. Turing devised a game in which an interrogator sits in a room apart from two other people. This person has to figure out, by asking questions via a keyboard, which of the other two is a man and which is a woman. Turing proposed that when a computer was substituted for the man behind the screen, if the performance of the interrogator remained the same, it would make sense to conceptualise both computers and people as, essentially, information processors. In accepting the logic of this test, many psychologists construct their research activities within a version of human ontology that is detached, mentalistic and emotionally isolated. Consequently, the importance of culture, material embodiment and the physical, dynamic, interactive nature of natural forms of human communication are ignored, and the complexity and richness of language and the negotiation of meaning are reduced to a basic input–output, questions and answers style process.

Shotter (1993, 1995) similarly argues:

> There is something very special about the nature of conversational activity which has been overshadowed by cognitive psychology's central focus upon the possession by individuals of inner mental

representations . . . by attending to the actions of isolated individuals . . . we have left the genuinely social in the background
unexplored.

(Shotter, 1995: 49–52)

Shotter characterises conversational activity as a 'joint action' where the
speakers are accountable to the others involved in the conversation, but
also, importantly, to a strange ethical 'Otherness', a socially constructed
audience beyond the immediately present entities (referred to by Bakhtin as
a 'Superaddressee' and by Goffman as the 'moral order'). He adds, 'Something is going on here [in dialogue] that cannot be understood by being
separated out into autonomously behaving parts in interaction with each
other . . . [it] ought to make us question the adequacy of our current
analytic forms of description' (Shotter, 1995: 53).

In the psychology of rape perception then, the focus is on individuals and
the internal sphere at the expense of examining the operation of dynamic
social and cultural processes, social structural inequalities (oppression,
power differentials) and material circumstances. Sampson argues that
cognitivism encourages psychologists to 'present a portrait of humanity in
which mental events, mental activities, mental operations, mental organisation and mental transformation are of greater importance than events,
activities, operations organisation or transformations in the external world'
(Sampson, 1981: 733). He further argues that the individualistic study of
mental operations promotes an attitude towards intervention which locates
problems and the responsibility for finding solutions in *individuals* outside
of any appreciation of how we are all embedded in wider social and structural contexts, promoting a culture of self-criticism (Sampson, 1977). In the
area of rape prevention this is well illustrated by studies such Myers *et al.*
(1984). Myers *et al.* examine women's vulnerability to rape based on their
mental health records (e.g. drug-taking and psychiatric history) and their
cognitive processes which exhibit external as opposed to internal locus of
control (the hypothesis being that although 'external women want to avoid
the assault as much as internal women, their cognitive processes do not
provide alternatives to cope with the situation' (Myers *et al.*, 1984: 73)).
They also examine personality dimensions, where 'women who successfully
resisted rape were higher on Dominance, Social Presence, Sociability and
Communality scales' (ibid.). The overall hypothesis of the study was that
'rapists select women for their apparent vulnerability and then proceed to
the "testing stage" in which they determine if the potential victim can be
intimidated' (ibid.). It is a short step from studies such as these to therapies
which attempt to rectify the victim's apparent lack of certain desirable
personality traits or her inappropriate lifestyle (containing as it may
episodes of drinking and/or drug-taking), or indeed which attempt to
inculcate in the victim a different attributional style. The actions of the

perpetrator, or the cultural conditions that produce them, are simply omitted, severely limiting possibilities for intervention.

The appropriateness of the theoretical assumptions and implications of attribution theory for the examination of causal reasoning about rape seems to go largely unquestioned in rape-perception research. Yet we have argued that the cultural grounding (in discourses that construct gender and sexuality) and the political significance (in terms of maintaining patriarchy) of reasoning about rape are inevitably backgrounded when researchers adopt attribution theory to examine sense-making about sexual violence. Attribution theory's refusal to treat victim testimony as anything other than 'neutral' in the first instance is problematic for feminist scholars and activists who campaign for the rights of rape victims to be heard, for their testimony to be routinely treated as likely to be *valid*, and to receive sympathy and justice. In the next chapter we examine in more detail how the notion that rape claims are to be treated as neutral prior to analysis of the 'facts' is also fiercely contested in discourse theory, which draws attention to the dynamic social construction of events and identities and its interconnection with accounting practices for rape.

Conclusions

Inspired by feminist writings, psychologists have generated empirical data to test feminist theory. These data have in turn been cited by feminists as substantiating their claims and have been integrated into the knowledge base for the advancement of theory . . . developments in psychology have added fuel to the feminist fire.
(Ward, 1995: 6–8)

[F]eminism and social psychology should be viewed as sisters in the pursuit of knowledge and in the precipitation of social change.
(Ward, 1995: 192)

In her review of feminist and social psychological research on attitudes to rape, Ward (1995) celebrates the mutually beneficial relationship of feminist scholarship and the experimental social psychology of rape perception. However, in spite of this very genuine attempt to validate and build bridges between the different frameworks, throughout her book feminist work on rape tends to be positioned as 'preliminary' to the serious and more systematic business of experimental psychological research. If the rules defining scientific method are rigorously and skilfully applied, it is believed that then, and only then, will the validity of the knowledge produced be guaranteed. This view in large part reflects the way in which notions of 'scientific rigour' and 'scientific knowledge' enjoy a privileged status in general within modern culture (Sherif, 1987; Hollway, 1989), linked as they are to notions of 'progression', 'enlightenment' and technological advancement (Polking-horne, 1992; Richardson and Fowers, 1997). Many psychologists argue that the application of rigorous empirical methods should be considered a *precondition* for making interventions that have the potential to enhance 'human relationships, the world of work and the creation of prosperity' (Gale, 1997: 11). The implication is that we can only really know something *for sure* via objective science, which in turn subtly downgrades 'claims' and 'assertions' based in qualitative data.

This sentiment is captured well in the following extract from Ward's book, *Attitudes to Rape*:

> Whilst acknowledging the significance of feminist theory, most psychologists would argue that these theoretical speculations require more empirical grounding . . . (Social psychologists) have tentatively embraced feminist theory and chosen to investigate it *in more depth*.
>
> (Ward, 1995: 36–37; our italics)

Experimentation is thus evaluated as a powerful investigative tool – rigorous and robust – with the capacity to test hypothesised cause and effect relationships. Rape-perception research, it is argued, therefore allows us to 'confidently' conclude that characteristics of the victim, the perpetrator and the situation affect perceptions and attributions about rape and also to show variations in degree of negativity according to demographic and occupational categories. Pollard (1992) concurs with this view and concludes that studies in the attribution of responsibility paradigm offer particularly reliable results in two areas. First, if women engage in behaviour deemed risky they may be perceived to be at fault, especially by subjects holding traditional gender role or 'sexist' attitudes, and second, prior 'romantic' involvement mitigates the perceived seriousness of the attack and may even be seen as offering justification for the attack. These findings are indeed broadly consistent with feminist theory on the relationship between hegemonic constructions of gender and heterosexuality and explanations for rape, and certainly may be rhetorically useful in arguing the case for improving the treatment of rape victims. Griffin and Phoenix (1994) have noted that precisely *because* of their positivist orientation, some findings may be easier to disseminate to relevant groups where findings from qualitative studies may be of less obvious operational relevance to the targeted populations. However, as we have argued above, there are considerable shortcomings and limitations associated with the rape-perception paradigm, and in this chapter we have started to critically evaluate the extent to which the rape-perception paradigm – grounded, as it is, in objectivist epistemology, attribution theory and a commitment to experimental methods – can contribute to feminist scholarship on accounting for rape. Ward argues that psychologists tackle research on rape perception in more 'depth' than feminist scholars, where the notion of depth is used essentially to refer to the employment of experimental methodology within a framework of objectivist epistemology. However, we argue that far from adding 'depth', psychological theory and research on rape perception in this tradition has added only limited momentum to the feminist goal of elucidating the social processes involved in the legitimation of rape. This is because attribution theory decontextualises, individualises and simplifies the processes of sense-making and argumentation when social participants build and sustain victim-blaming positions in accounts for rape. In terms of research methods, paper-and-pencil exercises of the type used in attribution experiments can also be roundly criticised for their poor ecological validity, prohibiting the exploration of spontaneous, unconstrained responses to rape claims (e.g. Potter and Wetherell, 1987; Antaki, 1994), and employing highly artificial, at worst stereotypical, independent variable categories in their experimental manipulations – hazard/risk is treated as objectively definable, and victim and perpetrator identities are pre-categorised and fixed by researchers, making it impossible to see how the dynamic construction of events and actors may be tied into (not separate from) the pragmatic business of attributing cause, fault and responsibility (Edwards and Potter, 1992).

As Pollard (1992) points out, an interesting feature of the findings in rape-perception studies is the tendency towards overall low mean scores on dependent measures. On the surface of it, this could be taken as a reassuring sign that feminist claims of widespread negativity towards rape victims in a rape-supportive culture are exaggerated. However, the tendency towards low mean scores could equally be an artefact of the methodological techniques employed. It seems plausible that the methodological instruments used in rape-perception research are not sensitive enough to capture the rhetorical subtlety of social reasoning about rape. The paper-and-pencil tasks prohibit exploration of the skilled interactional business of arguing and explaining in interaction (Antaki, 1994), and a response bias due to social desirability factors (wanting to maintain a positive image as a generally sympathetic observer) is also likely to be at work – though a detailed examination of the way in which participants do 'facework' (Goffman, 1967; Brown and Levinson, 1987) isn't possible with this methodology. The rape-perception paradigm thus risks underestimating the extent of rape-supportive reasoning and failing to analyse its forms.

Overall, our contention is that there is a lack of fit between the precepts and assumptions of liberal, psychological attribution theory and methods (human individuals are naïve scientists, processing the available information about alleged rape incidents logically and rationally in order to make attribution judgements) and the research programme suggested by early feminist scholarship on the social definition of rape – where the significance of the social construction of meaning in cultural and political context is highlighted. Our contention is that classic feminist scholarship on rape points in the direction of research based in critical applications of social constructionist discourse theory (rather than objectivist experimentation), which does have the potential to offer insight into the cultural construction and legitimation of sexual violence. It is interesting that discourse theory and research doesn't feature in Ward's 1995 review of research on attitudes toward rape; indeed feminist scholarship is aligned with ethnographic (observations, interviews, documents) action research and content analysis methodologies only. In the next chapter we build a case for the application of discourse theory and research in the study of accounting practices for rape, first by offering a detailed feminist critique of the scientific methods used in rape-perception research and, second, by discussing the approach to discourse theory and analysis which we utilise in the empirical chapters that follow.

Note

1. One difficulty with covariational relations between cause and effect is that these can sometimes produce spurious causes (for example, falsely concluding that a drop in a barometric reading causes a storm), although of course covariational relations do produce genuine causes as well (for example, that between touching a red-hot poker and burning one's hand), and several models have been proposed to show exactly how people judge covariational relations correctly. Specifically, they do so by using a variety of techniques, which guard against the possibility of deriving spurious causes. For example, work is continuing on the possibility that there may exist innate or acquired constraints governing which factors are likely to be considered causes so that covariation is evaluated only for factors that are psychologically prior to the target event (Cheng and Novick, 1991, 1992). Another model adopts the criterion of conditional independence, computing covariation between causes and the effect over a focal set – a set of events implied by a particular context (Cheng and Novick, 1990, 1991, 1992). All of these approaches have been found to be good predictors of rational and logical causal induction in humans. It is thus assumed in the present study that people are able to apply covariational rules correctly to derive covariational causality, although it is of course not known which particular type of mechanism they are using.

3

TOWARDS A FEMINIST DISCOURSE ANALYSIS OF ACCOUNTS FOR RAPE

Introduction

In our critical evaluation of the rape-perception paradigm in chapter 2, we argued that although positivist research within this tradition offers some support to the feminist concept of 'rape-supportive culture', it is ultimately limited in its ability to provide useful knowledge about the social production and legitimation of rape. We outlined problems with the disciplinary grounding of rape-perception research in the objectivist, liberal assumptions of classic attribution theory and its commitment to experimental methods. We argued that rape-perception research decontextualises, individualises and drastically oversimplifies the processes of sense-making and argumentation when social participants build and sustain victim-blaming positions in accounts for rape. In terms of research methods, we noted that paper-and-pencil exercises of the type used in attribution experiments prohibit the exploration of spontaneous, unconstrained responses, fix victim and perpetrator identities and treat hazard/risk is if it is objectively definable – making it impossible to see how the dynamic construction of events and actors may be tied into (not separate from) the pragmatic business of attributing cause, fault and responsibility (Edwards and Potter, 1992). Overall, we argued that the methods employed in rape-perception research might not be sensitive enough to capture the rhetorical subtlety of social reasoning about rape and thus are at risk of underestimating the extent of rape-supportive reasoning in rape-supportive cultures and of failing to analyse its forms. In this chapter we continue to develop our critique of the rape-perception paradigm and outline an alternative feminist standpoint, discourse analytic approach to accounting practices for rape.

In chapter 2, we introduced the concept of feminist reflexivity, noting that for feminist standpoint researchers (Harding, 1991), it is important to critically reflect on the practice and process of research and the disciplinary context in which a research programme is conducted (Wilkinson, 1988). As Sue Wilkinson's seminal paper on reflexivity outlines, in practice, this can involve analysis of the experience of researchers and participants throughout the research process, the theoretical, methodological and ideological foundations of knowledge production and the relationships between these factors. Critical reflection on the contexts and practices of knowledge production has been embraced by feminist scholarship to stress the intricate interrelationship between empirical research, social experience and the researcher's engagement (or not) with social concerns (Bhavnani, 1993; Harding, 1991; Parker, 1994) and to contextualise and problematise positivist truth claims. For reflexive researchers, there is no issue about whether epistemological and political values, commitments and biases impact on research activity, only over the extent to which they are acknowledged or made a focus of the research (Reicher, 1994; Crotty, 1998). Critical reflection on the production of knowledge is not commonly practised in positivistic psychologies (such as the rape-perception paradigm) where objectivity is the goal and where the validity or 'truth' status of knowledge is evaluated only in terms of adherence to particular institutionally sanctioned research procedures and statistical techniques, explicitly designed to remove researcher subjectivity from the research process (Sherif, 1987; Riger, 1992; Doherty and Malson, 1996; Willig, 2001).

In our critical evaluation of classic attribution theory as a theoretical resource for research on accounting for rape in chapter 2, we argued that rape-perception researchers have not been sufficiently reflexive in considering how reasoning about rape is located within a patriarchal society and how the basic tenets of classic attribution theory might reproduce, rather than challenge, the values and practices of patriarchy. In this chapter we continue our interrogation of the rape-perception paradigm by focusing in more detail on issues of research method and design and on the experience of research participants completing tasks in rape-perception experiments. In the first section we discuss a number of research practices, condoned within the traditional rape research programme, which feminist researchers are likely to find problematic. We argue that research participants in many of these studies are required to complete tasks that uncritically reproduce patriarchal assumptions about gender, sexuality and the causes of sexual violence. We argue that the completion of such tasks may be puzzling and potentially troubling for research participants (particularly for women) and could thus be seen to be ethically suspect and disempowering (Anderson and Ahmed, 2003). In the second section, we draw on discourse theory to discuss in more detail the problems with vignette methods as practised in rape-perception research for exploring accounting practices for rape. In the final section of the chapter, we are then in a position to move forward and outline the data collection and analysis methods employed in our own feminist discourse analysis of accounts for rape. Consistent with our commitment to feminist reflexivity, we attempt throughout to offer a critical commentary on our own research practice.

The experience of research participants in rape-perception research

Dependent measures focus on the victim

The number of dependent variables used to measure a participant's judge-ments of the victim and perpetrator can vary considerably in rape-perception studies. For example, in a study by Cann *et al.* (1979) six dependent variables were used to judge the rape victim, but only two to judge the perpetrator. The content of the dependent measures utilised in rape-perception studies also varies substantially between the victim and perpetrator. In Cann *et al.*, the victim was judged on such aspects as her 'behaviour on the night', 'type of person' that she is, her 'suggestive behaviour prior to the assault', 'her unconscious desire to be raped', her 'fault' and 'how believable her testimony is'. With respect to the perpe-trator, however, the participants were only asked to evaluate the degree to which he was at 'fault' and the length his sentence should be. In a study by Damrosch (1985), participants were asked to evaluate *only the victim* from 0 to 9 on a series of bipolar adjective scales similar to the ones described above: 'the extent of the victim's predisposition to get into situations like rape', 'victim's unconscious desire to be raped', 'subject's liking for the victim', 'victim's responsibility for the rape', 'likelihood that the same thing could happen to the subject', 'victim's need for therapy' and 'victim's carelessness'.

Participants in rape-perception studies such as these are therefore typically required to respond to the rape incident depicted by scrutinising and evaluating the behaviour of *the victim* and not the perpetrator. Thus, although many rape-perception studies undoubtedly reflect the researchers' genuine orientation to knowledge generation about rape (e.g. the aim in Damrosch (1985) was to examine nursing students' reactions to rape vic-tims because of the importance of health-care professionals' attitudes in influencing the physical and psychological care administered to rape victims), they nevertheless uncritically reflect back to the participants a pattern of reasoning about rape that is informed by patriarchal values: that women by and large play a contributory role in their own rape, that it is entirely appropriate to raise questions about the culpability and credibility of rape victims and that the legitimate focus for any investigation into the causality of rape is the character and behaviour of the *victim*, not the perpetrator. This may be puzzling to participants given that, for instance in this example, the vignette clearly depicts the assailant as agentic – he used a knife to drive the victim to a deserted spot where the assault took place, after which the rapist stranded the victim by driving away in her car. Studies employing dependent measures that focus on the victim and not the perpetrator, in a similar process to a legalistic one, therefore encourage the research participants to search for 'proxies for sluttishness' in the victim's character and behaviour (Childs and Ellison, 2000). As discussed in chapter

1, this may include dredging up the possibility of previous abortions, drug-taking history, mental health problems etc., where submission of such factors is deliberately intended to undermine the credibility of the victim, thereby undermining the veracity of a rape claim. Many rape-perception studies do not allow the participants to engage in an equal scrutiny of the perpetrator's character, motives and responsibility – should they wish to, and if they do wish to, it may be troubling to be prevented from doing so – nor do they legitimate this as an activity.

These issues can be further illustrated in another example. Shotland and Goodstein (1983) examined perceptions of the extent to which a rape may be perceived as a genuine function of the onset of resistance from the victim (early vs. medium vs. late), type of protest (verbal vs. verbal and physical) and degree of violence from the assailant (low force vs. moderate force). However, despite an extremely detailed description of the incident provided for participants where both the assailant and the victim play out a highly interactional dating situation, participants were only really asked to evaluate the victim and not the perpetrator. The dependent measures evaluating the victim comprised four items measuring her fault/responsibility for the rape (e.g. 'Diane is more responsible than Lee for the fact that intercourse occurred'), four items measuring her Desire for Sex scale (e.g. 'Diane wanted to have sexual intercourse with Lee'), while the perpetrator's possible motives and accountability were obliquely measured in only two items designed to test the participant's perception of the event as an act of normative sexual intercourse or as an act of aggression on the sexual body ('Lee behaved violently towards Diane') and ('Lee raped Diane'). Studies that use an equitable number of dependent measures to assess victim and participant blame include Anderson and Lyons (2005), which used two measures, one to assess victim blame and the other, worded identically, to assess perpetrator blame. Another variant for future studies to utilise when constructing an equitable experimental environment for their participants is to use free format, to ask participants to write, in their own words, about issues such as extraneous factors or blame issues in rape (Anderson, 2007).

Reasoning about 'rape' or 'alleged rape'

As discussed in chapter 2, rape-perception researchers claim that 'As a basic theoretical orientation, investigators in this area share the view that responsibility attributions can be conceived of as the end product of a judgmental process that is influenced to a significant extent by factors beyond the specific incident in question' (Krahé, 1991). The implication here therefore is that rape-perception researchers are actively engaged in an exploration of the factors that contribute to decisions about whether an alleged victim of rape can be categorised as a legitimate rape victim role claimant (i.e. the victim was raped and should not be held accountable) or not. We have already noted in chapter 1 that feminist scholars highlight the significance of the social definition of rape for the experience of rape victims who making public their victimisation, focusing on the way that stereotypical assumptions about gender and sexuality inform claims and counter-claims about the legitimacy of rape victimhood. A key observation in this writing therefore is that from the moment that a rape survivor makes a public declaration that s/he was raped, the truth status of that claim is likely to be treated as provisional, as an 'allegation' and will be scrutinised and debated. It is therefore crucial that that rape-perception researchers, if they are to analyse the social processes leading to an end product judgement of whether an individual will be granted legitimate rape victim status or not, refer to the incident in rape vignettes as an 'alleged rape'; only then can the task be seen to in any sense reflect the social process of dispute following the public declaration of rape.

In rape-perception studies there is in fact an inconsistency in the depiction of the incidents in rape vignettes as either an 'alleged rape' or 'rape'. We suggest that this inadequate attention to detail in the construction of rape vignettes and tasks may introduce another problematic implication about accountability for rape, leaving participants struggling to scrutinise and evaluate the victim's character and behaviour in cases where the incident is described as a 'rape'. For example, 'One night, while crossing the campus on her way from the library, she was accosted and raped' (Calhoun *et al.*, 1976). This implies that an end judgement has at least partly been reached *already*, that a rape has been committed and that the perpetrator is at fault. Participants are then typically asked to make a range of judgements (based on other information provided in the vignette) about the victim's responsibility for the attack (e.g. the degree to which the rape was caused by her behaviour or appearance on the night). Participants asked to make judgements about the blameworthiness and responsibility on the part of the victim for events described as 'rape' are essentially being invited to redistribute some of the blame away from the perpetrator back towards the victim (and, as discussed above, the dependent measures typically focus on the victim and not the perpetrator). Rape-perception research methods can therefore be argued to simply reproduce patriarchal assumptions that allegations of rape *are* problematic and continue to be problematic in spite of a judgement that the victim role claimant was indeed a victim of 'rape', a violent crime. On the one hand then, this experimental manipulation (requiring participants to scrutinise the victim in cases of 'rape') could be said to merely reflect society's tendency towards illogical and irrational victim-blaming – offering the potential to explore the contexts in which victim-blaming may increase or decrease in relation to this scenario. However, we started to interrogate this claim in chapter 2 from the perspective of discourse theory, and will continue to critically evaluate the extent to which the vignette method can offer insight into the rhetorical subtlety of social reasoning about rape in the second half of this chapter. The point we wish to make here is that for the research participants, the authority of the experimenter to establish the task as appropriate and ethical implies that it is right and proper to consider the accountability of rape victims and that they *should* perhaps be held responsible for regulating their own behaviour in actions such as rape. Little or no sensitivity is displayed towards participants' reactions and emotions when they are to be confronted with the task of being asked to 'blame' an apparently genuine victim. The participants may experience these tasks as disempowering because in a research study such as this, they are confronted *prima facie* with societal patriarchal assumptions that rape claims *are* problematic and will be treated as such in spite of claims to the contrary (i.e. by a woman, or even by a researcher who says she was raped). The possibility of challenging this view and of exploring arguments that challenge the patriarchal 'common sense' position is effectively denied to participants in these studies.

Measuring gender differences in sexual response to depictions of rape

There are a number of studies in the rape-perception literature that display a distinct lack of engagement with feminist theorising on the topic of sexual violence (Anderson and Doherty, 1997). We focus here on the questionable value of measuring gender differences in the degree of sexual arousal to rape depictions (e.g. Malamuth and Check, 1980a, 1980b) and more generally on the unreflexive presentation of sexualised versions of sexual assault. Check and Malamuth (1983) used three scenarios to measure high or low sex role stereotyped participants' reactions to 'sexual depictions' (Check and Malamuth, 1983: 344) – mutually consenting intercourse, stranger rape and acquaintance rape. The hypothesis was that individuals with more stereotyped sex role beliefs would show greater sexual arousal to rape if they perceived a rape victim as acting more favourably to the assault and (for men) report a greater likelihood of raping than low sex role stereotyped subjects.

The measurement of sexual arousal to rape depictions and the attempt to identify variables that differentiate among the general population on this measure is justified in the study thus:

> Recent research . . . suggested that rapists may be differentiated from nonrapists on the basis of sexual arousal measures. Specifically, rapists showed about equal levels of sexual arousal to both rape and consenting intercourse depictions, whereas nonrapists showed lower (inhibited) levels of arousal to rape relative to consenting-intercourse depictions . . . It is noteworthy that although researchers found overall differences in arousal to rape stimuli for rapists as compared to nonrapists, it has also been

52

observed in these studies that many normals do respond considerably to deviant film material involving rape. These experiments
have not, however, identified variables that distinguish among
individuals from the general population who do or do not become
sexually aroused by rape depictions.

(Check and Malamuth, 1983: 345–346)

Leaving the interesting turn of phrase aside for a moment, whereby non-
arousal to rape is considered to be an 'inhibited' response, no theoretical
reason is given here for why subject gender should be analysed as an
individual difference variable and thus *women's* sexual arousal measured in
response to images depicting sexual violence perpetrated against women, or
to images that are see-able as degrading women – no reason, that is, apart
from the possibility of being a member of the general category 'normals'
(i.e. non-rapists) (which may well be one of the very few times that women
have been described as such in the psychological literature – see Ussher,
1989; Wilkinson, 1997). In other words, as the authors themselves point
out, participant gender is explored as an individual differences variable
because it is something that *might* differentiate participants from one
another and which may (or may not) have an impact on the dependent
variable (in this case, sexual arousal, among others). In the absence of any
theorisation for its inclusion, it is clear that the authors are reacting to the
visibility of the gender variable (people are clearly demarcated in society
into male and female), 'shooting in the dark', by inputting this variable into
the equation to 'see what happens', rather than providing any sound
rationale for its inclusion. However, in seeking to measure women's sexual
arousal to depictions of rape, and in offering no rationale for this practice,
rape-perception researchers could also be accused of unreflexively buying
into and ultimately reproducing a commonly articulated argument in rape-
supportive discourse – that women may well secretly enjoy forced sexual
intercourse (Brownmiller, 1975).

In research tasks such as this, it is clear that the requirements of positivist
research design are being prioritised over the experience of research participants. We wish to make two points here. Firstly, in Check and
Malamuth's study, female participants are subjected to images of sexual
violence perpetrated against women, and required to consider their level of
sexual arousal, partly because of the requirements within positivist research
for the *counterbalancing of dependent and independent variables*. What we
mean by this here is that positivist research designs typically require
researchers to attend to the possible confounds in the study, one of which
may be a differential number of items used as dependent variables in two
conditions (which, given this requirement, make certain research designs
that we report here such as using nine dependent variables to measure
attributional reasoning about a rape victim but only two dependent

variables to assess attributional reasoning about the perpetrator, all the more surprising). It is possible that women's sexual arousal to images was measured in the study referred to above because researchers decided that they needed a category of 'women' in their design, to counterbalance the category of 'men', to counteract a possible accusation of a confound in the study of attempting to generalise from male-only data.

Second, there are serious problems related to the ecological validity of this kind of task, particularly the extent to which it can actually measure likely responses to an embodied *rape* scenario. Bronfenbrenner (1979) argues that social psychology research is too often conducted within artificial situations – far removed from the contexts and conventions of everyday communication. 'Subjects' are studied in isolation, stripped of their social roles and required to complete unfamiliar, meaningless tasks. Consider the following extract, where the authors point out certain shared features of three stories (all the stories require the participant to visualise the event from the perspective of the male actor; in both rape depictions the victim is female):

> First, in all three depictions, the woman was wearing the same ('enticing') clothing. . . . Second, both rape stories were identical in terms of the number of references to the woman's pain (e.g., 'She cries out in pain'). The rape depictions were also similar with respect to the man's overt sexual and aggressive actions during the actual rape (e.g., 'You are getting on top of her . . . You give her a hard slap and tell her to be quiet . . .).
>
> (Bronfenbrenner, 1979: 348)

The first point to note is the clear confound in the study. By including the description that the woman was wearing 'enticing' clothing (why was this included? It is difficult to see how the depictions would have suffered in the omission of this information), the authors are in danger of measuring participants' beliefs in a number of rape myths (women provoke rape, women are responsible for male sexual arousal, rape = sex), confounding the belief in the sex role stereotypes variable that they were hoping to measure. Second, the language used in the rape depictions is reminiscent of a pornographic story rather than a rape depiction. The authors position the research participant in the role of the rapist/lover protagonist in the vignettes, and this unhelpfully blurs the distinction between measuring sexual response to the experience of sexual fantasy, where an individual experiences a sense of control in relation to the scenario described (which in this example may or may not be subjectively arousing) and the embodied experience of rape, which, by definition involves the removal of consent, aggression and disempowerment. Feeling arousal in relation to one of these hypothetical scenarios is therefore not the same as feeling aroused by raping or being raped. As a result, the experience of being a research participant in this kind of study is more than likely to be confusing at best and troubling at worst. Within the 'rigours' of positivist research it would seem that there is no space to critically reflect on the theoretical implications of experimental tasks or on the possible impact of experiencing these tasks for participants. More recently, Bohner's (2001, 515) excerpt from the abstract states that, in his study, 'The hypothesis that the passive voice is used to put the actor in the background and the acted-upon person in the focus of discourse is tested in the realm of sexual violence. German university students (N = 67) watched a silent video segment depicting a rape whose circumstances, depending on condition, could or could not be easily interpreted in terms of rape myths'. We wonder what effects this type of research would have had on the research participants in this otherwise clearly engaging study.

The disempowering experience of participation in rape-perception research

In general, we argue that many of these problems occur because rape-perception researchers don't adequately reflect on the experience of research participants in terms of their location in a culture structured by gender power relations, in which rape claims are already trivialised and routinely disputed. In this context, participation in a rape-perception study is likely to be experienced as simply 'more of the same', leaving participants (particularly women) feeling disempowered, with no space to challenge or transform the standard victim-blaming views that they are effectively invited to reproduce. Problematic, unreflexive research practices are however sanctioned under the auspices of the search for objective truth and the personal and political implications of engaging in such research are disregarded.

Problems with the vignette method in rape-perception research

In large degree, the sciences have been enchanted by the myth that the assiduous application of rigorous method will yield sound fact – as if empirical methodology were some form of meat grinder from which truth could be turned out like so many sausages.

(Gergen, 1985: 273)

A literature proclaiming a 'crisis' in the discipline of social psychology gathered pace during the 1970s, expressing serious doubts about the values underlying psychological research, its methods and the relevance of the discipline to understanding social behaviour in real-world settings. One of the key issues was the widespread use of laboratory experiments and paper-and-pencil tests to collect human data. Allport, writing in the late

1960s, claimed that psychology was impoverished because of its obsession with experimental technique and with the production of 'snippets of empiricism' at the expense of theory and an awareness of the historical location of the discipline (Cherry, 1995). In chapter 2 we argued that in shackling itself to classic attribution theory, research on the social perception of rape placed an essentially decontextualised, individualised process of 'rational' information-processing at the heart of its enquiry. Rape-perception research can be further problematised for allowing the analysis of accounting practices for rape to become dictated by the tyrannies of experimental method and technique, methods unlikely to be able to offer much insight into the ways in which explanations for rape are built and defended in social interaction. In this section we expand on our critical discussion of the vignette method in rape-perception research which we embarked on in chapter 2. Our discussion revolves around two related issues, the presentation of the event to be explained and the restriction of response from participants in the studies.

As described in chapter 2, in rape-perception studies, a participant's task is to make a range of attribution judgements about a ready-frame event depicted in a vignette. We argue here that this is problematic because the static, objective presentation of the incident to be explained ignores the significance of the dynamic social construction of events, self and others in social life (including what people may or may not count as an offence in the first place) and sets up an unhelpful separation between the activities of event description and explanation (Edwards and Potter, 1992; Potter *et al.*, 1993). Social constructionists reject objectivist understandings of the relationship between reality and representation emphasising that meaning is not intrinsic to things in the world; there can be no meaning without *interpretation*: 'The world and objects in the world may be pregnant with potential meaning but actual meaning emerges only when consciousness engages with them' (Merleau-Ponty, cited in Crotty, 1998: 43). The metaphor of construction highlights notions of assembly and manufacture, emphasising that any description of events, activities or people could always have been otherwise (Edwards, 1997). In Potter's words:

> The world is not ready categorised by God or Nature in ways that we are all forced to accept. It is constituted, brought into being, in one way or another as people talk it, write it, argue it.
>
> (Potter, 1996: 98)

Social constructionists therefore emphasise that 'The terms in which the world is understood are social artefacts, products of historically situated exchanges between people' (Gergen, 1985: 267) and focus our attention on the critical significance that such forms of negotiated understanding have for social life (Billig, 1987). However, this vision of social life effectively disappears in rape-perception research, where the 'relevant things about this incident', including descriptions of the identities and characteristics of the actors, their behaviour and the nature of the event are provided by the researcher in advance, as if these matters were objectively definable and beyond dispute. In other words, the vignette is intended to stand as a simple reflection of what happened – the event to be explained – and the theoretical assumption underpinning its presentation is that the description straightforwardly depicts the event in neutral, universally meaningful terms. Furthermore, discourse theorists emphasise that separating the event description from the explanation in rape-perception studies does not reflect the skilful and dynamic way that accounting is done in social interaction. When people are discussing and accounting, the construction and evaluation of an event as problematic (or not) is not separate from the social activities of, for example, expressing an attitude, expressing an opinion or offering an explanation. Rather, accountability (including the speaker's accountability) is handled *via* event construction where certain versions of reality may be promoted over others in the context of communicative activity (Edwards and Potter, 1992). For example, rape-perception researchers utilise identity categories to describe the social actors in a vignette (e.g. in an attempt to manipulate a variable such as 'victim respectability'). However, rather than simply displaying a person's abstracted understanding of the world 'as it is', discourse theorists argue that categorisation can be usefully understood as a social practice (Condor, 1988; Edwards, 1991). 'Categorisation is something that we do, in talk, in order to accomplish social actions (persuasion, blamings, denials, refutations, accusations etc.)' (Edwards, 1991: 517). Identity categories in vignettes then can't be conceptualised as neutral descriptors that, in theory, accurately depict the 'kind of person' an actor in a vignette actually *is*, as if this were a matter of straightforward objective description, beyond dispute. The category selection already performs explanatory work (Condor, 1988; Edwards, 1991). In Luginbhul and Mulin's study, for example, the subjects were presented with depictions of an alleged rape perpetrated on a 'nun' as opposed to a 'topless dancer'. These descriptions aren't neutral, they already do some accounting and evaluation work by invoking cultural stereotypes and norms of femininity and sexuality. The point is that by providing the categorisations in advance in the body of the vignette, and then offering no opportunity to dispute the categories selected, rape-perception research makes it impossible to see how in social interaction participants may or may not spontaneously invoke an identity category in the course of their sense-making activities, their understanding of the category selected (the implications and connotations it carries; see Wowk, 1984), whether the particular labels selected by researchers are viewed as relevant or not in a discussion of an alleged rape incident and indeed how category selections made by participants might be implicated in social action. Edwards and Potter also point out that in talk-in-interaction the activities of world-making (versions of what the world is like and the events that happen in it) and self-making (versions of identity, for self and others) are intricately intermeshed (Edwards and Potter, 1992):

> Speakers need to develop an account of the circumstances, in the form of event descriptions, such that specific psychological attributions will be sensible and warranted . . . it is necessary to build a convincing description of the context of the action. Put simply, to build a version of mind, one has to build a version of world.
>
> (Edwards and Potter, 1992: 142)

The significance of this insight in relation to accounting for rape will become evident in the next chapter, where we examine accounts for female rape. As we shall see, participants jointly construct versions of context, both local circumstances and cultural context, in which it appears 'reasonable' to attribute negative traits to the alleged victim, undermining her credibility particularly in relation to alleged carelessness, naïvety or risk-taking. Overall then, experimental research artificially restricts social performance and makes the variability in social performance – an important feature of open-ended conversation that is intimately connected to talk's action orientation – invisible (Lalljee *et al.*, 1984; Potter and Wetherell, 1987; Potter and Wetherell, 1988). Potential responses are constrained into just a few options, pre-selected by the researcher. This means that:

> The possibility of a respondent giving contrasting views on a topic [expressing] ambivalence, flexible opinions . . . and inconsistent responses [is] ruled out by the response format.
>
> (Potter and Wetherell, 1987: 40)

We argued in chapter 2 that rape-perception research grounded in classic attribution theory is problematic because of the over-simplified model of language, the decontextualised model of personhood at its heart and the backgrounding of social critique, particularly feminist analysis on social regulation and the legitimation of rape. This impoverished view of language and social interaction spills over into the methodological practice of measuring quantitative responses to vignettes, on dimensions selected and defined by the researcher. Participants are not permitted to dispute or discuss the elements of a rape scenario, nor can they set the agenda for discussion. This means that we can't see how, in interaction, explanations may be forwarded by social actors and perhaps supported or refuted in hedged or even contradictory terms, as potentially unsympathetic or victim-blaming arguments are built and speakers attend to their 'public face' (Goffman, 1967).

Towards textual analysis

The explanatory locus of human action shifts from the interior
region of mind to the processes and structure of human interaction.

(Gergen, 1985: 271)

We have so far seen how social constructionists problematise objectivist
psychology for misleading us about the appropriate location for the study
of psychological phenomena, placing cognitions and emotions 'inside'
individual heads rather than 'outside', *between* people, in social interaction
(Parker, 1997). Essentially, the turn to the text in psychology has been an
attempt to resist this 'inside-out' approach by tracing mental categories
(constructions of identity, cognitions and emotions), event description and
subjective experience to networks of social relations and discourse (Burman
and Parker, 1993; Parker, 1997). In social constructionist psychologies, an
alternative epistemology and ontology of psychological phenomena is on
offer (Edwards and Potter, 1992; Crotty, 1996) which emphasises that the
social world is constituted in text, consisting of discursive action located in
conversations and forms of negotiated meaning (Van Langenhove, 1995).
In working with an individualistic model of personhood, psychology has
treated people and mental processes as if they could in principle be
separated from culture and history (Kvale, 1992a, 1992b). The turn towards
analysis of text and talk therefore attempts to remedy the dualist separation
of the individual and the social in traditional psychology, promising a form
of analysis that can better comment on the intersection between cultural
sense-making resources, social activity and subjectivity. This involves a
radical refocusing of research activity – the measurement and description
of mental processes is rejected in favour of the study of 'discursive
practices'. Text is treated as the phenomenon of interest in its own right,
where the action is, rather than something to be 'read through' in the
assumption that it represents a truth about the psychological characteristics
of the speaker or their material situation, that is somehow beyond textual
representation.

Data collection analytic methodology

In the final section of this chapter we describe the data collection and
analysis methods utilised for our feminist discourse analysis of accounts for
rape in the two empirical chapters that follow.

Participants

Men and women, in dyads, were asked to discuss incidents of female or
male rape. Thirty male/female dyads discussed the female rape incident and

thirty male/female dyads discussed the male rape incident. Given that this research intended to ask people to talk about rape, a sensitive topic for most people, it was decided to invite participants who already knew each other, rather than strangers, who would thus feel comfortable in each other's company while discussing this issue. Women and men walking together on the street outside the Psychology departments at Sheffield and Birmingham universities were approached and asked to participate in research concerning opinions on rape (approximately 70% of the participants were students with ages ranging between 18 and 45; the mean age was 21.5 years). The participants were involved in various forms of relationship with each other; most frequently, they were dating couples, and friends and acquaintances. No other instructions were issued at this stage. Full anonymity was guaranteed and the participants were informed that they were free to leave at their discretion.

The research task

The participants were shown to a room with a tape recorder set up and ready for use. They were asked to read a description of an incident (see below) and then discuss it, reaching a 'conclusion' if possible (the exact nature of the conclusion was not specified). This instruction was designed to limit the discussions to a reasonable length. (Some pilot testing of the incident found that one dyad had a very wide-ranging discussion for over two hours. This particular conversation was not used in the final research project because its length was so different to the other conversations.) The final dataset consisted of conversations lasting on average 15 minutes and conducted without the researcher's presence.

It may appear paradoxical that we chose to ask participants to read a vignette, given the criticisms of the vignette method that we outline above and in the preceding chapter. However, the type of research presented here is very different to the vignette studies that we have reviewed. This vignette reproduces, much more closely than the experimental vignette studies, a realistic situation whereby somebody might read about an incident of sexual violence in the media and then discuss it. To record these types of discussions unobtrusively would contravene ethical guidelines. As such, our task mirrors the 'real life' situation of talk about rape much more closely than the paper-and-pencil tasks typically given to participants in rape-perception studies. The collection of open-ended conversations also avoids the problems of response restriction in experimental research that we discussed above. In addition, the incident provides the participants with a starting point, a focus or 'springboard' for their conversations in the form of a description of an incident presented in the form of a newspaper report of an alleged rape – a practical solution to generating a number of conversations on the topic of rape. The practice of providing a catalyst to generate conversation on a focused topic is now fairly common in social research and is typical of the 'focus group' method. Focus groups have proved to be a popular qualitative method, used to investigate sense-making on sensitive issues or subjects about which little is known. This method has been used widely in the arena of sexuality and sexual violence, for example in the study of sexual refusals among adolescents and sexual risk-taking (Frith, 1999). The method allows participants to discuss issues in their own language, to raise new issues not anticipated by the researcher and to interact with each other spontaneously.

Participants were asked to read a vignette that parallels an incident which occurred in 1997 in the UK and which was widely reported in the media. The key features of the incident (e.g. the victim taking a short cut, the victim being suddenly accosted and dragged away from the main path) were preserved in the vignette, although the description was shorter than the original newspaper article. Below is an example of the female rape vignette.

A 22 year old single woman testified in court that she was raped in the campus of a middle-sized university where she was attending as a full-time student. On the evening of the attack, the woman had taken a short-cut home through the campus after attending a dance class. The alleged rape took place at 9.30 p.m., when the woman was attacked and dragged away from the main path and sexually assaulted. The woman told the court that she was aware of a man walking behind her but this had not aroused any suspicion. The woman's screams from the attack were heard by a passer-by who chased the attacker away. This passer-by subsequently identified the accused in the police line up. The woman had been raped once before about one year prior to this attack. It was known that no other women had been sexually assaulted on the campus in the past 6 months before this alleged attack took place.

The vignette was not intended to represent a 'typical' rape, or indeed, some kind of neutral description (of course, there is no such thing as a 'neutral' description; all description *describes*, even one that calls itself 'neutral') where participants extract certain features from it, 'cognitivise' them and then produce their own judgement devoid of any of the original descriptive features; rather it is one possible version of a rape, which provides a starting point for discussion. However, bearing in mind the discussion above on the problems with the vignette method in rape-perception research, a potential drawback in our method is that we as researchers have also presented the participants with a version of the event to be explained, and the particular details provided will inevitably impact on both the scope of the conversations and the explanations offered (Antaki, 1994). It is therefore vitally important to consider, as part of the analysis, *how* the details in the event description are taken up, ignored or elaborated upon as the participants make sense of the event described and deal with issues of accountability. This is exactly what we do here. As such, although the vignette will contain certain features that will skew the conversations towards a particular trajectory (and in experimental research, these would be construed as biases), in our research, these features (such as a description of the rape as an 'alleged rape' or the description of the victim as a full-time university student) do not constitute biases but are integral to the vignette, to be deployed in particular ways (which are also, of course, analysed) as the participants wish.

For example, the conversational data analysed in this book were initially collected for a doctoral thesis on rape perception that examined gender differences in uses of covariation information in spontaneous talk (Anderson, 1996). For this reason, two versions of the vignette were used which had two different configurations of covariation information embedded in the more general description of the incident of rape. One scenario contained the information that the victim had been raped once before prior to the assault (consistency over time) and that no other rapes had occurred in the area (an 'atypical event'). The second scenario contained the information that the victim had been raped before and that other rapes *had* occurred in the area (a 'typical' event). The two scenarios also manipulated the gender of the victim. In the accounting for male rape study in chapter 5, we present analyses of data generated by the second scenario only, where it is noted in the vignette that the victim had been 'raped before'. Interestingly, attribution theory predicts that this covariation information will tend to produce attributions of responsibility to the circumstances of the assault rather than to the victim. However, as we shall see, the participants work with this information in a way that offers some insight into the cultural resources available for making sense of an incident of alleged rape. We shall see how the 'raped before information' prompts them to speculate on the alleged victim's sexuality, to question the status of the incident as 'rape' and, ultimately, to apportion responsibility back in the direction of the victim (Doherty and Anderson, 2004).

In our analysis of the conversations we also made an explicit attempt to grapple with the experience of the participants in the research, inasmuch as we could trace this through the 'task talk', which was part and parcel of the conversations recorded. Issues such as, 'what are we supposed to do?' and, 'what kinds of things do you think they're looking for?' were very much live concerns for those that took part in the research. Instead of ignoring this element of the data, we have attended to it as a vital clue to some of the impression management activities that the participants engage in e.g. maintaining face as a 'good citizen' or a 'good research subject' as they engage with the task. The task commentary also offers an insight into how the participants made sense of the event we presented *as an offence to be accounted for* or not. There are various factors in the event description that, on the surface, makes it perceptable as an offence – and as a particular kind of offence: a violent 'stranger rape'. For example, the victim's testimony that she was 'raped' is noted. The event is constructed as problematic via the description of the victim's 'screams', which was treated as serious and acted upon by a 'passer-by'. The alleged perpetrator is categorised as the 'attacker', positioning agency for the event as described with the perpe-trator. However, the participants don't always make sense of these elements as straightforward indicators that the event described should be treated as problematic, or as how accountability should be handled. As we shall see in the analysis chapters, the participants are equally capable of constructing normative, 'neutralising' interpretations of the event depicted and, as they do so, offering us insight into cultural understandings of gender, sexuality and sexual violence that may be mobilised in accounts for alleged rape.

Feminist standpoint

The critical analyses and research presented in this book are explicitly informed by a feminist standpoint. At its heart, this means that we as researchers are committed to challenging and transforming oppression and to putting women's lives on the research agenda (e.g. see Harding, 1991; Griffin, 1995). Feminist standpoint research is 'passionate scholarship', explicitly driven by politics (DuBois, 1983) and informed by a cultural, political and ideological reading of the context of interaction and everyday experience. Our aim is to examine, make explicit and (if necessary) chal-lenge the discursive practices that shape the experience of rape victims in the aftermath of rape (Lees, 1993; Doherty and Anderson, 1998), and this aim is underpinned by existing feminist scholarship on the negative experience of rape victims in the aftermath of rape and feminist theory on sexual violence and patriarchy. In this sense the discourse analyses that follow start from a concern with the societal and a wish to deconstruct relations of power to see how they are underpinned by discursive forms (see Parker, 1992). Our research is explicitly grounded in the ongoing political struggle for improved treatment and services for rape victims, and our hope is that our analysis of accounting practices for rape may go some way towards informing that struggle (see Wilkinson and Kitzinger, 1995). In scrutinising 'the practical reasoning through which the taken-for-granted world is accomplished (and resisted) and the resources members have for sustaining a social world' (Kitzinger, 2000: 173) we aim to trace the rela-tionship of accounting practices for rape to power relations and the fabric of everyday life. As reflexive researchers then, we place our feminist credentials up front, within an arena where they can be agreed with or argued against (Doherty, 1995; Gill, 1995).

Discourse analysis

According to Edwards and Potter, certain things, once the province of cognitive psychology (like memory and attribution) now stand revealed as essentially reports which do discursive duties . . . representing the speaker as an accountable member of society . . . through the promotion of credentials as a factually unimpeachable observer, arriving at truthful explanation only after navigating through the tricky waters of self-interest.

(Antaki, 1994: 41)

Our approach to the discourse analyses presented here is informed by our reading of discursive psychology (e.g. Edley, 2000; Wetherell, 1998; Edwards, 1997; Potter, 1996; Wilkinson and Kitzinger, 1995; Potter and Wetherell, 1995; Wood and Rennie, 1994; Burman and Parker, 1993; Edwards and Potter, 1992; Wetherell and Potter, 1992; Parker, 1992; Gavey, 1989; Potter and Wetherell, 1987; Billig, 1987) and work on accountability and the moral order rooted in discourse pragmatics and ethnomethodology (e.g. Goffman, 1967; Watson, 1978; Watson, 1983; Scully and Morolla, 1984; Wowk, 1984; Lee, 1984; Brown and Levinson, 1987; Scully, 1990; Antaki, 1994).

Grounded in social constructionist epistemology, discourse analysis starts from the assumption that descriptions of events, people, groups, institutions and psychological phenomena are *versions*, which should be treated as open-ended and flexible. Analysis thus involves a search for actual or potential variability in construction and speculation on the function of particular formulations as they appear in interactional sequence. The construction of meaning is thus understood as intermeshed with the accomplishment of social action. As Parker argues, 'When we seem to be merely describing a state of affairs, our commentary always has other effects; it plays a part it legitimizing or challenging, supporting or ironizing, endorsing or subverting what it describes' (Parker, 1997: 290). Analytically, a focus on social action involves interpretation of the localised social activity and ideological work accomplished by constructing one particular version rather than another.

Ethnomethodology and its empirical discipline – conversation analysis (CA) – can help with the practical interpretation of the pragmatics of talk-in-interaction. Ethnomethodology reminds us that the meaning of utterances is indexical – related to the precise context of use. In CA, 'context' tends to refer to the specifics of the interaction in which participants are engaged – the 'micro-context' – which is understood as 'endogenously grounded', i.e. based in participant's understandings (Schegloff, 1997; Widdicombe, 1995). This draws our attention as analysts to the way in which each utterance is interpreted by participants in the context of the conversational turn that preceded it and the way that each turn also forms the context for the talk that follows it (Heritage, 1984). In terms of analytic practice, the point is that participants make available to the analyst a basis in the data for claiming what the intersubjective understanding is of prior utterances, 'for as they display it to one another, we can see it too' (Schegloff, 1984; cited in Edwards, 1997: 101). The availability of participants' 'readings' of each other's talk therefore means that analysis of what an utterance is doing can be based in a reading of how participants themselves respond to it in subsequent turns. Although sensitive to the importance of interactional structure and sequence as context, the analyses presented here do range further in their interpretation of social action by locating the participant's sense-making practices in wider historical, cultural and ideological context and by speculating on their relationship to institutional power (Wilkinson and Kitzinger, 1995; Wetherell, 1998).

Discourse analysts are also sensitive to the rhetorical organisation of arguments and opinions and the many discursive strategies that can make an argument or explanation seem factual or persuasive, including attention to the speaker's construction of their credentials as, for example, 'qualified', 'neutral' or 'sympathetic' observers. The Discourse Action Model (Edwards and Potter, 1992) draws particular analytic attention to a speaker's concerns about their own accountability to the views that they express or action being discussed. Antaki notes that an explanation can play a vital role in propping up or rescuing a speaker's social accountability (1994: 42). As analysts we can see how social actors display sensitivity to societal norms and expectations in the development of arguments, carefully structuring (in ways that are endemic to the culture) the delivery of an opinion to, for example, avoid possible accusations of 'interestedness', 'investment', 'spite' or 'harshness'. When blame, fault or responsibility gets assigned to persons or groups, speakers are generally likely to be concerned with 'how they look'. Goffman's writings on the central role of 'face work' in the dynamics of social interaction, and its more contemporary treatment in politeness theory (e.g. Brown and Levinson, 1987), are highly relevant here. Using a dramaturgical metaphor, Goffman argued that social actors are in the business of performing and present a 'public self' on the stage of everyday life, and we use a range of linguistic and behavioural displays to present a positive self-image, or 'face', to the social world, attending to and renewing the constraints of the moral order.

We also examine the interpretative resources that are mobilised in the text (Potter and Wetherell, 1995; Wetherell, 1998). In the Discursive Psychology literature systems of content, coherent ways of talking about objects, subjects and events in the world are referred to as 'interpretative repertoires' (Potter and Wetherell, 1987; Wetherell and Potter, 1988; Edley, 2000). These are conceived as the 'building blocks' of sense-making, the range of interpretative resources ('cultural themes', arguments and assumptions) that can be utilised in the course of social interaction and which form the 'common sense' basis for shared understanding. An interpretative repertoire is constituted from a limited range of lexical items, stylistic constructions and the use of a range of metaphors (Potter and Reicher, 1987). Selections can be made from available repertoires to suit the occasion and function to which the discourse is put (Potter *et al.*, 1990).

Repertoires are in use when constructing descriptions of people, groups, objects, institutions and events and when offering opinions, evaluations and explanations. Our analysis therefore involves clarifying and discussing the interpretative resources that members draw on and the development of a critical commentary on the cultural significance of the discursive patterns and resources in play. In Antaki's words:

> Explanations lock together as a means of constituting the social world . . . and constitute the people who navigate through it. To understand accounts properly one has to dismantle them to show their inner assembly and points at which they latch onto the outer world.

> (Antaki, 1994: 116)

In chapter 1 we discussed feminist writings on sexual violence and noted that a key theme in this literature is the significance of socially constructed understandings of gender and heterosexuality in providing a socially approved vocabulary of motive for the legitimation of rape. In other words, the exchange of explanations in the exoneration of rape will have a vital role to play in regulating the moral order in relation to gender power relations. In the discourse analyses that follow we pay close attention to the cultural themes and argumentative resources that are invoked in the accounts for rape, particularly in relation to the construction of gender and sexuality, and to their function in the unfolding interactional sequence in 'the setting up or knocking down of social realities . . . to promote some position in the context of the talk' (Antaki, 1994: 120–121).

To summarise, interpretation of the data presented in the next three chapters proceeds by attending to the detail of the descriptions and explanations presented. The aim is to make the constructed status and action orientation of the accounts explicit, to trace the argumentative threads, to discuss the features of rhetorical organisation and to document and discuss the sense-making resources that the participants utilise in their conversations. Attention is paid throughout to the sequential organisation of the conversational extracts in which the versions of self, world and others emerge.

4

TALKING ABOUT FEMALE RAPE: THE SOCIAL CONSTRUCTION OF HAZARD/ RISK AND ACCOUNTABILITY

Introduction

In chapter 1, we discussed early feminist scholarship on the social definition of rape, examining in some detail Burt and Estep's 1981 paper on the social construction of victimhood. They argue that definitions of what counts as 'rape' and who is to be treated as a 'genuine' victim – innocent rather than accountable – are constructed in discourse and practices that reflect the social, political and cultural conditions of society. In this chapter we explore this argument further by examining the social construction of victimhood in conversations about female rape. Burt and Estep (1981) identified several potential arguments that participants might offer to challenge a sexual assault claim. To recap, they identified three strategies: (1) suggest that 'what happened' was consensual as opposed to coerced intercourse (deny the rape claim), (2) concede that coerced intercourse probably did occur but minimise the significance of the event by down-playing the severity of rape in general or its impact on particular kinds of 'open territory' victims (i.e. accept the rape claim but deny that the victim suffered or deserves justice), or (3) accuse the victim role claimant of recklessness in precipitating the attack or failing to prevent it. In the data corpus examined here, the participants routinely accuse the rape victims of reckless behaviour, and we became fascinated with the apparent status of this argument for the participants as a 'satisfactory', 'good enough' or common sense explanation for the rape incident they were asked to discuss (see chapter 3). In this chapter, we attempt to unpick this form of argument in detail, focusing on how it is constructed to seem 'reasonable' or per-suasive, and examine how it is underpinned by cultural sense-making resources that construct and legitimate hegemonic forms of heterosexual gender relations (see chapter 1) and neo-liberal notions of ideal citizenship. Central to our discussion will be the theoretical assertions that notions of hazard/risk are socially constructed and that accusations of recklessness are therefore intimately connected to the social construction of hazard/risk. This will allow us to bring into sharp focus how the positioning of rape victims as 'risk takers' is a social construction as opposed to being – as it is treated in much talk about rape – an objective fact, and will lead us to speculate on the consequences of this construction for the experience of rape victims in the aftermath of rape and for the maintenance of patriarchal gender relations.

The social construction of hazard/risk and recklessness

The relationship between risk and individual responsibility is a central theme in neo-liberal culture and, as we will argue, informs argumentative strategies that function to position rape victims as culpable and blame-worthy in cases of alleged rape. We therefore turn first to a discussion of the social construction of hazard/risk and notions of recklessness before looking at how, in neo-liberal culture, the 'ideal citizen' is defined as reflexive and responsible in relation to risk assessment and risk avoidance.

Nick Fox outlines a number of sociological 'models' of the 'risk/hazard opposition' (Fox, 1999), and this discussion is useful in building our appreciation of the socially constructed nature of hazard (the circumstances which lead to the occurrence)/risk (the likelihood of a negative occurrence). The first position, termed 'realist or materialist', suggests that the underlying ontology of a hazard is real, material and objectively knowable and that a calculation of risk maps directly onto the hazard. This position underlies practices of risk management and assessment where strategies (policies, preventative measures or education) may be devised to minimise the likelihood of the hazard manifesting itself into a negative outcome. In other words, this approach assumes that a formal 'scientific' analysis of risks is possible. In chapter 6, we shall see how metaphors from science, medicine and mathematics are mobilised in particular to describe and discuss the female rape incident. These metaphorical vehicles enable female rape to be constructed as a material 'hazard', an objectively describable event amenable to a 'scientific' analysis of the risk of occurrence. One practical upshot of this is that the perpetrator gets configured as a material hazard to be avoided by the person construed as 'at risk', rather than as a responsible agent in his own right, which deflects responsibility away from the perpetrator towards the alleged victim.

The second position is what Fox terms 'culturalist'. Here, risks are opposed to 'hazards'. Hazards are seen as natural and neutral, whereas risks become the value-laden judgements of those concerned about the hazard: what is considered 'risky' is constructed by interested parties. The hazards however are understood as 'real' and objectively describable. This leads to an interest in the process of risk perception focusing on the kinds of knowledges and politics that inform perceptions of risk. Douglas argues that the risks people tend to focus on are to do with the way individuals construct their understanding of the world and their place within it. What becomes considered a risk, its causes and its magnitude, depends upon membership of and identification with the culture (Douglas, 1992). Different perspectives lead to different understandings of what constitutes an 'acceptable risk' and thus also to judgements about whether an individual overstepped the line into the territory of 'unacceptable risk-taking'. This also highlights how the 'risk-taking individual' can take on a moral character (Fox, 1999: 208) in neo-liberal culture – we are held morally accountable to prevailing cultural norms and standards for what counts as unacceptably 'risky' behaviour.

The 'postmodern' position on hazard/risk goes one step further than the culturalist position to argue that hazards themselves are social fabrications. In other words, situations, objects and subjects are considered to be inherently 'inert'; their construction as hazards is contingent on the immediate situation and wider institutional or political interests in play. Judgements about what counts as hazardous may utilise knowledges about what is deemed serious or trivial, probable or unlikely, but will always be evaluative. It is not simply 'outlooks on risks' therefore that are dependent on the social milieu, but hazards themselves: both risks and hazards are 'cultural products'. Further, if hazards themselves are constructed from contingent and partial descriptions of the world, then the attribution of riskiness is:

> grounded not in objective estimation, but entirely upon what Foucault calls power/knowledge; the 'knowledgeability' which both discursively constructs objects and confirms the authority of the person claiming the knowledge.
>
> (Fox, 1999: 210)

Practices of risk assessment, from this position, not only construct the risks and hazards but also establish the subjectivity of those it addresses as individuals or populations 'at risk', and the 'subjectivities which are created around risk . . . are relative and grounded in discursive fabrications of what is to be positively or negatively valued' (Fox, 1999: 216). One potentially powerful implication of all this is that it is not adequate to point out which phenomena are 'really hazardous' or to assume that, by making claims about where the 'real' harm is, we are necessarily acting in anybody's best interests. As Fox argues, taking 'risks' may, in some circumstances, 'be an opportunity to become other' (Fox, 1999: 217) – an insight which feminist activists are acutely aware of. Participation in 'reclaiming the night' demonstrations, for example, displays a refusal to buy into the patriarchal norm that the streets are 'hazardous' for women, who are construed as at risk from sexual predators and as responsible for avoiding this hazard. In 'taking the risk' of going out at night, we become other to the stereotypically feminine subject, refusing to be positioned as passive, vulnerable and excluded from public life. We also register a challenge to the premises on which the construction of the 'hazard' are built in the first place – recognising that in patriarchal society, the construction of sexual violence related hazard/risk plays a key role in the maintenance of gender power relations and gendered norms of behaviour (also see discussion in chapter 1).

Neo-liberal culture, self-reliance and individual responsibility

Ericson *et al.* (2000) claim that neo-liberalism, understood as a 'restructured global form of capitalism', can be viewed as a model for governance 'beyond the state', comprising five basic assumptions that link to the constitution of the 'risk-taking' subject. The first basic assumption in this model is that the state has a minimal role. Good citizens are assumed to be rational, informed and active agents, able to use self-restraint and with a will and a capacity to self-govern. Second, the global free market is positioned as central to economic growth, security and prosperity, and the social sphere is re-defined as a similar form of economic domain. Third, in this context notions of 'hazard/risk', risk-taking and individual responsibility play an important conceptual role in the management and avoidance of diverse 'hazards' at an individual, local and global level. Certain forms of risk-taking behaviour, especially in the economic sphere, are actively encouraged. Entrepreneurs, for example, are imagined as glamorous, risk-taking cultural hero/ines with the foresight and confidence to pursue a business venture in conditions when costs may be known but rewards are uncertain (Jennings, 1994). However, in neo-liberal culture the relationship between risk-taking and individual responsibility for the consequences is always crystal clear, even in the case of culturally valued activities such as entrepreneurial business ventures – 'good entrepreneurs' must bear the responsibility for business failure and must not expect to be rescued from the consequences of a failed venture by a philanthropic State (Doherty, 2000).

Fourth, individual responsibility is emphasised and expected. Each person becomes their own 'political economy', making informed consumer choices, not only about goods and services but also about matters of personal security, health and well-being. Beck (1992) suggests that living in a 'risk society' involves experiencing pressure to be aware of the possibilities and uncertainties of any course of action, where individuals are confronted with a range of alternatives, especially in relation to lifestyle. 'Good citizens' constituted in relation to this 'climate of risk' are expected to be self-reflexive subjects, actively engaging with and taking responsibility for shaping their own biographies. Finally, within a framework of 'responsible risk-taking' there is the tendency to perceive differences and inequalities that arise more as matters of personal choice rather than being influenced by external, more structural factors beyond the control of the individual

(Ericson *et al.*, 2000). Individualist philosophy characterises the values and philosophy of the capitalist world and is a predominant theme, descriptive of a 'cultural ethos' in the West. Edward Sampson, for example, argues that:

> Our culture emphasizes individuality, in particular a kind of individual self-sufficiency that describes an extreme of the individualistic dimension . . . although self-contained individualism is an extreme, it is not unreasonable as a description of an emerging cultural ideal.
>
> (Sampson, 1977: 769)

Indeed, from 1979 onwards, we in Britain have witnessed a sustained political attempt to nurture this cultural ideal in both public and private life. A key part of the New Right and latterly the New Labour agendas has been to nurture a 'British' spirit of free enterprise and sense of initiative (Hall and Jacques, 1983; Corner and Harvey, 1991a, 1991b; Hutton, 1997; Doherty, 2000). We are encouraged to embrace individualist values and take our place in an 'enterprise culture' as reflexive, self-reliant, self-responsible, initiative-takers. We are expected to take responsibility in becoming educated and knowledgeable in relation to 'hazard/risk', street wise and flexible enough to cope with life transitions and crises.

Petersen (1996), building on the work of Castel (1991), suggests neo-liberalism requires individuals to regulate their own health and safety through self-examination, self-care and self-improvement – limiting demands for state intervention or institutional support and emphasising an individual's responsibility to protect themselves from hazard/risk. Individuals are expected to adopt 'safe' lifestyles and behaviours, and avoid whatever is deemed hazardous, and this is now a commonplace theme in political and media discourse. Within this framework, victimisation can be understood as a case of individuals recklessly 'choosing' to expose themselves to the 'dangers' of society. It is up to us to become more responsible for taking measures to protect ourselves from misfortune, and those failing to do so, it will be argued, have no one to blame but themselves. As we shall see in the analysis of talk about female rape that follows, this form of argument is frequently mobilised when accounting for rape, to construct the alleged victim as culpable and blameworthy.

Analysis

In chapter 3, we described the data collection methodology used to create the database of conversations to be analysed in this book in some detail. We also discussed our feminist standpoint and the key theoretical influences on our approach to discourse analysis. In this chapter we present an analysis of the conversations about the female rape vignette. As noted in the introduction, in these conversations the alleged victim is routinely accused of reckless behaviour and found culpable in relation to the rape perpetrated against her. We focus here on the social construction of hazard/ risk and responsibility in relation to the alleged rape. As we shall see, the participants draw on the details provided in the vignette but also go beyond the basic information provided to build a picture of the circumstances of the alleged rape incident and construct its status as a predictable 'hazard' by drawing on their cultural knowledge, including understandings of gender, sexuality and sexual violence. We also examine the construction of victim and perpetrator identities in relation to the construction of the context and the rape event.

In discussing the social construction of identity we employ an ethno-methodological orientation, focusing on the action-orientation of the identity categories in use. The concept of 'membership categorisation' is an important feature of ethnomethodologically informed analyses of identity (e.g. Antaki and Widdicombe, 1998a; Beattie and Doherty, 1995a, 1995b; Billig, 1985; Billig, 1987; Condor, 1988; Doherty and Anderson, 1998; Jayusi, 1984; Lee, 1984; Moir, 1993; Potter, 1988a, 1988b; Potter and Halliday, 1990; Watson, 1978; Watson, 1983; Watson and Weinberg, 1982; Wowk, 1984). In this work, 'to have an identity' means to be cast into a category with associated characteristics or features (Antaki and Widdi-combe, 1998b). Membership categorisations are common-sense units of identification for referring to people in talk (Sacks, 1972). Certain activities are conventionally seen to go with or be bound to a membership category, for example the activity 'crying' is conventionally considered to be bound to the category 'baby' (Sacks, 1974). Implicit reference can be made to a membership category by outlining the activities or attributes conventionally associated with it, without the category being explicitly mentioned. Conversely, it is also possible to make inferences about people and their behaviour on the basis of the membership categories that are used to describe them (Wowk, 1984). There are always a number of different categories available which could potentially be applied to an individual. Following Sacks, both Condor (1988) and Edwards (1991) argue that the selection made should be understood not as a representation of a pre-formed cognition that straightforwardly maps onto an ontological reality, but only with reference to the functional context of the utterance – as an occasioned, indexical phenomenon which is consequential in the ongoing interaction and (adopting a critical perspective) which may also have wider consequences for the maintenance of societal power relations.

This orientation is in stark contrast to the theoretical assumptions about identity underlying research on attitudes and attribution in the cognitive social psychology paradigm, discussed and critically evaluated in chapter 2. In this work, it is assumed that identity can be conceptualised as internally owned, ontologically real and related to the production of consistencies in behaviour (Widdicombe, 1998). Research concerns tend to revolve around identifying and describing the elements of an individual's identity (e.g. in terms of attitudinal constructs or attributional style) or perhaps making distinctions between different types of identity (e.g. the 'victim-prone' type, the 'victim-blaming' type etc.). We are not suggesting that rape-supportive culture is perpetuated by a few 'bad' or prejudiced individuals. Our focus is on the effects and consequences of discursive resources and practices which are culturally available and institutionally sanctioned. The treatment of identity in our analyses therefore focuses on the interactional management of identity – on the way in which the ascription to self or others of an identity characteristic or type is situated, variable and very much a live topic for discussion and debate in the context of social interaction (Antaki and Widdicombe, 1998a; Sacks, 1984; Widdicombe, 1995; Widdicombe and Wooffitt, 1990; Wooffitt, 1992).

We start by presenting three conversational extracts, using these extracts to explore first how the nature of the 'hazard/risk' confronting the alleged victim is constructed in the accounts. We will argue that the discussions construct rape/rapists in the public sphere as a hazard which is onto-logically real, objectively knowable and predictable, gendered and intransi-gent (if regrettable). We then examine the construction of the alleged victim and perpetrator identities in this context, focusing on the significance for the participants of the issue of 'hazard/risk' awareness on the part of the victim. Throughout we discuss how this constructive work relates to the management of accountability for the alleged rape (/ indicates a pause; [ ] overlapping speech).

Extract 1
1. Vernon: well yeah so here we're saying that she should have probably been aware of this and not [been so foolish] as to take a short cut but even so
2. Sally: maybe / she yeah it does / seem that way doesn't, they should be able to I think
3. Vernon: yeah but even so / people should be able to to walk about in freedom but
4. Sally: but the trouble is you can't nowadays can you / I mean it's too dangerous
5. Vernon: well
6. Sally: I mean people are forever telling you on television you know whatever you don't
7. Vernon: yeah I think people are becoming more and more aware of it

Extract 2
1. John: you would have thought she would have been aware of the danger wouldn't you

2. Debbie: yeah it does seem like / you know it was a silly thing to do really
3. John: yeah it does seem a bit strange I mean / I agree with you / I mean but yeah like I said
4. Debbie: but you can't can you that's the trouble / people should be able to walk about without being attacked but given that / it's a violent it's a violent society that we live in / er / people have to be aware of the dangers I mean it's no good just walking about with her head in the clouds is it

Extract 3
1. Alison: yeah but I dunno it reflects that women always have to be careful I mean I know blokes get beaten up and stuff but / you know you can still walk home and stuff like that
2. Frank: oh well yeah I know it's not fair but it's / life innit
3. Alison: mm / I mean so that implies that this poor woman has to spend her whole life looking over her shoulder and (inaudible)
4. Frank: [no not at all] but if you walk back take the lit way where it's like well lit up instead of taking this huge short cut across the badly lit field or whatever

In the extracts above the speakers jointly develop a version of the context and circumstances of the rape event – in terms of general societal conditions 'nowadays' (extract 1, turn 4) and in terms of the details of location – both of these activities contribute to the social construction of the 'hazard/risk' facing the alleged victim. The characterisation offered is of a society which is generally 'dangerous' (extract 1, turn 4; extract 2, turn 4) and 'violent' (extract 2, turn 4), a place where people run the risk of being 'attacked' (extract 2, turn 4) or 'beaten up' (extract 3, turn 1). The nature of the danger and the manner of attack are, however, constructed as *gendered*, a view which reflects the participant's cultural understanding of 'hazard/risk' for men and women. Feminist scholars have long argued that the specific nature and consequences of perceived threats in the public sphere are different for men and women. For example, in her seminal analysis of rape, culture and the maintenance of patriarchy, Susan Griffin suggested that there is an 'unnamed fear' which, 'relentlessly figures as a daily part of every woman's consciousness' (Griffin, 1971: 27) – the fear of rape. The social belief that the fear of rape exerts a powerful means of social control over all women, often leading to the adoption of behaviours such as not going out alone (Riger and Gordon, 1981) or feeling pressure to engage in and/or take responsibility for risk assessment and avoidance practices, is alluded to in extract 3: although, 'blokes get beaten up and stuff' (extract 3, turn 1) this is construed as different from the constant concern for their safety that women experience, who 'always have to be careful' (extract 3, turn 1). It is further argued that the risk of 'getting beaten up' does not necessarily restrict men's behaviour in a general way: 'you can still walk home and stuff' (extract 3, turn 1). There were several examples of participants arguing along the same lines in both the female and male rape data corpus, e.g. 'I mean it's a thing that you always think, as a bloke walking on your own, that you would be alright, the worst that can happen to you is that you might get mugged or something' (Male Rape, Conversation 11).

We now turn to an analysis of the next layer of context in these accounts – the construction of the geographical location of the alleged rape as 'hazardous'. It is worth reminding ourselves at this point about the details of location embedded in the vignette (see also chapter 3). It was reported that the event took place at:

> the campus of a middle-sized university where she was attending as a full-time student . . . the woman had taken a short-cut home through the campus after attending a dance class . . . the woman was attacked and dragged away from the main path and sexually assaulted.

The main features of location reported in the vignette therefore are (1) that the rape took place in a university setting and (2) that the route taken was a main path through the university campus, a route which, it is noted, was a quicker route home for the alleged victim than not walking through the campus. The sense-making activities of the participants in relation to the construct 'short-cut' are particularly interesting here. In extract 1, turn 1, 'taking a short-cut' is evaluated as 'foolish'. The cultural understanding of 'short-cut' in play here is explicated in extract 3, turn 4 where the alleged victim's route is described as a 'huge short cut across the badly lit field'. Her route home is therefore re-imagined as dark, remote and out of the institutional context of the university campus – features which are culturally understood as potentially signalling danger. Darkness in itself is a powerful cultural signifier of fear and danger, invoking childhood fairytales and myths of 'things that go bump in the night' or monsters that lurk in the deep dark forest or the bogey man under the bed. The construction and evaluation of this version of the route is emphasised by contrasting it with an alternative hypothetical route that the speaker suggests the victim *should* have taken, 'the lit way where it's well lit up'. Here, light as a cultural signifier of safety and clarity is in play. The disappearance in these accounts of certain features of the university setting, which *could* have been highlighted, is also interesting in terms of the social construction of 'hazard/ risk'. The participants could just as easily have constructed the university as marked by several features leading to an evaluation of the setting as 'safe' or relatively low risk (Anderson and Doherty, 1996, 1997). For example, they could have argued that the central route through the university was likely to have been, or should have been, protected by a university security operation, that is well lit, patrolled possibly, with CCTV even. They could have argued that it is perfectly reasonable to take a shorter route home; they could point out that they would have done the same thing in the circumstances. To underline the plausibility of these suggestions, it should be noted that this type of construction was indeed relatively common in the conversations about the male-rape incident. In these accounts, taking the route as described in the vignette was evaluated as 'understandable' rather than 'foolish' and in terms of accountability for the rape, the institution, rather than the alleged victim, was more likely to be held directly or at least partly responsible for the series of reported attacks on campus; accused of failing in their duty of care to the students. For example:

Male Rape Conversation 10
1. James: I think the most worrying point is security especially for this university and that for people in general that they don't feel safe walking across what should be a pretty safe place, that is the campus of the university and it shows the dangers of this sort of thing happening wherever you are

Male Rape Conversation 11
1. Holly: Yes, I mean you could I suppose find another way to go, but it might have been the quickest way to walk through the campus or whatever
2. Oliver: Sometimes it's just not avoidable, I mean if it's normally the, like, if it's an area where there's normal lighting, and the lighting's gone, from power failure or like the lamp has been vandalised or something there's nothing you can do

Overall, in the conversations about female rape discussed here, the implication is that the geographical landscape can be straightforwardly mapped out into different categories of location that have an objective, material reality – 'dangerous' places and 'safe' places (where the scene of the alleged rape on the university campus is constructed here as a 'dangerous' high-risk place) and that the identification of each is as easy as knowing the difference between light and dark.

A construction of the rapist as hazard is also embedded in the notion of the 'short-cut' as discussed above. In extract 3, turn 4, for example, the rapist takes on the cultural significance of the 'bogey man', a shadowy, sub-human figure lying in wait to pounce on potential victims – in this case maybe from behind a large tree or a hedge in the dimly lit field. Overall, we can see that the participants are also drawing on and reproducing a cultural rape myth that plays a key role in constructions of the 'classic stranger rape' scenario: that rape is overwhelmingly a crime perpetrated by psycho-pathic (sub-human, out of control) rapists lurking in dark, unpopulated, public spaces.

The social construction of the 'hazard/risk' in this scenario is therefore built up from a number of argumentative strategies: construct the societal context as in general 'dangerous' and 'violent' (a place where we need to be generally vigilant but where the nature of 'hazard/risk' is gendered); con-struct the geographical location of the alleged rape as 'dangerous'; and locate the rapist as a predictable shadowy, subhuman, figure in this type of location. The 'hazard' is also constructed in these accounts as intransigent, if regrettable. In each of the conversations above we see evidence of a form of reasoning called 'pragmatic realism' (Wetherell and Potter, 1988, 1989, 1992) (extract 1, turns 2–4; extract 2, turn 4; extract 3, turn 2). This form of argument suggests that there are commonly accepted practical constraints that may act to restrict our freedom of movement and choice. Pointing this out plays a central role in constructing the identity of the participants themselves as they discuss the rape vignette. It functions to position the speakers first as 'sensible' because they are 'realistic' enough to recognise the constraints 'out there' beyond the control of ordinary folk which 'inevitably' inhibit one's freedom – or in this case, of course, in particular the freedom of women – and second, by expressing regret about these constraints, it also positions them as reasonable and 'worldly wise', for example 'I know it's not fair but it's life innit'. This is a particularly robust piece of rhetoric as it operates as a closed argument against the possibility of social change: 'people should be able to to walk about in freedom but but the trouble is you can't nowadays can you / I mean it's too dangerous' (extract 1, turns 3–4). In other words, the participants in all the extracts above reproduce a cultural understanding of risk in relation to rape that acknowledges that women's freedom of movement may in practice be restricted. The cultural reaction to that state of affairs is to argue that we all just have to be 'sensible' about it – recognise it, accept it and work within the situation as best we can, rather than to suggest that 'something should be done' to restore equality between men and women in this regard. And if the situation is constructed as unchangeable, that then becomes a powerful platform from which to argue that the individuals 'at risk' must become responsible and vigilant in their 'risk' assessment and avoidance practices.

Michael Billig's work on rhetoric reminds us that descriptions have an argumentative quality with regard to what someone else might say. Ver-sions of reality – like the one we have been unpicking above – always counter, explicitly or implicitly, real or potential alternative arguments, containing a silent endorsement of particular concepts at the expense of alternatives. He argues that the meaning of a piece of discourse, its 'plain sense' (or logos) must be understood in terms of the views being countered, its 'argumentative sense' (or anti-logos) (Billig, 1987, 1988a, 1988b). In other words, discourse which seems to be arguing for one point may contain implicit meanings, which could be made explicit to argue for the counter-point (Billig *et al.*, 1988). Even accounts which claim or appear to be neutral or unbiased can be examined in terms of the position/s that they indirectly argue against. This is because 'common sense' is comprised of conflicting moral evaluations which enable opposing moral judgements to be made (Billig *et al.*, 1988). This also enables us to see how the seeds of resistance to a prevailing, 'taken-for-granted' or culturally dominant position are present in the cultural sense-making resources.

In the above extracts we can see how the 'common sense' position developed is rooted in both cultural understandings of gender, sexuality and violence and neo-liberal concepts stressing individual responsibility and conservatism, back-grounding the social values of institutional, social and collective responsibility. Nevertheless, the counter theme is recoverable, present within the articulation of the major theme, revealed by the presence of qualifications.

Extract 1
2. Sally: maybe / she yeah it does / seem that way doesn't, *they should be able to I think*
3. Vernon: yeah but even so / *people should be able to to walk about in freedom* but
4. Sally: but the trouble is you can't nowadays can you / I mean it's too dangerous

Extract 2
4. Debbie: but you can't can you that's the trouble / *people should be able to walk about without being attacked* but given that / it's a violent it's a violent society that we live in / er / people have to be aware of the dangers I mean it's no good just walking about with her head in the clouds is it

In extracts 1 and 2, the participants explicitly mobilise the contrary common-sense theme – that women should be able to walk about without fear of attack – which is then immediately disclaimed to make way for an articulation of the dominant theme, that this is in fact impossible for 'sensible' folk like themselves – folk who don't walk about with their 'head in the clouds' (extract 2, turn 4) and who heed the 'expert' warnings to be risk aware that are, it is argued, ever-present in the culture:

Extract 1, turns 6–7
6. Sally: I mean *people are forever telling you on television* you know whatever you don't
7. Vernon: yeah I think people *are becoming more and more aware* of it

In other words, the conversations about female rape are characterised by the presence of opposing cultural themes, which enable an argument to be formulated in the first place. In extract 3, turn 3 Alison's resistance to the emerging 'common-sense' victim-blaming argument is a little more developed still:

Extract 3
2. Frank: oh well yeah I know it's not fair but it's / life innit
3. Alison: *mm / I mean so that implies that this poor woman has to spend her whole life looking over her shoulder and* (inaudible)
4. Frank: [no not at all] but if you walk back take the lit way where it's like well lit up instead of taking this huge short cut across the badly lit field or whatever

Alison responds to Frank's 'common sense' conclusion – that the restriction of movement and freedom for women may not be fair, but nevertheless it is a non-negotiable, non-challengeable feature of life – by clarifying and re-stressing the extent of the unfairness and reduced quality of life for women (and this woman in particular) that this view would entail, 'this poor woman has to spend her whole life looking over her shoulder'. Frank's response is to hold the dominant cultural 'common sense' line, re-stressing that the way to *not live in fear* is for individuals deemed 'at risk' to take individual responsibility for engaging in personal risk assessment and risk avoidance strategies. So, although, the possibility of countering the 'common sense' position constructed above is there, in practice the evidence in this data corpus of conversations about female rape suggests that the common sense position is dominant and fairly robust against attempts to resist it.

To summarise so far, the social construction of the 'hazard/risk' facing the alleged victim on her way home is constructed as extreme, gendered, inevitable and, ultimately as we will now discuss, as foreseeable and avoidable. As we will see, the issue of the alleged victim's awareness of the 'hazard/risk' so constructed becomes crucial in the categorisation of the alleged victim and the management of accountability for the alleged rape.

Extract 1
1. Vernon: well yeah so here we're saying that *she should have probably been aware of this* and not [been so foolish] as to take a short cut but even so

Extract 2
1. John: *you would have thought she would have been aware of the danger wouldn't you*
2. Debbie: yeah it does seem like / you know it was a silly thing to do really

The participants in extracts 1 and 2 argue that the alleged victim should have been *aware* of the 'hazard/risk', the 'danger' as constructed in these accounts. They accuse her therefore of failing in her responsibility to be a reflexive, knowledgeable citizen in relation to issues of personal security and/or of deliberately choosing to ignore the 'hazard/risk' that 'common sense' dictates she has a responsibility to understand, recognise and avoid. The participants single her out as negligent in this respect by contrasting her action with their own hypothetical actions in the same situation and by arguing that the risk of sexual violence for women has the status of knowledge in the public domain (extract 1, turns 6–7) (i.e. they argue that it is 'reasonable' to expect that this woman was aware of the 'hazard/risk' so constructed and its implications). She is thus positioned as deliberately 'reckless' or recklessly naïve in failing to avoid rape victimisation and is categorised in the accounts as 'foolish' (extract 1, turn 2), 'silly' (extract 2, turn 2) and also 'naïve' through the suggestion that she walks about 'with her head in the clouds' (extract 2, turn 4). Identity categorisations of this nature were extremely common in the data corpus of conversations about female rape, and it is worth drawing attention to the constructive work that is going on here. The alleged victim could have been categorised in a number of ways (e.g. perhaps as 'sensible' for taking a short cut because it's quicker, or as 'unlucky' for being 'in the wrong place at the wrong time'). As discussed in the introduction, the category selected is related to the accomplishment of social action (Wowk, 1984; Edwards, 1991). The invocation of these particular category attributes makes available inferences about 'what kind of victim' is under discussion – one who can be accepted as 'genuine', unaccountable victim (Burt and Estep, 1981), an individual who suffered through no fault of her own – or one who is identifiable as accountable for 'what happened' (cf. Beattie and Doherty, 1995a, 1995b). The reference to traits such as 'silly', 'stupid' and naïve are tied to and index the latter of these two membership categories: 'accountable victim'. The implication is that she is accountable for the attack perpetrated against her because of her alleged 'stupidity' and 'recklessness'.

This analysis also indicates how in social interaction the construction of versions of identity, mind and reality are highly intermeshed and mutually implicative (Edwards, 1997) or, put another way, how 'world-making' and 'self-making' are in practice intricately related (Edwards and Potter, 1992). The negative traits attributed to the alleged victim appear 'reasonable' partly because of the particular, constructed features of the setting as hazardous, in which the alleged rape takes place. In these accounts, it is argued that she consciously selected an 'obviously dangerous' route home (ignoring or failing to recognise the 'danger') when 'safer alternatives' were available. This enables the participants to imply that she 'placed herself' in the path of a rapist or, as some participants articulate elsewhere in the data corpus, that she 'self-induced' the rape.

Overall, the analysis shows that in discussing the alleged rape incident the participants overwhelmingly focus on the behaviour and personal characteristics of the victim and not the perpetrator. As we argued above, the perpetrator figures implicitly as part of the hazard to be avoided in the re-imagination of the location of the rape as in a 'badly lit field' or as part and parcel of the 'hazard/risk' of 'short cuts', rather than as an accountable agent in his own right. It is implied that the victim only has herself to blame because she *placed herself* in the path of a 'hazard'. As Burt and Estep (1981) noted, if a victim role claimant can be accused of being 'wilfully reckless' with their personal safety and moral reputation, then they can also be positioned as culpable for rape victimisation. And this is how the alleged victim in these conversations stands accused – the participants argue that she is 'out of place', literally a 'bad girl' for being unaccompanied in the masculine sphere of public life and also a 'bad neo-liberal citizen' for failing in her responsibility to engage in 'risk' assessment and avoidance strategies.

At the heart of this argument is the conviction that we as individuals *have it in our power* to avoid victimisation and that individual reflexivity and awareness about 'hazard/risk' is *the single biggest factor* in securing personal safety. What does it therefore take to be constructed as a genuine claimant on the victim role in patriarchal, neo-liberal culture? Our analysis indicates that a key factor in being granted 'ideal victim' status is likely to be whether the victim role claimant can be positioned as *not aware* of the 'hazard/risk' associated with sexual victimisation, as constructed within our culture, and for it also to be argued that it is 'reasonable' or 'understandable' for the victim to not be 'risk aware'. Evidence suggests that this is probably unlikely in most cases – after all, there is always the possibility of arguing that the victim 'should have' been aware, particularly in the case of female victims who are socialised into a culture which holds women responsible for the regulation of male sexuality. To underline this point, in the next chapter we will see how in the case of male rape, victims constructed as heterosexual are culturally exempt from the responsibility of 'hazard/risk' awareness in relation to sexual violence, resulting in more acceptance on the part of the participants that they are 'genuine', unaccountable victims and resulting in more apportionment of sympathy to this category of victim than either to female victims or to male victims positioned as 'gay'.

It would seem that alleged 'hazard/risk' awareness confers a moral responsibility to enter into practices of risk assessment and avoidance and that failure to do so – evidenced by becoming a victim – provides a cultural warrant to deny the victim sympathy, resources and justice because, it is argued, they only have themselves to blame. All of the participants in our study orient to this framework of moral accountability in some form, for example in claiming that they would not be so complacent in their duty to keep themselves safe, in criticising the victim for failing to do so, but also in planting the occasional seeds of resistance to victim-blaming positions, e.g. in arguments that the institution is accountable, that becoming a victim is just plain bad luck or that taking a short cut is a practical option. The link between risk awareness and responsibility in our culture is incredibly strong, so strong that in cases of rape it appears to preclude any extended discussion of the rapist as agent in the act of rape. The rapist may be constructed as at fault or as guilty (i.e. in general the rape claim *per se* is not disputed in these conversations, and rape is clearly evaluated as 'wrong') but, unlike the victim, not as *responsible* – he appears as a sub-human figure, without agency, control and the power to reflect.

Conclusions

In this chapter we analysed the participant's practices of event description focusing on the social construction of 'hazard/risk' and the identities of the alleged victim and rapist. We showed how the victim is constructed as responsible for her victimisation because of her 'recklessness' and how this argument is sustained by and reproduces patriarchal and neo-liberal 'common sense' values and beliefs. She is positioned as culpable in failing in her duty to be a 'good woman' and an 'ideal self-governing, self-responsible neo-liberal citizen' in relation to her health, safety and prosperity. The rapist effectively disappears from these accounts – he features only as a sub-human figure without agency, control and the power to reflect – merely part of the 'hazard/risk' that the alleged victim must deal with. A number of material consequences flow from an emphasis on the victim's character and behaviour in accounts for rape. If victims are the focus of explanation, then they also become the targets for intervention. This results in a preoccupation with the regulation of the behaviour of 'foolish' or 'wayward' women whilst the seriousness of rape as a violent and oppressive crime is ignored, rape victims receive inadequate support and rapists continue to go unpunished.

TALKING ABOUT MALE RAPE:
WHO SUFFERS MOST?

Introduction

In 1994 the Criminal Justice and Public Order Act redefined rape within English Law to take account of male as well as female victims. Crime statistics show that in the UK in 1995, 150 such offences against men were recorded, rising to 231 in 1996[1] (Adler, 2000). It is widely recognised, however, that official statistics on male rape greatly underestimate the number of actual incidences of non-consensual sex between adult men.[2] The first major UK epidemiological study reported an incidence figure for male rape of 3% in the general population (Coxell *et al.*, 1999) and there is evidence to suggest that this figure may be much higher when sampled in gay communities (Coxell *et al.*, 1999; Hickson *et al.*, 1994) or in college populations (Struckman-Johnson and Struckman-Johnson, 1994).

Male rape survivors describe their experience of rape as life-threatening, de-humanising and humiliating (e.g. Groth and Burgess, 1980; Kaufman *et al.*, 1980; Goyer and Eddleman, 1984; Myers, 1989; Garnets *et al.*, 1990). The clinical literature indicates that survivors can experience long-lasting and severe physical and psychological reactions, including post-traumatic stress disorder (Isely and Gehrenbeck-Shim, 1997; Rogers, 1997; Turner, 2000) and disruption in their social and sexual identity and relationships. Yet, the majority of male rapes are never reported to the authorities or to friends and family members. Coxell *et al.* (1999) found that only 2 of the 71 adult males who reported non-consensual sex in their study had told the police about the incident. Hillman *et al.* (1990) and King and Woollett (1997) found that only 12% and 15% 'respectively' of the participants in their studies (contacted in both cases via the male rape crisis organisation 'Survivors') had reported the incident to the police. The American Medical Association characterises male rape as a 'silent-violent epidemic' (1995) and Lees argues that male rape is, 'one of the most underreported serious crimes in Britain' (Lees, 1997: 89). There is a consensus in the UK and US male rape literature that the sexual victimisation of men is a serious, yet largely 'invisible' problem in society (Isely, 1998). Overwhelmingly, male rape survivors remain silent, hidden and isolated (Donaldson, 1990; McMullen, 1990; Rochman, 1991; Scarce, 1997; Davies, 2000), often without counselling or medical support (Hillman *et al.*, 1990).

According to the literature, there are several powerful 'report defense elements' (McMullen, 1990) that prohibit the reporting of a male rape experience, most of which have to do with actual or perceived societal responses. Survivors' accounts indicate that normative expectations about masculinity discourage men from reporting sexual victimisation for fear of being ridiculed as weak or inadequate. Some survivors remain silent rather than risk being labelled as a 'closet homosexual', bi-sexual or as promiscuous and thus somehow 'deserving' of rape (Scarce, 1997; Ussher, 1997; West, 2000). Social stigmatisation of victims in the aftermath of rape has been identified as a form of 'secondary victimisation' (Williams, 1984) and has been directly linked to the under-reporting of rape and post-rape trauma. As such, closer investigation of societal responses to male rape is a pressing concern.

In the main, psychologists have approached this task from within the social cognition paradigm. A small number of experimental studies on rape perception, examining interpretations of the causes of male rape or describing and measuring attitudes towards male rape, have now entered the literature. In a typical causal attribution study, male and female participants are required to read one of several hypothetical rape descriptions in which variables thought to influence attribution judgements (e.g. gender of victim, 'respectability', familiarity with assailant) are manipulated. Participants are then asked to indicate their level of agreement or disagreement with a range of statements to measure issues such as the apportionment of blame, fault or responsibility, attributions of causality, judgements about what 'type of person' the victim is and the victim's likely response to the rape experience (e.g. the amount of pleasure or trauma the victim experienced).

The findings from this type of study indicate that, as in female rape (Pollard, 1992), participants tend to assign fairly modest levels of responsibility to victims. Nevertheless, despite the relatively low overall mean scores this research has highlighted a number of fairly consistent findings indicating a pattern in attribution judgements according to the gender of observers and characteristics and behaviour of the depicted victim. For example, in terms of observer gender, most studies show that men tend to attribute more blame to male rape victims than women do (McCaul *et al.*, 1990; Whatley and Riggio, 1993; Mitchell *et al.*, 1999) and McCaul *et al.*'s research showed that male observers are more likely than female observers to judge that any rape victim (male or female) derives sexual pleasure from a rape attack (McCaul *et al.*, 1990).

In terms of the characteristics and behaviour of victims, male victims tend to be blamed relatively less than female victims. This may be because men are not expected to foresee rape as a potential occurrence as readily as female victims are (McCaul *et al.*, 1990; Schneider *et al.*, 1994; Perrott and Webber, 1996; Anderson, 1999). On the other hand, it is a commonplace assumption that women should restrict their behaviour according to societal expectations of 'respectable femininity' (dress modestly, don't go out unaccompanied at night etc.) to regulate male desire and 'prevent' rape (Griffin, 1971; Riger and Gordon, 1981). Perrott and Webber (1996) found that male victims (more than female victims) are held responsible for rape on account of their behaviour during an attack (e.g. observers think that men should be able to fight off attackers or escape from the scene), whereas female victims are attributed more blame on account of their internal characteristics (e.g. observers think that women are more likely to put themselves in jeopardy than are men).

There is also a small literature on attitudes towards male rape where, most notably, the level of support in different populations or occupational groups for a limited range of explicitly stated, researcher-defined 'myths' about male rape[3] (e.g. 'adult males only get raped in prison'; 'most men who are raped are homosexuals' or 'men are too strong to be overpowered') is measured. Burt defined rape myths in relation to female rape as, 'prejudicial, stereotyped or false beliefs about rape, rape victims and rapists' (Burt, 1980: 217). Rape myths are considered to contribute to the cultural acceptance of sexual violence (and the maintenance of patriarchy) by framing rape as a sexual rather than violent act and by providing a repertoire of justification and exoneration for acts of rape (Brownmiller, 1975; Burt, 1980; Russell, 1982; Scully, 1990; Ussher, 1997; Doherty and Anderson, 1998).

The results from these studies tend to indicate fairly low levels of agreement with the rape myths as presented but show that there are significant differences in level of agreement with the different rape myth statements and between different categories of respondents. For example, Tewksbury and Adkins (1992) found that, amongst emergency room personnel, parents more strongly reject myths that imply a degree of victim blame ('men who are raped are homosexual'; 'a gay man who goes to another man's home on a first date implies willingness to have sex') than do non-parents. Tewksbury and Adkins suggest that this is because parents are more likely to view individuals as equally vulnerable.

Struckman-Johnson and Struckman-Johnson (1992) report significant differences in degree of rape-myth acceptance according to the gender of observers and the sex of the perpetrator depicted in the rape-myth statements. Female respondents were more extreme than the male respondents in their disagreement with the male rape-myth statements, but all participants responded less sympathetically when the perpetrator was depicted as a woman. Smith *et al.* (1988) also showed that men tend to be rated as less deserving of sympathy when raped by a female than when raped by a male stranger.

As was argued in chapter 4, although rape perception studies such as these are useful in providing a systematic examination of the factors that affect the perception of rape events and in allowing a comparison of the views held about rape according to demographic location or professional status, they are limited in their ability to offer insight into dynamic accounting practices for male rape in social interaction. We want to explore in detail the way in which, in social interaction, attitudes, beliefs and explanations are skilfully constructed and defended as part of broader activity sequences such as evaluating the experience of the actors in an event or subtly exonerating the actions of an alleged perpetrator.

The analysis that follows is based on unconstrained discussion on the topic of male rape, and we treat the accounts offered as constructive and action-oriented. Our central concern is to explore whether and how mundane accounting practices produce or resist a 'rape supportive' social order in relation to the sexual victimisation of men.

Constructions of gender, sexuality and the experience of rape victims

The aim of this analysis is to explore the 'socially approved vocabularies' (Antaki, 1994) or culturally shared 'interpretative repertoires' (Potter and Wetherell, 1987; Wetherell and Potter, 1988; Edley, 2000) utilised in the construction and evaluation of male rape. Particular attention is paid to the speakers' manipulation of membership category labels and descriptions of membership features (Wowk, 1984; Antaki and Widdicombe, 1998). The analysis explores how the participants display and ascribe category memberships to themselves and the actors in the vignette. We consider how the deployment of identity categories is connected to the accomplishment of interactional business, such as the management of motives and reasons for what they say and do (Edwards, 1998). Throughout, analytic attention is paid to the social and rhetorical organisation of the unfolding accounts (Antaki, 1994; Wetherell, 1998; Kitzinger, 2000).

Extract 1
1. Fay: Have you seen *Pulp Fiction*?
2. Sam: Yeah
3. Fay: It reminds me of that where that man gets raped
4. Sam: Oh yeah, I know what you mean
5. Fay: That's disgusting, it's really horrible
6. Sam: Do you think it's worse a man getting raped than a women getting raped?
7. Fay: No, no because I can't imagine a man getting raped but I can think of a women getting raped. Well I can't but it means more to me

thinking of a woman getting raped and it probably means more to you thinking of a man getting raped

8. Sam: Yeah, I don't know
9. Fay: What about you?
10. Sam: It's just really pretty horrible anyway isn't it (Fay: oh yeah) you can't really put a measure on it cos like, I mean I suppose it's not as bad as being murdered in a way because you have a life afterwards
11. Fay: But it's not really a life is it
12. Sam: Well it is, I mean I think you can live through that sort of thing. I mean I know a girl that got raped (Fay: oh my God) and she's fine really you know, she's fine really she's just a normal person
13. Fay: Oh that's really good
14. Sam: And I think most people are but it's just a really traumatic incident when it actually happens
15. Fay: Yeah yeah, it's got to leave bad memories but I mean it could almost be worse for a man because it must be so hard to talk about it for a man
16. Sam: Well yes I suppose it's the fact that if you're a heterosexual man being raped then that would seem to be worse. It's weird, it's hard to say quite why
17. Fay: You couldn't
18. Sam: I mean partially there's the social thing of you'd be less likely to get support from people. I mean I don't know if you really would or not but you get the feeling perhaps that because of all the macho image and all that stuff and like people might take it more as, you know a joke or something even though it's not at all
19. Fay: And it's just not publicised that kind of thing is it, a man getting raped
20. Sam: I don't know
21. Fay: Well, people are much more aware of women being raped and can probably talk about it
22. Sam: Well many more women do get raped I think
23. Fay: Yeah. I've not got – I mean you know what you said before about, it's easier, I mean harder for a heterosexual man to talk about it. You know, if it's happened to him. I've not really got anything against homosexual men
24. Sam: Well no
25. Fay: That's all. Just get that bit straight
26. Sam: Yeah, no I don't have a problem with it but erm, the point I was making more was that, I mean not even necessarily just a heterosexual man but someone who is to some degree homophobic or something, it would be more traumatic than, although I don't know if it really would because it's still someone forcing sex on you you know, which would be nightmarish

27. Fay: I can see your point though, because they're not going to experience that sort of thing before, it's going to be one heck of a shock

At the start of this extract Fay and Sam discover a shared point of reference for their discussion of male rape. They establish that they have both seen the film *Pulp Fiction* in which an incident of male rape is depicted. Fay evaluates the rape in *Pulp Fiction* as 'disgusting' and 'really horrible' (turn 5). This comment prompts Sam to ask Fay whether she thinks a man getting raped is 'worse' than a 'woman getting raped' (turn 6). Fay does not offer a direct answer to Sam's question. She instead claims that she 'can't imagine a man getting raped'. She argues that, as a woman, she is not in a position to make a judgement about the experience of rape for men. Sam agrees that male rape 'means more to him' (turn 7), but hedges that agreement with the addition of 'I don't know'. This weak agreement with Fay's assertion (that, as a man, male rape surely means more to Sam) functions to keep the discussion of the relative severity of male and female rape 'live'. In the next turn it prompts Fay to invite Sam to express his views on the matter. She does this by reflecting Sam's original question (posed in turn 6) back to him, 'What about you?' (turn 9).

At this point, the floor is wide open for Sam to offer his view on whether the experience of rape is worse for men or for women. However, he declines the opportunity to make this evaluation and instead offers the view that all rape is 'pretty horrible anyway' (turn 10). He resists the notion that it is possible to quantify and rank the severity of any particular rape experience in comparison to others by arguing that, 'you can't really put a measure on it' (turn 10). Thus, having initially raised for discussion the issue of whether rape is 'worse' for men or women (in turn 6), Sam now puts forward a possible counter-argument, that all rape experiences must be treated as equally bad. This argument is developed and sustained by grouping rape experiences together for comparison to other forms of assault, such as murder. In this case, rape is evaluated as 'not as bad' as murder because 'you have a life afterwards'.

The articulation of the argument that all rapes should be treated as equally 'traumatic' plays an important role in the construction of speaker identity in this part of the conversation. Sam displays himself as the kind of person who appreciates the grave nature of rape, as the kind of person who is, in principle, equally sympathetic to all categories of rape victim. Having established credentials as a basically 'sympathetic' person, the way is paved for the re-introduction of Sam's still hanging question from turn 6: whether it is worse for a man getting raped than a woman. Sam and Fay can now embark on a discussion of the reasons why rape 'could almost be worse' for men, without appearing unduly unsympathetic towards any other category of victim.

In the first half of the extract, the participants discuss rape in relation to the generic categories of 'men' and 'women'. Turn 16, however, marks a crucial point in the discussion. Sam introduces the idea that the *sexuality* of a male rape victim may be a significant factor when making judgements about the severity of a rape experience. The proposition that rape may be 'worse' for a man is thus refined by Sam to suggest that rape for *heterosexual* men is worse than for women and, by implication, homosexual men.[4] In the rest of the extract, arguments are presented first that heterosexual male rape victims will suffer more ridicule at the hands of society and second that the rape act itself will be more traumatic for heterosexual men than it is for other categories of victims. We will deal with the construction and consequences of these two arguments in turn.

Fay suggests in turn 15 that rape may 'almost be worse for a man because it must be so hard to talk about it for a man'. In turn 18 Sam develops this line of argument by suggesting that heterosexual men are less likely to get 'support from people' because of 'all the macho image and all that stuff . . . people might take it more as a joke or something'. Sam thus suggests that, in becoming a victim of rape, heterosexual men are likely to be perceived as 'less than men'. This is because they are likely to be judged as having departed from hegemonic (Connell, 1995) norms for masculinity. Cultural expectations dictate that 'macho' men exhibit strength, autonomy and sexual aggression. By definition then, 'macho' men cannot also be victims. Sam builds an image of 'society' where, in this context, 'people' are likely to ridicule heterosexual male rape victims for failing in their duties to be 'real men'. Sam, however, carefully distances himself from this view. He locates the tendency to ridicule heterosexual male rape victims as something endemic to a general category of 'people' 'out there' rather than as something about himself. He also explicitly states that male rape isn't a joke. In this way he is able to distance himself away from charges of being a member of the 'unsympathetic majority' that hold stereotypical views of acceptable male conduct. Sam's credentials as a basically sympathetic and enlightened speaker are thus maintained.

Over the course of turns 15–22, Sam and Fay develop an argument that rape is 'worse' for heterosexual men than for women or gay men because heterosexual men are less likely to receive support from society. In turn 23 Fay explicitly orients to the possibility that this argument may make her appear unduly unsympathetic to gay male rape victims. She emphatically states 'I've not really got anything against homosexual men . . . that's all . . . Just get that bit straight'. Sam enthusiastically agrees (turns 24–26) that he also 'does not have a problem with it' (i.e. homosexual men and homosexuality). Sam and Fay thus anticipate, and deny, any possible charges that their particular concern for *heterosexual* men is motivated by homophobia.

In turn 26 the topic switches from the issue of the likely public response to male rape victims to the experience of the rape act itself. Sam suggests that for a 'heterosexual' victim or for a victim 'who is to some degree homophobic or something', the rape act would be 'more traumatic'. Immediately following this utterance, Sam also articulates the contrary view, that forced sex, under any circumstances, is 'nightmarish'. This offers Fay the opportunity of agreeing with either of these points of view, which are presented as provisional, and the opportunity for Sam of retracting either of them. In turn 27 she explicitly reflects back *her* understanding of Sam's developing central argument. She announces that she can see his point, i.e. that heterosexual men suffer more than other categories of rape victim, because 'they're not going to have experienced that sort of thing before' and thus, it will be 'one heck of a shock'. The formulation 'that sort of thing' is vague. However, it seems likely that Fay is referring to what is assumed to be the normative *sexual* practice of 'straight' and 'gay' men. The rape experience is judged to be 'worse' for heterosexual men because the physical act of rape is assumed to deviate from the normative sexual practice of 'straight' men. Conversely, it is assumed to replicate (or resemble) the normative sexual practice of 'gay' men.

In the next extract, the main topics for discussion are, once again, the experience of the rape act itself and society's response to male rape victims in the aftermath of rape.

Extract 2

1. Gary: I mean it's like a thing where I reckon, I suppose it gets to a heterosexual man that, I mean for a woman to be raped by a man, it's, it's a heterosexual act, whereas for a man to be raped by another man it's a homosexual act and I don't know, it it, not only, it destroys yourself and, sexuality as well really, erm, I don't
2. Sarah: Puts your own sexuality in your own mind perhaps
3. Gary: Yeah, yeah, also I mean in the rape of women I think that when a woman has been raped you can say all right, she's been raped by a man, sort of in most cases a man is bigger, stronger
4. Sarah: Yeah, it's coming down to the ableness, the issue that men are stronger than women generally, and so it's, if you're raped by another man
5. Gary: Yeah, and so if you're raped by another man then you'd think, people would say, 'you're a bloke why couldn't you fight them off, why couldn't you stop him from doing that'. It's words that normally you'd say, I mean oh well, you know

As in extract 1, victim gender and sexuality are raised by the participants as relevant factors when evaluating the impact of rape for different categories of victims. In turn 1, Gary suggests that rape 'gets to' a heterosexual man. In sketching out the reasons why, he compares the case of a woman raped by a man with the case of a man raped by a man. Gary constructs the former as 'a heterosexual act' and the latter as a 'homosexual act'. The participants once again draw a strong line between categories of sexual identity and sexual practice: heterosexuals do one thing (vaginal sex) and homosexuals do another (anal sex). This boundary is so firmly drawn that male on male rape is described as necessarily entailing the experience of a '*homosexual* act' and this experience is constructed as particularly 'destructive' for a heterosexual man, leading him to question his heterosexuality.

As in extract 1, the participants make sense of male rape within a phallocentric version of gender, sexuality and sexual practice, which is based in a model of reproductive biology (Weeks, 1986; Jackson, 1987; Nicolson, 1994). Within this framework, the idealised heterosexual male is constructed as potent and non-permeable, and 'normal' sexual activity is strictly defined as penetration of the female body by the phallus (Ussher, 1997; Wood, 2000). A clear distinction is made between 'heterosexuality' and 'homosexuality' as discrete categories of sexual identity, which in turn are considered to confer distinct forms of sexual practice, for example anal penetration is an activity that conventionally goes with the category 'homosexual'. It is important, however, to underline the socially constructed status of the sexual identity/practice categories that inform the accounts presented here. Anal penetration, for example, carries a range of different cultural meanings from 'sexual/desirable' to 'undesirable/ perverse'. However, it is far too simplistic to straightforwardly ascribe these meanings to gay men and heterosexual men/women respectively (Lees, 1997; Wood, 2000). Wood (2000) presents a range of evidence that suggests that anal sex is unappealing for some men who identify as gay, whereas some men and women identifying as heterosexual engage in activities which bring them anal pleasure. As Ussher similarly argues:

> we should ask the question whether this argument about the true biological cause of sexual orientation is a red herring. For what it assumes is that there is this simple distinction between heterosexuality and homosexuality, that gay men or lesbians are a homogenous group of people identifiably different from the heterosexual man or woman . . .
>
> (Ussher, 1997: 303–304)

> Making a primary distinction between heterosexual and homosexual identity or behaviour is a social decision, not a biological given . . .
>
> (Ussher, 1997: 305)

> This is not to say that 'homosexuality' does not exist . . . It is to question these very simple distinctions and to draw attention to the fact that in many cultures this is not a line used to distinguish and

divide people. It is the dominance of phallocentric heterosexual ideologies that dictates the narrow boundaries of sexual behaviour and desire for (and between) women and men . . . as Garber has argued, the public adoption of one sexual label or another is not, 'a *description* of a sex life, but an event within it . . . to narrate a sex life is itself a sexual performance.'

(Ussher, 1997: 306)

The experience of rape is judged by the participants to be worse for heterosexual men than it is for women and gay men because the rape act is assumed to deviate from socially constructed norms of sexual expression for men positioned as heterosexual, whereas it is assumed to replicate 'regular sex' for women and gay men. Male victims identified as heterosexual are argued to be particularly deserving of sympathy on these grounds. However, this argument also has the effect of diminishing the importance of rape and of trivialising its devastating effects for women, and men positioned as 'gay' (Anderson and Doherty, 1996; Ussher, 1997; Scarce, 1997). To argue that acts of rape replicate normative sexual acts is to minimise and deny the status of rape as an act of *violence*, a humiliating expression of power (Brownmiller, 1975; Burt and Estep, 1981). In his discussion of male rape, Scarce notes that the effect of this move is to 'reduce the tragedy of the rape of a gay man . . . the person has already experienced the physical act so it's no big deal' (1997: 64). However, as Ussher argues,

Sexual violence is 'sexual' in that the hatred is directed at the sexual body . . . or because the enactment of such violence often parodies that of a non-abusive sexual encounter. In every other way these are acts of violence, degradation and defilement – as far from a consensual sexual experience as most [victims] could ever possibly contemplate.

(Ussher, 1997: 420)

In turns 3–5 Gary and Sarah switch to a discussion of the way in which societal attitudes may also differently affect female and male victims of rape. Gary and Sarah agree that there is a plausible explanation for the victimisation of women by men in acts of rape: 'you can say, all right, she's been raped by a man . . .' who 'in most cases' is 'bigger, stronger'. Here, socially approved vocabularies of gender and sexuality are readily utilised to construct an account for the rape of women. This repertoire constructs men as 'stronger than women generally' (turn 4) and positions women as the 'natural' ('you can say alright') victims of more 'able' (turn 4) men.

Working with this understanding of gender relations, Gary then considers the possible response to male victims of rape. His opinion is prefaced by 'you'd think', which is then immediately repaired to 'people would say' (turn 5). This self-repair occurs at a crucial point in the conversation – it prefaces the expression of an opinion that could be interpreted as an overly harsh piece of victim-blaming, that a 'bloke' (archetypal 'real man') should be able to defend himself from a rapist. Male victims of rape, by implication, are positioned here as not 'blokes', as men who have, by definition, failed as men: 'you'd think, people would say, "you're a bloke why couldn't you fight them off, why couldn't you stop him from doing that"' (turn 5). The repair displays an orientation on the part of the speaker to be identified as neutral (if not sympathetic) towards male rape victims, which helps to maintain the rhetorical weight of the argument expressed (Potter, 1996). Gary accomplishes this by distancing himself from the more personal 'you'd think' and instead constructs the negative evaluation of male rape victims which follows as located in others, 'people would say'.

As in extract 1 then, rape is evaluated as worse for heterosexual men because first, the rape act is assumed to deviate from the normative sexual practice of heterosexual men and second, because 'society' is portrayed as unsympathetic towards men who violate the norms of masculinity. In the final extract presented, Chris also raises these two issues as relevant in response to Stella's question about whether male and female victims of rape are likely to be 'treated differently' (turn 1).

Extract 3

1. Stella: I wonder if you get treated differently if you're a man who's been raped rather than a women cause . . .?
2. Chris: I suppose because if you were a heterosexual male um, being raped by another male, although they'd be equally as traumatic and I'm not trying to differentiate between the two, um (Stella: There's an extra thing as well) the fact that you're being raped also by someone who's not of your sexual group I suppose, yeah for men because (a) in a way I suppose it's far more, this sounds a bit prejudiced but I would imagine that it's socially more accepted for a female to be a victim than for a man to be a victim (Stella: That's true) and therefore, with that in the back of his mind you've almost been emasculated (a) sexually and (b) sort of, I mean it smacks of machismo, but if you've been raped it's, for a man anyway, whether right or wrong you're going to feel really, I don't know, emasculated I think is the best way of saying it.
3. Stella: Yes, I know, you should have been able to stick up for yourself or something. Yes, it's true.

As in extracts 1 and 2, at the start of this conversation Chris similarly argues that the sexuality of male rape victims is a relevant factor when making a comparison between the treatment of male and female rape victims. Once again, it is argued that heterosexual men suffer more and are likely to be treated more harshly than other categories of rape victim. This potentially contentious view is produced *indirectly* using a 'two-sided' style of expression, where the speaker also disclaims the contentious statement. In turn 2 Chris denies that the rape of heterosexual men and women is different: 'they'd be equally as traumatic and I'm not trying to differentiate between the two' directly before sketching the reasons why the experience of male and female rape victims could be evaluated as different. Contentious views are frequently delivered in this way (e.g. see van Dijk, 1987; Griffin, 1989; Billig *et al.*, 1988; Edwards and Potter, 1992). The disclaiming utterance allows the speaker to avoid censure and here to establish credentials as the kind of person who appreciates the 'traumatic' nature of rape in general. Stella gives Chris a conversational 'green light' to go ahead and 'differentiate' (turn 3) the rape experiences of heterosexual men and women with her overlapping turn: 'There's an extra thing as well'.

His first point is that, for 'a heterosexual male', the perpetrator is someone 'who is not of your sexual group' (turn 2). It is therefore assumed that male rape offenders are necessarily 'homosexual', whereas female rape (by implication) is constructed as consistent with socially constructed norms of heterosexuality. Interestingly, statistics show that perpetrators of male rape are more commonly heterosexual. Male rape nevertheless tends to be constructed and explained as a 'homosexual problem', and as a sexually motivated crime, rather than as an expression of power and aggression (McMullen, 1990).

Chris prefaces the next portion of his argument – it is more socially accepted for women than men to be victims – with a form of 'stake confession' (Potter, 1996): 'This sounds a bit prejudiced but . . .'. This operates as an acknowledgment that the opinion he is about to voice could be treated as somewhat biased, here against female victims of sexual violence. As discussed below, it could easily be heard as normalising or even trivialising the victimisation of women. The stake confession displays the speaker as honest and objective, as someone who is *already aware* of the potentially contentious nature of the view that is nevertheless about to be put forward. As Potter argues, this is rhetorically powerful because it is disarming; 'it puts objectors in the position of making a point that has already been conceded' (Potter, 1996: 130).

Chris and Stella agree that men and women are going to be treated differently in the aftermath of rape because it is not as socially accepted for men to be victims. They argue that a male rape victim is 'going to feel really, I don't know, emasculated I think is the best way of saying it' (turn 2). The term 'emasculated' signals a departure from the script of hegemonic masculinity, where 'real men' are constructed as potent and the male body is constructed as non-permeable and 'endowed with physical closure' (Wood, 2000). The female body, by comparison, is constructed as penetrable and women are treated as *destined* to have their bodily integrity shattered. Male rape victims are therefore positioned as different from female rape victims in having transgressed both socially constructed gender boundaries and constructions of 'normal sex'. Chris and Stella thus argue that male rape victims suffer an 'extra trauma' compared to women in their experience of the rape act and that they will be treated differently to female victims because they will be judged to have failed (and may tell themselves that they have failed) in their masculine duty to 'stick up for themselves' (see turn 3). Chris carefully distances himself as the author of this latter view, building credentials as a neutral, convincing speaker on this topic. He acknowledges that to characterise male rape victims as 'emasculated' – as feeble and ineffective (feminised) – 'smacks of machismo'. In other words, this action is perhaps, in itself, an inappropriate (victim-blaming) display of masculinity. The contentious nature of Chris' description of male rape is also signalled by the hedged ('I don't know', turn 2), equivocal ('whether right or wrong') way in which the description is formulated.

Evaluating the experience of male rape: a 'hierarchy of suffering'

In extracts 1–3, we have seen that the participants raised two issues for discussion in response to the male rape vignette: the likely societal response to male rape victims in the aftermath of rape and the experience of the rape act itself. In both cases, the participants engage with these issues by comparing and evaluating the treatment and experience of different categories of rape victim. 'Men' are differentiated from 'women' as victims, and 'men' as a category are further differentiated according to sexuality: 'heterosexual' or 'gay'. A hierarchy of suffering is established whereby rape is judged to be worse (more 'horrible', 'disgusting', 'shocking' [extract 1], 'destructive' [extract 2], 'traumatic' [extract 3]) for heterosexual men than it is for women or gay men. Different degrees of sympathy are accorded to these different categories of victim on the basis of stereotypical assumptions regarding gender, sexual identity and sexual practice. The participants evaluate the experience of the depicted rape by making a comparison between the rape act and a 'regular' act of consensual sexual intercourse. In both cases, the participants draw on interpretative repertoires of phallocentric heterosexuality and stereotypical homosexuality to construct an understanding of what constitutes normative or regular sex and what, therefore, constitutes an act of rape (Anderson and Doherty, 1996; Ussher, 1997). In other words, sex and sex crimes are both socially constructed concepts that reflect hegemonic phallocentric representations of 'woman', 'man' and 'sex' (Ussher, 1997).

The starting point for these participants is to consider rape as primarily a *sexual* act, behaviour that is likely to be motivated by sexual desire. The central issue for them in evaluating the experience of rape is the extent to which the supposed rape act deviates from their understanding of normative sexual practice for the different categories of victim that they construct. If the experience of male-on-male rape is evaluated according to this criterion, the outlook for victims constructed as 'heterosexual' is reasonably positive. The evidence suggests that they will at least be judged to have genuinely suffered, but principally on the grounds that they are assumed to have experienced a sexual act that is foreign to them. However, judged against the same criterion, the devastating impact of rape as a violent assault for women, and men positioned as 'homosexual', is likely to be downgraded on the grounds that an experience of rape is assumed to be essentially the same as a consensual sexual act.

In support of this conclusion, Mitchell *et al.* (1999) similarly found that homosexual victims are rated as deriving more pleasure and experiencing fewer traumas from rape than heterosexual victims. In a similar vein, Smith *et al.* (1988) showed that male rape victims tend to be rated as less deserving of sympathy when raped by a female as opposed to a male stranger. McCaul *et al.* concluded that in general, conceptualising a specific act of rape more in a sexual versus a violent manner causes persons to blame the rape victim to a greater extent (McCaul *et al.*, 1990).

When making judgements about the severity of an experience of rape, the evidence therefore suggests that social participants discriminate between different categories of victim, and they do this primarily on the grounds of gender and sexual identity. Our study demonstrates that the issue of victim sexuality is raised spontaneously by the *participants* themselves as a relevant factor when making judgements in conversation about the experience of rape victims. If participants judge that an alleged rape matches the stereotype of 'regular sex' for a particular category of victim, then they are also likely to downgrade or dismiss its status as a violent assault and are likely to offer less sympathy and support for the victim than is appropriate in the context of violent assault.

In their typology of accounts, Semin and Manstead (1983) suggest that one possible way of justifying 'wrong-doing' may be to claim that the effect of an action has been misrepresented, for example by denying that injury has been sustained or by minimising the impact of an action. Our analysis demonstrates that social participants do actually use this form of account when reasoning about rape. The trauma of rape for gay men and for women is downgraded by stressing the supposed similarity of rape, in somatic terms, to acts of consensual sex. Ultimately, this form of account at least partially exonerates an alleged rapist who can be re-cast as merely stretching the boundaries of what has been constructed as normative, or at least regular, sexual conduct.

Validation of our analysis is provided by the way the participants themselves orient to the possibility that, in arguing that a rape experience is more severe for heterosexual men than it is for any other category of victim, they could be heard as unduly *unsympathetic* towards other rape victims.

This is evident in the way the participants build credentials as basically 'neutral' and 'sympathetic' speakers and in the way that the arguments are skilfully constructed to deny charges of being dismissive towards the rape of women and gay men.

In extracts 1–3, the participants also argue that, in becoming a rape victim, a heterosexual man will be perceived by 'society' as having departed from hegemonic masculinity. As such, it is argued that they will be forced to suffer in silence (extract 1), be ridiculed (extract 2) or ostracised as an emasculated man (extract 3). This finding is consistent with those of Perrott and Webber (1996), who showed that male rape victims tend to be held responsible for rape on account of their 'failure' to defend themselves from an attack or to otherwise escape from the situation. Hegemonic under-standings of femininity are mobilised to argue that victimisation is, on the other hand, an expected part of womanhood. The speakers' own position on the legitimacy of ridiculing male rape victims remains ambiguous. They distance themselves from the ridicule of male rape victims, skilfully avoid-ing charges of victim-blaming, but at the same time construct the ridicule of male rape victims as likely to be a commonplace activity.

We noted in chapter 2 that experimental paradigms for studying reason-ing about rape produce overall low mean scores on measures of victim blame and indicate low levels of acceptance of rape myth statements. However, our analysis shows that throughout their conversations, the par-ticipants display some awareness that a directly unsympathetic argument may be censured (Edwards and Potter, 1992) in that potentially contentious arguments were produced indirectly. It seems likely that experimental tasks that offer no room for distancing, equivocation or hedging in the produc-tion of an argument may also fail to appreciate the subtlety and complexity of rape-supportive discourse.

'He's either stupid, wanted it or is very vulnerable'

In the second half of this chapter, we examine three extracts where the participants deal more directly with the issue of accountability for the incident of male rape depicted in the vignette.

Extract 4
1. Mike: I was a bit suspicious when it was one man who raped him because I think that unless this chap who was allegedly raped, and he was enormously weaker than the other guy, there's no go considering the muscularness of like where he was raped, there's no-one going in there like unless he wants it, like
2. Clare: that's a terrible thing to say
3. Mike: I know

4. Clare: because he might have had a knife or something else
5. Mike: yes, exactly
6. Clare: holding it to him, or a gun. It doesn't say anything about a weapon does it?
7. Mike: That's the thing. I was just quite surprised 'cos there'd have to be some. Usually I think in male rapes there's either a group of men or you know, a threat here like, a weapon or something

In turn 1, Mike suggests that he was 'a bit suspicious' to learn from the vignette that the victim was attacked by a single perpetrator. The suspicion refers to the legitimacy of the alleged victim's claim to have been raped. Mike questions whether anal penetration is physically possible without consent: 'there's no go considering the muscularness of like where he was raped, there's no-one going in there like unless he wants it, like' (turn 1), unless the victim is 'enormously weaker' (turn 1) than his attacker. Victim weakness is offered here as an explanation for the occurrence of male rape. In these circumstances, Mike suggests that he could treat a rape claim as genuine and believable. It isn't clear here whether a rape victim would be found culpable in relation to the attack on account of weakness, but the analysis of extracts 1–3 above does suggest that a victim may at least be at risk of ridicule for having failed *as a man* to defend himself from an assault.

Mike argues that unless a victim is exceptionally weak, anal penetration could only be possible with consent, 'there's no-one going in there like unless he wants it, like' (turn 1). Here the male body is constructed as essentially non-penetrable, a central theme of hegemonic masculinity where the masculine body is constructed as a potent, non-permeable fortress (Wood, 2000). Mike reproduces this discourse to construct the anus as both a potential site of rupture for the non-permeable body and also as a guardian of hegemonic masculinity and heterosexuality, equipped to perform this role because of its muscularity, itself a characteristic of 'manliness'. In this account, a man can only be anally penetrated if he actively makes a choice to yield to a penetrator, and in so doing by implication set aside his manliness. Put another way, Mike argues that rape of the masculine body is literally not possible because anal penetration can only happen with consent. He therefore concludes that the alleged victim must have 'wanted it', the encounter was one of consensual sexual intercourse, and that his rape claim should not be believed.

Clare vehemently disagrees with this suggestion (turn 2) by pointing out that the alleged victim may have been forced to yield to his attacker, threatened by the presence of a weapon such as a knife or a gun (turns 4 and 6). Clare notes in turn 6 that the vignette does not specifically mention the presence of a weapon during the rape incident. Mike uses this as support for his argument that the legitimacy of the rape claim should therefore be treated as 'suspect': 'That's the thing' (turn 7). In this final turn of the extract, Mike rhetorically strengthens the argument presented in turn 1 by himself as knowledgeable on the topic of male rape, the procedure for which is constructed as standard and widely known by the use of the qualifier 'usually' and the pluralisation of male rape to 'rapes'.

Extract 5
1. Dan: This point about him being raped before
2. Jackie: Yeah
3. Dan: That's like, like you say you find it very strange
4. Jackie: Yeah it is quite
5. Dan: He's either got tendencies towards being gay, leads people on (Jackie: yeah) or is just very vulnerable

At the start of this extract, Dan draws attention to the 'raped once before' information from the vignette and both Dan and Jackie agree that this point is 'very strange' (turn 3) and later suggest that it is 'a bit weird'. This feature of the rape vignette is thus identified as puzzling, prompting specu-lation in turns 5 and 6 about why the victim may have been raped twice. Dan offers two solutions to the puzzle, which we'll deal with in turn.

First, he suggests that the victim may have 'tendencies towards being gay, leads people on' (turn 5). The formulation 'leads people on' transfers the agency and responsibility for the encounter from the alleged perpetrator to the alleged victim, redefining the victim as a provocateur who is given to deliberately misrepresenting his desires and intentions to others. The projection of a homosexual identity 'tendencies towards being gay' offers a sexual motivation for why the alleged victim may 'lead people on'. The formulation 'tendencies' suggests that the alleged victim is not openly gay, rather that his desire for other men is ordinarily kept private and hidden. This explanation therefore reconfigures what was originally depicted as a violent rape on an unsuspecting victim to a sexual encounter that was actively sought out by the alleged victim. The charge of rape is explained by implying that the alleged victim either 'cried rape' (to keep his 'tendencies' hidden) or withdrew his consent at the last moment ('leads people on'). Either way, in projecting a gay identity onto the alleged victim, sympathy is transferred from him to the alleged perpetrator, who is repositioned as the innocent and unsuspecting 'lover'. Dan therefore explains how the victim could have been raped twice by suggesting that the rape claims are deceitful and likely to be made habitually by a man who has repressed homosexual desire.

Negative stereotypes of homosexuality are invoked here to position the alleged victim as responsible for the events depicted in the vignette. Gay men are commonly depicted as predatory, engaging in public sex as part of a regular 'Martini' lifestyle, seeking out casual and covert pick-ups anytime, anyplace, anywhere. The circumstances of stranger rape as depicted in the rape vignette therefore get reformulated here as indicative of the normative gay sexual script, as a description of the way in which one would *expect* a young man to explore or express homosexual desire. In this way it is possible to see how the projection of a gay identity (onto any man) combined with the mobilisation of stereotypical understandings of homosexuality can swiftly lead to the dismissal of an accusation of male rape.

Second, Dan suggests that an alternative explanation might be that he is 'just very vulnerable'. Vulnerability is a stereotypically feminine quality, by definition, characteristic of individuals not able to defend themselves from physical or emotional assault. This explanation therefore once again mobilises the socially approved vocabulary of gender to argue that rape of the normative masculine body is simply not possible. The view expressed here is that victimisation only happens to effeminate individuals who are, necessarily, less than 'real men'. Being 'vulnerable' is thus offered here (as is 'weakness' in extract 4) as a plausible (if pitiable) explanation for rape victimhood and for repeat victimisation.

In the final data extract of this chapter, the participants once again project 'subconscious' homosexual desires onto the alleged victim as a way of making sense of and dismissing the rape claim in the vignette, and in addition we will see how accusations of victim stupidity and naïvety (such a familiar theme in chapter 4 where we examined accounts for female rape) emerge here in relation to male rape victims in the context of 'failure' to prevent a second rape.

Extract 6
1. Fiona: It doesn't say, but even so, to be raped once you'd have thought, I wouldn't walk, if I'd been raped I wouldn't be walking through a dimly lit area by myself (Tony: no) without any alarm (Tony: Exactly) he was obviously like, in his gym kit, or whatever (Tony: Yes) and like to not look round, it's all a bit bizarre really
2. Tony: Yes, it is, it is very odd, I mean either he's very naïve or he's making something up or he wants to be raped, I mean I don't know I mean
3. Fiona: Yeah, he wanted it to happen
4. Tony: Yes, yes that would seem a fairly logical conclusion
5. Fiona: Yes
6. Tony: Yes, actually that would seem the most logical conclusion

[17 turns omitted]

7. Tony: Well anyway, my conclusion is that either he's very stupid or more probably he was asking for it, or hoping that it would happen.
8. Fiona: Arh, I think that's pretty harsh, um. I think he was extremely stupid and maybe naïve. I don't know, I can't believe he was that naïve

but I don't know, maybe he thought because male rapes don't happen as often that he wouldn't be raped again. I mean the thing is, it can't, yes I don't understand at all why he did it basically, cause it is such a stupid thing to do. So it is possible that he, yes he was, yes, maybe he

9. Tony: Maybe he's just
10. Fiona: Maybe he was sub-consciously, he wanted it
11. Tony: Maybe he's maybe he's just a really really sort of um, what's the word, um, maybe he was just really curious to find out
12. Fiona: But it depends cause, it depends what happened after he last got raped, say he got raped last time he got loads of sympathy
13. Tony: Maybe he's homosexual and he's really embarrassed about his sexuality and er, hoping that some guy comes on to him at 9.30 on the campus, no I'm serious, maybe he actually was hoping it happened, maybe he's really interested and curious and excited by it
14. Fiona: But that's such an extreme way to do it
15. Tony: Oh it is, um, I mean, if you, if you
16. Fiona: Yes, I suppose, because if you don't know his background about it
17. Tony: If you were 22, you were single
18. Fiona: Yes, but also you don't know
19. Tony: And if you were homosexual you'd be
20. Fiona: You don't know any background about him either, you could, he might be gay
21. Tony: Yes, I reckon the fact that he is 22, single and gay, and he's a erm, looking for it

At the start of the extract, Fiona speculates on the impact that being raped once before ought to have made on the alleged victim. She compares her own likely actions in such circumstances with the victim's behaviour, positioning herself as conforming to a 'common sense' position in contrast to the alleged victim, whose alleged actions (walking alone in a 'dimly lit' area, wearing a 'gym kit', not carrying an alarm, lack of suspicion towards a man walking behind) are constructed as 'bizarre' (turn 1) and 'odd' (turn 2).

Masculine sexuality is routinely constructed as dangerous and uncontrollable, and the message that women need to be vigilant at all times against the risk of sexual attack is part and parcel of gender socialisation. As we saw in chapter 4, female rape victims are held responsible for rapes perpetrated against them, on the grounds that they failed to take 'sensible' precautions to prevent a 'foreseeable' rape. Central to this argument is the erroneous but 'common sense' view that the circumstances of rape are entirely predictable and thus easily preventable by the 'average sensible woman'. In rape-supportive discourse, mere awareness of the risk of rape creates a 'reasonable' obligation to view oneself as a potential victim and to regulate one's behaviour according to societal norms for risk reduction, which in practice plays a part in the maintenance of gender relationships in patriarchy. The link between risk awareness and victim responsibility is so strong in our culture that in the aftermath of rape, it is the rape *victim's* behaviour that is scrutinised for evidence of 'recklessness' in a world that is constructed as full of obvious and preventable dangers (Doherty and Anderson, 1998). Constructing an alleged victim's behaviour as reckless enables participants to categorise the victim as 'stupid' (as in turns 7 and 8 above) or 'naïve' (as in turn 2 above), as beneath contempt and thus blameworthy, 'rapeworthy' even, without this seeming like an overly harsh conclusion.

In considering the case of male sexual victimisation, Fiona and Tony argue that the victim's previous experience of rape should have created awareness in him that the sexual victimisation of men is possible. In the context of this awareness, they locate the cause of the rape in the victim's naïvety or stupidity, completely sidelining the agency of the perpetrator in the incident described. Indeed Tony and Fiona find the *victim's* behaviour so reprehensible ('very stupid', 'extremely stupid', 'such a stupid thing to do') and so beyond comprehension ('I don't understand why he did it basically') that they consider that two other explanations for the rape claim are equally plausible – 'he's making something up' (turn 2), i.e. he 'cried rape'; or 'he wants to be raped' (turn 2), i.e. 'yeah, he wanted it to happen' (turn 3); 'more probably he was asking for it, or hoping it would happen' (turn 7).

In turn 8, Fiona unequivocally accuses the alleged victim of stupidity, but initially resists Tony's alternative explanation that the victim was hoping that the 'rape' would happen as 'pretty harsh'. Throughout the rest of the extract Tony expands and strengthens his argument that the victim 'wanted it' and Fiona continues to offer some resistance to this view – e.g. by making the lesser charge that he only 'subconsciously' wanted it (line 10); by suggesting that the rape claim may be motivated by a desire for sympathy (turn 12) or by reminding Tony (turns 16 and 20) that they are merely speculating on the alleged victim's sexuality – until she eventually offers some weak support of Tony's position, 'you could, he might be gay' (turn 20). The remainder of the analysis of this extract will focus on the construction and consequences of categorising the alleged victim as gay.

Tony speculates that the alleged victim was 'just really curious to find out' (turn 11 and also turn 13) and articulates the possibility that the vignette depicts a homosexual man 'embarrassed' about his sexuality (turn 13). This construction of the victim's psychological state as 'embarrassed' then works both as an explanation for why the victim might be actively seeking sex in public places with anonymous men ('hoping some guy comes on to him') and as an explanation for the rape claim. Fiona questions the validity of Tony's argument by insisting that this would surely be 'an extreme way to do it', that is, express one's sexuality. Tony agrees with

Fiona but in a final flourish to his unfolding argument asserts that on the contrary, this would be normative 'cruising' behaviour for a young, single, gay man.

Thus, once again, the participants make the sexuality of the victim a relevant factor in discussing, defining and evaluating the incident described in the vignette. Here, the projection of a homosexual identity onto the victim works as a strategy to discredit the victim's rape claim. Indeed his very status as a rape victim is called into question by reformulating the events in the vignette from an alleged rape into a sexually motivated encounter that was actively desired by the alleged victim. The participants mobilise gay stereotypes to reframe the rape incident depicted in the vignette as typical sexual behaviour for gay men who are either embarrassed by their sexuality and later 'cry rape' or who are constructed as desiring public, anonymous sex, presumably because it feeds into a self-destructive wish to be brutalised.

Discussion

The aim of this chapter was to explore whether and how mundane conversational accounting practices reproduce or resist a 'rape supportive' social order in relation to the sexual victimisation of men. We have examined the ways in which social participants raise and discuss issues relating to victim experience and accountability for an alleged incident of male rape depicted in a rape vignette.

When making judgements about the severity of an experience of rape, the evidence suggests that social participants discriminate between different categories of victim and they do this primarily on the grounds of gender and sexual identity. In focusing on the somatic aspects of rape, the participants construe rape as primarily a *sexual* act. The central issue for them in evaluating the experience of rape is the extent to which the supposed rape act deviates from their understanding of normative sexual practice for the different categories of victim that they construct. Consequently, the status of rape as an extreme act of *violence*, albeit perpetrated on the sexual body, remains hidden. We saw how, under these circumstances, victims constructed as 'heterosexual' are likely to be judged to have genuinely suffered, principally on the grounds that they are assumed to have experienced a sexual act that is foreign to them. Judged against the same criterion, victims categorised as 'gay' or 'women' in comparison are likely to receive rather less sympathy on the grounds that an experience of rape for them is assumed to be essentially the same as a consensual sexual act. We further argued that it is too simplistic to assume that particular sexual acts necessarily 'go with' categories of sexual identity. As McMullen argues in relation to the rape of men identifying as gay:

103

It is a mistaken notion that all gay people actively and passively enjoy anal intercourse. Many do not. People believe that because they are gay, somehow the rape is less severe than if they had been heterosexual. It is not. Rape is rape.

(McMullen, 1990: 50)

The devastating impact of rape as a violent assault for all victims is overlooked in much of the discourse analysed. The view that rape is not damaging because it's 'only sex' has been identified by many feminist scholars as contributing to the construction and maintenance of a rape-supportive culture (Ward, 1995; Gavey, 2005). Reframing rape as 'sex' serves to minimise the violence and severity of a rape experience and also normalises the alleged perpetrator's behaviour.

In the second half of the chapter we examined three extracts that touch on issues of accountability. We saw how the alleged victims were positioned as responsible for the events depicted in the vignette in several ways. In extract 4 it was argued that rape of the masculine body is literally not possible because anal penetration can only happen with consent. The participants conclude that the alleged victim must therefore have 'wanted it', that the encounter was one of consensual sexual intercourse, and that his rape claim should not be believed. Second it is suggested that a male rape victim might be 'weak' or 'just very vulnerable', that sexual victimisation only happens to effeminate individuals who are, necessarily, less than 'real men'. Being 'vulnerable' is offered as a plausible (if pitiable) explanation for male rape.

We also saw how, like female victims (Burt and Estep, 1981; Doherty and Anderson, 1998) a male rape victim can be constructed as 'stupid' and/or 'naïve' and thus responsible for rape on the grounds that he did not prevent the attack. In this way, victims are positioned negatively, as 'deserving' of what they got. It is interesting to note that this occurred readily in response to a vignette that, according to attribution theory, would be more likely to produce attributions of responsibility to the circumstances and not the victim (Anderson, 1996). The focus remains squarely on the victim as provocateur rather than on the rapist. It is important to recognise that rape is never deserved and that most of us have very little real control over the environment that we inhabit. The unquestioned link, so much in evidence in the discourse analysed here, between risk awareness, victim responsibility and victim blame needs to be firmly challenged if we are to move to a situation in which victims of rape are adequately supported.

Finally, we saw how the projection of a gay identity onto an alleged victim (and this may happen to any victim, regardless of his sexual identity) results in reframing the depicted rape as a consensual sexual encounter. The participants mobilise negative gay stereotypes to redefine the rape incident depicted in the vignette as typical sexual behaviour for gay men who are either embarrassed by their sexuality and later 'cry rape' or who are constructed as actively desiring public, anonymous and violent sex.

In the accounts of rape examined in this chapter, it is evident that gay men are culturally designed to be 'unrapeable'. On the one hand, the experience of rape is constructed as less severe for gay men than it is for victims positioned as heterosexual, and on the other, the projection of a gay identity onto an alleged victim effectively reframes an alleged rape as a normative sexual encounter for gay men. The evidence from an anonymous victim survey carried out by Lees (1997) indicates that the police often believe that rape is less traumatic for gay men and don't treat rape claims made by victims positioned as 'gay' seriously. Our analysis provides some support for this finding by demonstrating the discursive strategies by which rape victims that are openly (or obviously) gay, or victims who are positioned as gay, are likely to be discredited and treated unsympathetically.

There are clear implications here for education and training in institutional and everyday contexts. The message that 'rape is rape', whatever the gender or supposed sexual identity of the victim, needs to be firmly and repeatedly underlined if rape victims are to receive appropriate support or justice.

Notes

1. In comparison to 4986 and 5759 recorded cases of rapes perpetrated against women in 1995 and 1996 respectively.
2. There is some evidence to suggest that men report sexual victimisation even less frequently than women do (Pino and Meier, 1999).
3. Gleaned from discussions in the broader male rape literature on the incidence and characteristics of male rape, survivor's accounts, and modelled on existing items in Attitudes Towards Rape scales.
4. The distinction between 'heterosexual' and 'homosexual' as categories of victim is explicitly made in turn 23.
5. It should be noted that the description of the scene as 'dimly lit' and the suggestions that the victim was wearing his 'gym kit' and not carrying a rape alarm go beyond the details actually provided in the vignette.

6

METAPHORS IN
CONVERSATION ABOUT
FEMALE AND MALE RAPE

Metaphor, identity and the management of accountability

In this chapter, we examine the role of metaphor in talk about sexual violence. Metaphors are a significant feature of people's talk about their everyday lives and experiences (Gibbs and Franks, 2002). Lakoff and Johnson (1980) argue that our ordinary conceptual system is fundamentally metaphorical and that metaphors play a central role in defining our everyday realities (whole organisations have devoted significant amounts of time to studying the concept, testifying to its importance. See, for example, the Metaphor Analysis Project, based in the north of England, funded by ESRC's National Centre for Research Methodology (http://creet.open.ac.uk/projects/metaphor-analysis/index.cfm)). The essence of a metaphor is understanding and experiencing one kind of thing in terms of another (Lakoff and Johnson, 1980) and metaphors thus exploit imaginative connections which are shared within a culture and which link the familiar with the unfamiliar in the act of sense-making (Adams *et al.*, 1995). Metaphors are cultural-meaning systems that function as resources for understanding social experience or phenomena and can be likened to a filter or a lens through which we view social life; they are cultural resources, in other words, that can tell us how (and whether) to see natural objects and events (Oakley, 1974; Crotty, 1998).

Metaphors allow us to comprehend one aspect of a concept in terms of another, but in so doing, metaphorical concepts offer a particular or partial understanding of the phenomena in question, hiding or highlighting different aspects of the events or people under discussion. Kirmayer (1992: 332) points out that metaphors are not simply a literary trope but, in their invitation to think 'A is B', they involve a process of discovery or invention and are essentially creative of meaning. Metaphors are asymmetrical analogies, applying only certain features of the vehicle (the 'B' in the 'A is B' expression) to the topic. For example, 'surgeons are butchers' is distinct from 'butchers are surgeons' – each metaphorical expression draws on salient features of the vehicle to highlight latent features of the topic. In the context of social interaction, topic and vehicle always interact, colouring each other to determine which of the many potential features of each can be related and are relevant to the context and intention.

Metaphors can restructure a whole domain, generating a network of 'entailments', which highlight and make coherent (or 'true') certain aspects of our experience and suggesting certain actions rather than others:

> In all aspects of life . . . we define our reality in terms of metaphors and then proceed to act on the basis of metaphors. We draw inferences, set goals, make commitments and execute plans, all on the basis of how we in part structure our experience, consciously and unconsciously, by means of metaphor . . . metaphors highlight and make coherent our pasts, our present activities and our dreams, hopes and goals as well.
>
> (Lakoff and Johnson, 1980: 158, 233)

People construct meaning as they actively engage with the world they are interpreting (Crotty, 1998), and talk about the world and events has a 'could have been otherwise' quality (Edwards, 1997). Discursive psychologists connect this variability in descriptive practices to the context of dynamic social action (Potter and Wetherell, 1987; Edwards and Potter, 1992). Social participants manage versions of events and psychological themes to fit the demands of practical situations, including the management of accountability. The act of constructing and sustaining a version of the world from selected interpretative resources, such as metaphors, at the same time has the potential to obscure or deny alternative versions of events or identities. In this sense, alternative descriptions don't just differ from each other – they have an *argumentative quality* (Billig, 1987), containing a silent endorsement of particular concepts or views at the expense of alternatives (Billig, 1985; Gergen, 1985). An analysis of the use of metaphor in social interaction is thus an important element in understanding the constructive processes and rhetorical dynamics at work in an account and can offer a way of understanding how subtle features of language can construct and maintain social relationships and power relations (Adams *et al.*, 1995) and be implicated in the interactional management of identity and accountability (Doherty, 2000).

For example, consider the metaphors in play when accounting for business failure (Doherty, 2000). In this study, failing businesses and business people were metaphorically described as 'drowning' and as 'under assault', and business struggle was metaphorically represented by deploying climbing or journey metaphors.

Sean: There's too many places *going under* and they're big places
June: Well we're here and *struggling* you know we're *just managing to keep our heads above water* at the moment

107

The metaphor 'being in business is swimming' graphically represents the experience of small business ownership in a particular way; it offers a way of describing and accounting for business success and failure which in turn has implications for challenging or sustaining the prevailing ideologies that promote entrepreneurship and implies certain courses of action rather than others. Within this metaphorical frame success in business is to 'stay afloat' and failure is imagined as a 'struggle' to not 'go under', drown, to keep one's 'head above the water'. The notion of struggle against a force that threatens to engulf in these small business owners' accounts constructs a version of self as *trying*, trying very hard, and as *actively* engaged in the exhausting task of business maintenance. In terms of accountability, this partially negotiates responsibility for business troubles away from the businessperson and engenders sympathy – the businessperson is imagined as kicking against the elements with their last ounce of strength, doing their level best, in a determined effort to survive in a hostile environment. A number of actions also follow on from this metaphorical construction of life in business. If an individual is doing everything they can to help themselves, to keep from drowning, then it is culturally conventional, i.e. only fair, to expect to be offered a 'life-line', to be rescued or supported. External support and rescue agencies in the form of lenient banks or government policies thus enter the metaphorical frame as a new cast of characters – 'life guards' or 'life boat operators' maybe – who *ought to be* ready and waiting, morally or professionally obliged to move in response to distress signals from valiant 'swimmers' who have strayed into 'dangerous waters'. In practice then, the 'being in business is swimming' metaphor can be utilised by small business owners to account for business struggles in a way that avoids accusations of laziness and also to challenge the individualist ideological zeitgeist by suggesting that there should be limitations to the self-reliance expected of small business 'entrepreneurs'.

Another metaphorical frame at work in the business people's accounts was 'being in business is a fight', where business troubles were metaphorically represented as an assault against the person. In the following examples, the business people construct an image of self as victims of an external aggressor who can dish out a 'big blow' or put a 'stranglehold' on the business leaving them 'stuffed':

Sally: We had a *big blow* in September when we didn't get the [name of charity] money . . . so that gone it obviously left a very *big hole* and it also left a very *big gap* in all the provisions for the special schools as well . . . so erm that was *a blow*

Mark: If the work doesn't come in in great abundance (Kathy: mm mm) to to pay for that then you're stuffed

Mark: And rising interest rates just put a *stranglehold* on it

In Mark's account for the failure of his old company he describes how rising interest rates put a 'stranglehold' on the business, representing the business as the innocent victim of an economic policy that was metaphorically 'murderous'. The agent of failure in these accounts is constructed as external to the business and as aggressive and indiscriminate. In terms of managing accountability for business struggle then, this metaphorical frame functions to place responsibility outside of the business and the business persons who construct a version of self as 'minding their own business', only to be stopped in their tracks, assaulted by forces out of their control.

Feminist standpoint research on metaphor

Of considerable relevance to this chapter is the research on metaphors that has been conducted from the standpoint of feminist theory, particularly focusing on the role of metaphors in the maintenance of gender power relations (Stanley, 1977; Penelope, 1990). Numerous studies have documented the relationship between language and gender relations, and some of this work has specifically considered the role of metaphor in the identification and treatment of women in language and society (Weatherall and Walton, 1999). For example, sexual metaphors for women such as 'doll' (women as playthings), fox (women as sly animals) and sexual objects such as 'piece of ass', as well as the pervasive 'male as active, women as passive' construction of sentences about heterosexual activity both construct and delimit our understanding of gender and sexuality. Furthermore, metaphors such as these are part of the 'patriarchal universe of discourse' (Stanley, 1977), which form a pervasive sex-stereotyped conceptual framework used to understand and guide interactions between men and women. In their study concerning metaphors about sexual experience Weatherall and Walton (1999) found that the metaphors analysed in their sample reflected male dominance in sexual relations in the form of the 'active male, passive female' bias (e.g. 'he broke her in') and in terms of the objectification of women (e.g. 'she's a bit of crumpet').

A few studies have also focused on the relationship between metaphor and sexual violence, although these are considerably fewer in number than feminist theory's focus on metaphors and gender inequality. Metaphors which are mobilised to talk about women and relationships can have several effects such as justifying violence, concealing abuse and supporting entitlement to positions of power (Adams *et al.*, 1995). This latter study about the metaphorical construction of male violence towards women showed that the metaphors used by male participants frequently objectified women, e.g. 'when she came along she was just about *everything in the package* that I could want', and subjugated women, e.g. *'there's one boss* and that's me and end of story'.

Analysis of metaphor in conversations about female and male rape

Although there has been some recent interest in metaphors about sexual violence and more studies are now emerging in this area, few studies have explicitly considered metaphors used to talk about female and male rape, and none have compared the two. In this analysis, we use the previous data sets analysed in chapters 4 and 5 to examine the metaphorical construction of people, events and other themes of interest to the participants. We consider how these construct agency and accountability (both of the 'victims' in the rape and of the speakers themselves) when they discuss the female and male rape episodes.

As in previous chapters, the analysis that follows is based on unconstrained discussion on the topic of male rape, and we treat the accounts offered as constructive and action-oriented. Our central concern here is to document how male and female rape is talked about metaphorically. In particular, we focus on how the 'target domains' (Weatherall and Walton, 1999) of the victim, rapist and incident were talked about and which generative root metaphors (the vehicles, or source domains, e.g. rapist as being engaged on a journey – see Table 1) were used to construct meaning in relation to these target domains. We will argue that the mobilisation of metaphorical frames functions to construct the character and motivation of the alleged victim and rapist, as well as the experience and impact of male and female rape in different ways, with differing implications for the management of accountability and apportionment of blame and sympathy.

Metaphorical constructions of the incident

1. Science (female rape) vs. supernatural (male rape)

In this section we discuss and contrast the metaphorical vehicles used to give meaning to the incidents of female and male rape. The participants frequently described and discussed the female rape incident using a 'scientific' metaphorical frame – mobilising mathematical, statistical or medical language and concepts. For example:

Ben: Oh yeah, of course, but I mean, it's got *parallels* with like, with Aids, I mean, you know, if you don't take precautions at all then you're leaving yourself more open to the chances of getting Aids and in this case, of being raped

Sarah: That's right, and as we've just discussed, the *odds* are she wasn't raped in this sort of scenario

Simon: It's still, it's still, you've still increasing the *probability* of you being raped, you're not going to, increasing it from perhaps few, you're not *doubling your chance* or anything like that, but you're

110

Table 1 Target domains and root metaphors in talk about female and male rape

FEMALE RAPE			MALE RAPE		
Incident	*Victim*	*Rapist*	*Incident*	*Victim*	*Rapist*
Science	*Religion*	*Undercover agent*	*Paranormal/Supernatural*	*Broken/damaged*	*Journey*
e.g. *Math/Statistic* e.g. 'odds', 'probability', 'chance'	Female rape victim as 'fallen woman', 'nun'	Jumps out, pluck out, lurking, rapist as 'stalker'	Male rape as spooky, nightmarish, scary, hideous, bizarre, weird, freakish	Male rape victim as 'scarred', 'dented ego', 'shaken', 'shattered'	Rapist as 'driven to it', on a 'power trip'
e.g. *Geometry*	*Advert*		*Electric*	*Attracting force*	
Parallels, peripheral	e.g. 'sign on head'		Incident as 'shocking', a 'jolt'	Male rape victim as 'magnet', 'target', 'beacon'	
e.g. *Medicine*	*Mental illness*		*Catastrophe/Crisis*		
Symptoms, prevention better than cure	Female rape victim as 'not in right mind', 'daft', 'paranoid', 'going crazy', negative 'state of mind'		e.g. 'end of world', 'trauma'		

increasing the *probability* from, you know, one in 1000 to one in 500 or something like that

Susan: Oh yeah, I mean, you've gotta, it's all very well saying, you know, she's got the right, but you can't take the *chance*, can you?

Sarah: I mean, obviously the person at fault in all of this is the rapist yeah, and I don't really understand anything about the psychology of rape but I mean, you've gotta, we all know *prevention is better than cure* and rather than taking these minor steps to avoid women getting themselves in the situation

Ben: Try and get the *symptoms* and not the, I don't know, yeah

By contrast, male rape was frequently described and discussed by using terms and concepts from a 'supernatural/paranormal' metaphorical frame, e.g. male rape as 'spooky', 'nightmarish', 'scary', 'bizarre', 'weird' and 'freakish'. For example:

Sam: Yeah, no I don't have a problem with it but erm, the point I was making more was that, I mean not even necessarily just a hetero-sexual man but someone who is to some degree homophobic or something, it would be more traumatic than, although I don't know if it really would because it's still someone forcing sex on you you know, which would be *nightmarish*

David: Yeah, it's *weird*, you usually, you don't usually hear about, I mean, it's quite sad that you hear about women getting raped quite often

Sally: I don't think . . . it's a bit *scary* really. At least we've got little attack alarms in the office

Mike: I think that is quite *frightening* actually because being a young bloke like that guy's a year older than me, it is quite *spooky* because you don't get much stuff about male raping in the news

In mobilising the metaphorical vehicle of science to describe and discuss the target domain of female rape incidents, female rape is construed as mathematically predictable, and as knowable and describable in objective terms. This sense-making is in stark contrast to the construction of incidents of male rape, which are more frequently described by mobilising the meta-phorical vehicle of the paranormal or the supernatural, which functions to place male rape incidents in the realm of the unknowable, the otherworldly and the unpredictable. This is an interesting finding given that men, male affairs and masculinity have traditionally been associated with characteris-tics implied by science – objectivity, rationality, predictability and control.

The contrasting metaphorical frames described above can be thought of as cultural resources that enable the participants to construct and make sense of male and female rape in contrasting ways and which also play a key role in the management of accountability for the alleged incidents. The metaphorical vehicles of science and mathematics enable female rape to be constructed as a material 'hazard', an objectively describable event amenable to a 'scientific' analysis of the risk of occurrence. This construction of hazard/risk can function to emphasise the 'moral character of the risky individual' (Fox, 1999: 208) by adding weight to the suggestion that individuals have a responsibility to engage in practices of risk assessment and risk reduction. Victimhood is understood as a consequence of the failure to take this responsibility seriously, which can lead to victim-blaming. In the extracts above, female rape victimhood is thus imagined as under the control of a prospective victim who is subtly charged with the responsibility for being 'risk aware' and for engaging in practices that will reduce the risk of rape. This construction of rape as a material hazard also serves to direct accountability for the rape away from the perpetrator, who is configured as part of the hazard to be avoided by the person construed as 'at risk', *rather than as a responsible agent in his own right*. In these accounts, the female victim of rape is cast into the stereotypically feminine role of the irrational, illogical and, literally, unreasonable woman, by definition incapable of recognising hazards or of engaging in a scientific analysis of risk. However, from a postmodern perspective, the claimed objectivity of risk assessment is of course illusory (Fox, 1999). As we have argued elsewhere in this book, judgements about who, what or which behaviours are dangerous and who is at risk are always culturally contingent, located in, and playing a role in the maintenance of relations of power.

This point is brought into sharp focus when we examine the very different metaphorical vehicle of the paranormal/supernatural that the participants mobilise to make sense of risk and responsibility in relation to the target domain of male rape incidents. In contrast to the science and mathematics metaphors, this metaphorical framework construes male rape as a phenomenon that is not amenable to scientific analysis, which is unpredictable and subject to quirky, spooky and unexpected forces. Consequently, the accountability of male rape victims and perpetrators is handled very differently to the way it is handled in female rape incidents. The male victim is cast as an individual who couldn't reasonably be expected to have predicted or prevented the attack and this functions to position him as relatively blameless in relation to his victimhood. For example, a description of the occurrence of a male rape incident as 'freakish' carries the implication that it is an event that contravenes the natural order of things (being a 'freak of nature'), which can't be expected to conform to the rational and logical 'laws of science' in a predictable way. As such, male rape is construed as unavoidable and a male rape victim can be positioned as 'unlucky' rather than as accountable for his victim status.

Consistent with this social reasoning, in the analysis of conversations about male rape in chapter 5 we showed how the participants made the 'raped before' status of the alleged victim in the vignette a significant factor in their discussions about the sexuality and accountability of the male rape victims. This information was treated as evidence of a *pattern* in the occurrence of male rape, and this was argued by the participants to confer responsibility on the part of the dual rape victim to treat male rape as a predictable hazard and thus to be more 'risk aware' and to adopt 'reasonable' risk aversion strategies.

Metaphorical constructions of the victim

2. Female 'advertisements' vs. male 'magnets'

A number of metaphorical frames were mobilised to characterise the target domain of the rape victims in the vignettes, and once again, the metaphorical concepts utilised also carry different implications for the management of accountability. The female rape victims were often depicted as active agents in precipitating or provoking the rape, whereas male victims were frequently positioned as passive and vulnerable. A particularly interesting example of this is the description of a female rape victim as having 'advertised' herself for rape or as placing a 'sign on (or above) her head':

Stan: I mean, she was like, she might as well have just *written it up on a big sign and placed it above her head* saying . . .

This construction of the female rape victim is entirely consistent with the construction of rape as a material hazard amenable to a scientific analysis of risk, as discussed in the section above. In the above example, it is graphically suggested that she deliberately advertised herself as 'rapeable' by putting a sign on her head. In these constructs then, not only is the female victim construed as an irrational or illogical woman for failing to recognise a hazard and take steps to avoid it, she is cast as a *deliberate* risk-taker who actively invited or provoked the attack against her. This establishes her status as a reckless, culpable individual, fully accountable for the rape incident. Once again, the notion of the rapist as an active agent in the rape is rendered invisible – he can't be blamed for simply taking what was unambiguously (even willingly) offered. Indeed, the metaphorical vehicle of advertising entails the concept of 'products' (potential victims) being competitively displayed in terms of their distinct value to the target market (the rapist). In this way, the construct of the woman as 'advert' also implies consent on the part of the victim, subtly reframing the event as one that could or perhaps should be viewed as a consensual, sexual encounter. At this point it should be remembered that the participants are discussing an event that was described in the vignette as a violent assault: 'the woman was attacked and dragged away from the main path and sexually assaulted'.

This analysis of agency and accountability is also consistent with the frequent references made in the female rape conversations (and more widely) to the notion that female rape can be explained by arguing that rape victims put themselves in a position to be raped (also see Doherty and Anderson, 1998), e.g.

Frank: I mean, there's no pointer as to whether it was the same man is there, I mean, it's just the situations that make it probably more likely to occur, more likely for people so inclined to do it, I don't know, what would you say about, *could you have put yourself in that position*, what would you do?

Sarah: I mean, obviously the person at fault in all of this is the rapist yeah, and I don't really understand anything about the psychology of rape but I mean, you've gotta, we all know prevention is better than cure and rather than taking these minor steps *to avoid women getting themselves in the situation*

By contrast, male rape victims were frequently categorised in ways that imply they are passive and helpless in relation to the occurrence of the rape. For example, one male rape victim was depicted as a 'magnet':

Caroline: Poor guy. He's a *magnet* for it

This categorisation implies that the victim possessed an attracting quality 'for rape', but in contrast to the metaphorical identity category 'advertisement', not in a way that could be construed as a deliberate act of provocation or recklessness. Here the connection is imagined as a matter of irresistible attraction between two attracting forces (one negative and one positive) merely passively obeying the laws of physics. The power of attraction is thus construed as out of the *conscious* control of either the victim or the perpetrator. This positions a male rape victim as vulnerable to attack if in the proximity of a rapist and, importantly, also positions the rapist as vulnerable to committing rape if in the proximity of a 'magnetic' potential victim. Culpability for the rape disappears from the door of both the victim and the rapist in this account as both parties are construed as out of conscious control of their powerful magnetism rather than as active agents in causing the rape.

    The objectifying effects of the 'magnet', or elsewhere, the 'beacon' or 'target' metaphorical identity concepts for male rape victims has the potential then to work favourably in terms of the apportionment of sympathy, blame and responsibility. However, there is also a contradiction here between the male rape victim constructed as 'vulnerable/passive' and traditional notions of masculinity, where real, authentic men are more usually imagined as potent agents in control of their own fate and as capable of aggressively defending the self against the threat of physical assault. There are potential threats therefore to the masculine identity of the male rape victim categorised in these terms. As discussed in chapter 5, the participants often explained the male rape incident in the vignette by speculating that the victim may be weak, vulnerable, quite possibly gay or all three. So, although these 'objectifying' metaphors serve to legitimise the victim status of the male victim – a real victim is a passive object of action and not an active subject – they also lay the victim open to ridicule and to charges of being 'other' to the hegemonic masculine male.

3. Male rape as catastrophic, male rape victims as physically or psychologically broken or wounded vs. female rape victims as 'fallen women'

Metaphors describing the impact of male rape on the victim focused on the effects of the experience as being like a serious wound leaving a permanent scar or like a breakage, or a catastrophe. For example:

Richard: No but, you've got to admit to most heterosexual men, I'm sure that would be, I don't know
Sarah: The *end of the world*
Dawn: Yeah, I've only ever read about it once before, in a magazine, about a man telling how he's been raped, but I would have thought that for a man to be raped they would've they'd feel as if they couldn't protect themselves, and it'd probably kind of *scar them quite deeply*
Dawn: Yeah, exactly, *dent* their ego and stuff

These metaphorical descriptions of the impact of rape interestingly construe the act of rape itself quite clearly as a physical and/or psychological assault on the person, an extreme act with extreme negative effects. A discussion of female rape in these terms was notably absent in the conversations examined by us, and feminist scholars have long argued that the typical cultural response to rape is to minimise the severity of the experience or to reframe it as a normative sexual (potentially pleasurable) encounter (see chapters 1 and 5). Here, the metaphor of the 'scar' is mobilised to suggest that the experience of male rape is like receiving a physical wound, with immediate and intense initial traumatic impact, but also with the capacity to leave a permanent trace of that trauma with the victim. This is consistent with categorisations of the male rape victim (see analysis above) that construe him as vulnerable to attack – breakable and fragile.

On the other hand, some of the participants treat female rape much more matter-of-factly (although note that Sharon's response below could be heard as a sarcastic challenge to Tom's view), e.g.

Tom: I know it sounds awful but it happens, I mean, when you hear that a woman has been raped, it's like, somebody's been mugged, somebody's been raped, same thing

Sharon: Oh right, yeah, it's like what did you have for lunch

Female victims were quite often categorised as 'damaged goods', e.g. as mentally ill, 'mad' or stupid, but in the accounts for female rape it is important to note that an alleged psychological defect tends to function as a causal explanation for the occurrence of the rape itself rather than being discussed as a possible impact of the experience, engendering sympathy and expressions of support. Note, for example, how in the extracts below the female victim's alleged psychological state is used to position her as at least partly culpable for the rape perpetrated against her and as not deserving of sympathy. In the extracts, 'daft' implies a certain naïvety and/or reckless-ness on the part of the victim as does the construct 'head in the clouds', whereas 'not in her right mind' invokes the more extreme construct of insanity as an explanation for the victim's decision to walk home across the university campus described in the vignette:

Steve;:   Yeah well that's, it's not her own fault or anything but I mean, it's a bit *daft* innit really

William: So I mean, I wouldn't, I mean, anybody in their *right mind* won't go walking down a dark street if people have been sexu-ally assaulted down there before

Debbie: People have to be aware of the dangers I mean it's no *good just walking about with her head in the clouds is it?*

Metaphorical constructions of the papist

4. Rapist: subterranean lurker vs. power-hungry explorer

FEMALE RAPE

Shaun: I mean you couldn't, can't just *pluck* someone off a *main* road and rape them

Shaun: She should have stuck to the main routes . . . therefore being more in the public eye in that the rapist would be less likely to *jump on her* or whatever

The target domain of the rapist was also construed differently in the accounts for female and male rape. The vignette description of the rape that the participants were asked to comment on can be seen as an example of a classic 'stranger rape' (Anderson, 2007). However, it is interesting to observe how the participants amplify this stereotypical scenario by adding layers of meaning to the actions and characters described in the metaphors that they use. In the case of female rape, deploying the metaphorical vehicle of the subterranean dweller or undercover operator portrayed the rapist's actions or 'M.O.' as covert, stealthy and unpredictable. The rapist was frequently depicted as 'lurking', ready and willing to pounce from the shadow realm and 'pluck' a victim off the street. These constructs don't particularly add anything in terms of sketching in any possible motivation on the part of the rapist as agent or position him as responsible for his actions by appealing to stereotypically masculine rationality. In fact, they position the rapist as a sub-human fiend or monster whose actions cannot be explained by appeal to notions of acceptable human conduct. So, although the fiend/monster can be construed as at fault for his actions, this identity construct does not position him as responsible. We make inferences about people and their behaviour on the basis of the membership categories used to describe them (Wowk, 1984). The category 'fiend' entails inferences about motivation by conjuring up notions of a primeval, dark driving force, irresistible and compelling, determining the behaviour of the rapist. The responsibility for the rape is directed back towards the victim, who is positioned as culpable for failing to avoid the uncontrollable 'fiend/monster', i.e. for failing to deploy 'adequate' risk assessment and risk-avoidance practices.

In the extracts below, it is taken for granted that women are unquestionably and consistently at risk from 'sex fiends and monsters lurking in dark unpopulated places', constructed as an objective, material hazard. What is particularly interesting in accounts for female rape (as is the case here) is the move on the part of the participants to actively construe or even reframe the circumstances of a reported rape incident in these terms (see also chapter 4). In our data, for example, the scene of the rape in the vignette, the university campus, was variously re-imagined, even as a 'short cut across a badly lit field'. As Edwards and Potter (1992) have argued, constructions of identity and circumstances are intricately intermeshed such that here features of the setting in which the attack took place are constructed or imagined (as dark, unpopulated etc.) in such a way that the categorisation of the rapist as a 'fiend' appears coherent or even to be a common-sense assumption because that 'character' appears to fit into that 'scene'. Once this descriptive work has been accomplished, rape can then be argued to be essentially avoidable by women – all they have to do is avoid the places where 'we all know that rapists lurk' – and rape victims, by definition, can be positioned as culpable for failing to avoid the rapist.

MALE RAPE

Geoff: It's a *power trip*, isn't it, scaring them

In contrast to the depiction of the rapist in the accounts for female rape as subhuman and outside of human society, the motivation of the rapist in the male rape discussions was often addressed more explicitly in stereotypically masculine terms. In the above extract, for example, the rapist is described as on a 'power trip'. Here, the motivation for rape is constructed as arising from an active personal desire to scare the victim, and scaring the victim is linked to the notion of a 'power trip', i.e. being on a metaphorical journey towards gratification from the experience of power and authority over the victim. The metaphor 'trip' implies active agency on the part of the rapist and depicts rape as a staged process that must be planned and executed in much the same way as a literal geographic journey or expedition. This also places the rapist of men as much more visible and in the public domain of human affairs in contrast to the lurking sub-human fiend who populates the accounts of female rape. This metaphorical construction of the rapist's motivations positions him as much more clearly culpable, as an active agent in the planning and execution of the rape and as prepared to terrorise a victim for personal gratification. It is interesting that agentic metaphorical constructions of the rapist were most frequently observed in the accounts for male rape, but specifically also in conversations where the participants assume the victim to be a heterosexual male (cf. chapter 5). Constructions of rape that emphasise the violent and aggressive nature of the experience of rape for victims and which position the rapist as an active agent in perpetrating the rape were notably absent in the discussions of female rape and in the discussions of male rape where the victim was assumed to be gay.

Discussion

In this chapter we examined the role of metaphor in the sense-making practices of social participants as they discuss an alleged rape of a female victim and a male victim. Metaphors allow us to comprehend one aspect of a concept in terms of another and, in the process, metaphorical concepts offer us a particular or partial understanding of the phenomena in question, hiding or highlighting different aspects of the events or people under discussion. We argued that metaphor is a subtle feature of language that plays an interesting role in constructing the meaning of social relationships, in constructing and maintaining power relations (Adams *et al.*, 1995) and in the interactional management of identity and accountability. In the analysis presented here we focused on how the 'target domains' (Weatherall and Walton, 1999) of the victim, rapist and incident were talked about in both female and male rape cases and which generative root metaphors (the vehicles, or source domains) were used to construct meaning in relation to these target domains.

Some of the source domains that we analysed here have been found in previous research. For example, the 'stealthy' rapist vehicle has a prominent place in feminist analyses of gender relations, sexuality and sexual violence (Ussher, 1989). However, the present analysis also identified source domains that have not been discussed in previous research, for example the scientific metaphorical vehicle used to discuss and describe the circumstances of female rape and the supernatural metaphorical framework used to describe aspects of male rape incidents. This is an interesting finding, not least because of the way in which these metaphors appear to reverse commonly mobilised sense-making resources used to construct understandings of gender relations and sexual violence. In contradiction to normative understandings of normative femininity and womanhood, notions of the logical, rational and sensible were used to construct notions of desirable behaviour on the part of women in their navigation of the world in general and in particular their understanding of hazard/risk in relation to rape victimhood. On the other hand, rape for male victims was constructed as in the realms of the supernatural and the unpredictable. Men positioned in this metaphorical framework are not expected by social participants to conform to the expectations of normative masculine conduct – to be able to rationally predict and control events in the world – and as such were relieved of the responsibility to enter into a 'scientific' analysis of hazard/risk in relation to rape and to practise risk-avoidance strategies. Also unusual was the reversal of the ways in which the metaphors used here by the participants cast the female victim in an active role in her relationship to the rape perpetrated against her (e.g. the metaphorical description of the victim as advertising herself as rapeworthy or as foolhardy in ignoring the risk of rape) while objectifying and pacifying male victims of rape (e.g. male victim as magnet; fragile and breakable goods).

The findings of this analysis of the metaphors that social participants use to construct an understanding of identity and accountability in cases of rape appear to a certain extent to be contrary to feminist analyses of the metaphorical constructs used to make sense of gender relations in everyday situations (i.e. those treated as consistent with the gendered moral order). Metaphors about heteronormative sexual experience, for example, are usually more straightforwardly consistent with the patriarchal universe of discourse (Penelope, 1990) – a pervasive, *sex-stereotyped* conceptual framework, used by people to understand women and men, and guide social interactions with them. Here men are more often constructed as agents in sexual relations than are women (e.g. 'he broke her in'), whereas women are objectified more often than men (e.g. 'she's a bit of crumpet') (Weatherall and Walton, 1999). Similar findings were reported in Adams *et al.* (1995) in men's discussions about their physical violence towards their female partners (the men were undergoing a stopping-violence programme). Metaphors based on social hierarchies such as 'man as king, woman as subject' (man as king of his castle) or 'man as boss, woman as employee' were prevalent in these discussions as were metaphors that objectified women, including 'man as owner, woman as commodity' and 'man as parent, woman as child'.

Discussion and dispute in relation to identity and accountability are commonplace in sexual violence talk, and feminist analysis emphasises that the patriarchal universe of discourse generally works to weigh expressions, descriptions and discussions in sexual violence talk against women in favour of men, maintaining rather than challenging the status quo of the patriarchal order. Although the metaphorical constructions of the target domains of the victim, rapist and circumstances of the rape reported here reverse the stereotypical construction of masculine agency and feminine passivity, the metaphorical frames mobilised do still function to maintain patriarchal gender power relations. In general, the metaphors underpinning linguistic descriptions of female and male rape appear to undermine entitlements to sympathy for female compared to male victims and to maintain a victim-blaming orientation, particularly towards female victims and male victims positioned as gay (cf. chapter 5). The participants construct female rape as an objective hazard using scientific metaphors and cast women in the role of logician or rational scientist in the calculation of risk in relation to the hazard so constructed. Victims of rape can then be positioned as blameworthy on grounds of recklessness, stupidity or madness. The rapist is constructed as part of the hazard to be avoided rather than as an agent in the rape and, at the same time, as unaccountable for the rape due to his subhuman monster/beast status. Male rape on the other hand is imagined as unknowable and unpredictable, and heterosexual victims are positioned as unblameworthy – it isn't reasonable to expect someone to manage risk in relation to an 'unknowable' hazard. The rapist tends to be positioned as agentic in the rape, and overall the participants show more concern for the well-being of the victim in the aftermath of rape, construing him as vulnerable, fragile and breakable. This is not to suggest that male rape victims categorised as heterosexual received great support and understanding through the metaphors used – describing the male victim's experience as 'spooky' or 'nightmarish' is not particularly supportive. However, it certainly appears to us that through one of the major features of metaphorical constructions, namely their subtlety and indirectness, constructions of accountability and sympathy were harsher with respect to female rape than male rape. The use of these metaphors promotes a multilevel response from listeners which can serve to both camouflage and signal various messages (Adams *et al.*, 1995) – here, of inequitable treatment of female and male rape victims in terms of accountability and blame. Many of the metaphors associated with female rape, relative to male rape, were part of speech acts that communicated negative affect about women and their experience of violence such as rape victims mad/mentally ill or as agentic in her own rape. This conclusion is consistent with Weatherall and Walton's (1999) study of metaphors used to talk about sex and sexuality. They found that nearly half of the utterances that included sex metaphors were part of speech acts that communicated negative affect (e.g. insults, accusations) about women and women's sexuality. Taken together, these findings are also consistent with Pfaff *et al.*'s (1997) suggestion that metaphors frequently function as euphemisms (to make a difficult topic more socially acceptable) or as dysphemisms (to make a topic more offensive, sometimes in a humorous way).

The metaphorical devices analysed here refer to just one part of a broad range of rhetorical devices that could have been examined in relation to how people talk about female and male rape. We chose to focus on metaphors not only because of their inventive and creative nature, but also because of the ways in which they are so evocative in constructing versions of contexts and intention in cases of alleged rape. As such, we have seen how people have creatively and organically, through the use of metaphor, been able to lay blame and accountability inequitably with respect to female and male rape, turning deeply-held archetypes and stereotypes (e.g. the male as active, female as passive stereotype of masculinity and femininity) on their head, to enable them to activate the female victim and pacify the male, yet still maintain the patriarchal order. It would be fruitful for future research to consider further the role that not only metaphors, but also other rhetorical devices which are used to make up interpretative repertoires – such as synedoche (a reference which substitutes either a species for a genus, i.e. a part for a whole, or a genus for a species, i.e. a whole for a part) or metonymy (substitution of something which has come to be associated with the intended object) – play in constructing and accounting for sexual violence.

7

CONCLUSIONS

Throughout this book, we have argued for the importance of examining social responses to sexual violence in a context where rape claims are seldom met with a clear, supportive and positive response. A cultural climate of secondary victimisation in the aftermath of rape can be detrimental to a victim's psychological and physical health, and can impact on decisions to report an incident of rape, to investigate a rape allegation and to convict an alleged rapist if a case comes to trial. Claimants to 'genuine sexual assault victim' status routinely encounter a range of social and institutional barriers and struggle to receive sympathy, adequate resources or justice.

In chapter 1 we highlighted and discussed a key tenet of feminist scholarship on rape and society – that rape is both socially produced and socially legitimated. Feminist scholars draw our attention to the close connection between normative constructions of heterosexuality, the normalisation of aggression in hegemonic forms of masculinity and the maintenance of patriarchal gender power relations, and the way in which socially constructed understandings of gender and heterosexuality provide a socially approved vocabulary of motive for legitimating rape in social interaction, practices that sanction and normalise sexually violent encounters. This theoretical orientation establishes the social definition of rape as central to understanding and improving the experience and treatment of rape victims. We spent some time reviewing Burt and Estep's (1981) landmark discussion on the social definition of rape and argued that a powerful research agenda was suggested in this early work – to explore *precisely how* definitions of what counts as 'rape' and who is to be treated as a 'genuine' victim are constructed in discourse and practices that reflect the social, political and cultural conditions of society.

In chapter 2 we examined how mainstream social psychology responded to the challenge of investigating social responses to rape by operating within the well-established social-perception research tradition. We saw how, within this framework, the practice of explaining is individualised and decontextualised – treated as an internal, cognitive-perceptual process that can be meaningfully studied from an objectivist standpoint using experimental research and survey methodologies. One of our central arguments throughout this book has been that if we are to meaningfully explore the social definition of rape and the impact of these practices on the maintenance of gender power relations, we must dispense with experimentalism and turn to a research framework informed by social constructionist epistemology and feminist practice where the significance of the social construction of meaning in cultural and political context is placed centre stage.

Although it has been argued that socio-cognitive social psychology and feminist scholarship exist in a symbiotic relationship (Ward, 1995), we suggested that this assertion is problematic for a number of reasons. For one thing, qualitative research (frequently employed by feminist scholars in sexual-violence research) is too often relegated as 'preliminary' to the 'serious' and 'more systematic' business of experimental psychological research where quantitative rape-perception research is privileged as providing robust 'factual' knowledge about societal responses to rape. However, behind the rhetoric of scientific method and 'progress', there are considerable shortcomings and limitations associated with the rape-perception paradigm. The appropriateness of the theoretical assumptions and implications of attribution theory for the examination of causal reasoning about rape, for example, seems to go largely unquestioned in rape-perception research. Yet we argued that the cultural grounding (in discourses that construct gender and sexuality) and the political significance (in terms of maintaining patriarchy) of reasoning about rape are inevitably backgrounded when researchers adopt attribution theory to examine sense-making about sexual violence. Attribution theory's refusal to treat victim testimony as anything other than 'neutral' in the first instance is particularly problematic for feminist scholars and activists who campaign for the rights of rape victims to be heard, for their testimony to be routinely treated as likely to be *valid*, and to receive sympathy and justice.

Furthermore, in terms of research methods, we argued that paper-and-pencil exercises of the type used in attribution experiments have poor ecological validity, prohibiting the exploration of spontaneous, unconstrained responses to rape claims, and employing highly artificial, at worst stereotypical, independent variable categories in their experimental manipulations – hazard/risk is treated as objectively definable, and victim and perpetrator identities are pre-categorised and fixed by researchers, making it impossible to see how the dynamic construction of events and actors is tied into (not separate from) the pragmatic business of attributing cause, fault and responsibility (see analysis in chapter 4). The methodological instruments used in rape-perception research are simply not sensitive enough to capture the rhetorical subtlety of social reasoning about rape. The paper-and-pencil tasks prohibit exploration of the skilled interactional business of arguing and explaining in interaction, particularly in contexts where the pressure to be accountable to the social norms of open-mindedness, fairness and supportiveness are foregrounded (see particularly the analysis in chapter 5). In chapter 3 we also suggested that rape-perception researchers may not adequately reflect on *the experience of research participants* in terms of their location in a culture structured by gender power relations, in which rape claims are already trivialised and routinely disputed. In this context, participation in a rape-perception study, where participants are invited to consider the accountability of rape victims, gives research participants little space to challenge or transform standard victim-blaming views, a potentially troubling situation at worst and confusing at best for those participants not inclined to simply comply with the wishes of the researcher. Overall, we contend that rape-perception research is at risk of underestimating the extent of rape-supportive reasoning and also, through its adherence to experimental tasks, of failing to analyse the subtlety and political significance of its forms.

We presented three empirical chapters examining conversational interaction focused on cases of female and male rape, which we analysed from a feminist, social constructionist standpoint, exploring how language may construct and promote multilevel conceptualisations of rape and its victims, and how it can serve to both camouflage and signal various messages, working to maintain or challenge rape-supportive culture. Our findings highlighted a number of discursive practices and sense-making resources that serve to sustain and justify a lack of support for *some categories of rape victim* and to normalise and defend the actions of *some categories of perpetrator*. We examined participants' discursive orientation to the subtle, positive face-maintaining, construction of victim-blaming arguments and demonstrated that rape-supportive discourse is underpinned by deeply ingrained cultural sense-making resources that construct and legitimate hegemonic forms of heterosexual gender relations and also neo-liberal notions of ideal citizenship.

In chapter 4 we looked at conversations about female rape where the participants routinely accused the victim of 'reckless' risk-taking behaviour and found her accountable for the rape on these grounds. Our theoretical position on the social construction of hazard/risk and responsibility in relation to rape prompted us to examine the ways in which the participants built a picture of the context of the alleged rape incident and speculated on the identities and motivations of the victim and perpetrator in the vignette. We demonstrated that these two elements of constructive work are *intermeshed and mutually implicative* (cf. Edwards and Potter, 1992). For example, rapists can only be convincingly imagined as a 'predictable hazard' and victims as 'foolish and naïve' if they are contextualised by the participants in an environment constructed as objective, manageable and predictable (cf. chapter 4 on the construction of the environment categorised into objectively knowable 'safe'/'dangerous' routes). The social construction of the 'hazard/risk' facing the alleged victim on her way home was constructed as extreme, gendered, inevitable and, ultimately, as foreseeable and avoidable. We saw how the issue of the alleged victim's awareness of the 'hazard/risk' so constructed became crucial in the categorisation of the alleged victim and the management of accountability for the alleged rape. Participants' references to traits such as 'silly', 'stupid' and naïve indexed the membership category 'accountable victim', mobilising the implication that she was accountable for the attack, perpetrated against her largely because of her alleged 'stupidity' and 'recklessness'. The perpetrator exists as a shadowy figure in these accounts, appearing only implicitly as part of the 'hazard/risk' to be avoided by good women and self-responsible citizens in the big bad world, rather than as an accountable agent in his own right.

In chapter 5, we turned to a discussion of the male rape, focusing on the way in which participants discuss issues relating to the victim's experience of rape, and how these issues impact on the apportionment of sympathy and accountability. We showed in our analyses how participants spontaneously compared and evaluated the treatment and experience of different categories of rape victim. 'Men' were differentiated from 'women' as victims and 'men' as a category were further differentiated according to their hypothesised sexual orientation. A 'hierarchy of suffering' was established where rape was judged to be worse for heterosexual men than for women, or male victims constructed as gay. In this chapter, we approached the analysis from a theoretical position that views norms of sexual expression and sexual identity as socially constructed, reflecting hegemonic phallocentric representations of gender and heterosexuality. We discussed theory that disrupts the common-sense assumption that norms in relation to sexual acts are inexorably tied into categories of sexual identity. We showed how participants mobilise discourse to argue for the similarity of the acts of rape and consensual intercourse for certain categories of victim – for 'women' and for 'gay men'. Based on this assertion, rape was argued by the participants to be less traumatic for gay and bi-sexual men and for women than for heterosexual men. Rape was evaluated as being significantly worse for heterosexual men because it is assumed to deviate from their normative heterosexual practice. We went on to speculate that if the rape is evaluated primarily as a sexual act and, in somatic terms, as similar to 'normative' consensual sexual intercourse, the violent nature of rape as an assault on the sexual body can remain hidden and the devastating effects of rape for women, and men positioned as homosexual, can be easily dismissed. Reframing rape as 'sex' serves to minimise the violence and severity of a rape experience and also normalises the alleged perpetrator's behaviour.

We also examined in detail how the construction of male rape victims as accountable for the rape was intermeshed with the construction of his sexuality as 'gay' (and of course this may happen to any victim, regardless of his sexual practice). For example, it was argued that rape of the masculine body is literally not possible because anal penetration can only happen with consent. The participants concluded that the alleged victim must therefore have 'wanted it' (again, tying this assumption unproblematically to the assertion that his sexual identity is fixed and homosexual). The 'raped before' information from the vignette is taken up in these accounts to position the victim as responsible for rape prevention. Again, we saw how alleged knowledge of the mere possibility of sexual victimisation is treated as sufficient grounds in our neo-liberal culture to position a rape victim as responsible for preventing an attack and culpable for one's victimisation. And if the victim wasn't 'stupid', the participants argue, then maybe he 'wanted it'. The projection of a gay identity onto an alleged victim was also mobilised to reframe the depicted rape as a consensual sexual encounter. Gay stereotypes informed the redefinition of the rape incident as typical sexual behaviour for gay men, who are either embarrassed by their sexuality and later 'cry rape' or who are constructed as actively desiring public, anonymous and violent 'sex'. In the accounts of rape examined in this chapter, it is evident that gay men are culturally designed to be 'unrapeable'. On the one hand, the experience of rape is constructed as less severe for gay men than it is for victims positioned as heterosexual and, on the other, the projection of a gay identity onto an alleged victim effectively reframes an alleged rape as a normative sexual encounter for gay men.

In our data corpus, it was in the context of discussions about male rape that the argument that rape is 'just sex' was mobilised, in the service of minimising the severity of the experience of rape for women and gay men, for whom it was assumed that rape is similar to normative sex. But how can so much blurring, ambiguity and confusion exist in the minds of cultural members over what counts as consensual sex? How can there be any doubt that rape is a violent assault and likely to be experienced as an assault by all victims? At this point, shouldn't we be stepping back and raising a very large question mark over what passes for 'normal sex' (Gavey, 2005)? Nicola Gavey argues that heterosexual norms emphasise (and romanticise) female passivity (placing the emphasis on women meeting men's needs and constructing sex as penetration – the coital imperative). In this model the absence of women's active desire or pleasure is treated as *normative*, and the coital imperative precludes any exploration of sexuality other than this particular sexual act, strictly limited to vaginal or anal penetration for normative heterosex or male-on-male gay sex respectively.

Our analysis of the conversations about male rape provides empirical support for the range of critical scholarship, which argues that the cultural construction of sexual norms provides a framework for defining what rape is. As Weeks argues, 'the capacities of the body are given meaning only in social relations' (Weeks, 2003: 7) which tell us what sex is, ought to be and could be; who can do what to whom and how; and which sexual norms also define the boundaries of what is to be counted as deviant. If female passivity is the norm then, ignoring women's 'apparent' lack of consent is also normative and can become, in Gavey's term, 'the perfect cover story' for rape. In our data, more general norms for hegemonic masculinity also played a key role in defining appropriate conduct for male rape victims and directed participants towards constructing the victim as effeminate and, in some cases, in all likelihood 'gay', which in turn, mobilising stereotypes of sexual norms for gay men, led to speculation that he may not have been raped at all.

There must therefore be a clear place in rape-prevention strategy for the destabilisation of gender and sexuality norms. As Gavey argues in the case of preventing of sexual violence against adult women, 'a recognition of the important place of women's sexual desire is important in thinking through the prevention of sexual violence' (2005: 114). In terms of challenging the culture of victim-blaming documented in this book, there must also be an equally clear place for the destabilisation of 'common sense' views that so readily link 'risk' awareness to victim culpability.

In chapter 6, our central concern was to document how male and female rape is talked about metaphorically. In particular, we focused on how the 'target domains' (Weatherall and Walton, 1999) of the victim, rapist and incident were talked about and which generative root metaphors (the vehicles, or source domains, e.g. rapist as being engaged on a journey) were used to construct meaning in relation to these target domains. We argued that metaphorical frames function to construct the character and moti-vation of the alleged victim and rapist and the actual rape experience in different ways in the cases of male and female rape, with differing impli-cations for the management of accountability and apportionment of blame and sympathy. The analysis highlighted source domains that have not been discussed in previous research. For example we saw how a 'science' meta-phorical vehicle was used to discuss and describe the circumstances of female rape and a 'supernatural' metaphorical framework was used to describe aspects of male rape incidents. We argued that these metaphorical constructions reversed the commonly mobilised sense-making resources used to construct understandings of gender relations and sexual violence. For example, notions of the logical, rational and sensible subject were used to construct desirable behaviour on the part of women in their navigation of the world in general and their understanding of 'hazard/risk' in relation to rape victimhood in particular. On the other hand, rape for male victims was constructed as in the realms of the supernatural and the unpredictable. This reversal held some important consequences. Men positioned in this metaphorical framework are not expected to conform to the expectations of normative masculine conduct – to be able to rationally predict and control events in the world – and as such were relieved of the responsibility to enter into a 'scientific' analysis of 'hazard/risk' in relation to rape and to practice risk-avoidance strategies. However, the 'scientific rationality' subject position for women was used to cast her into an active role in her relationship to the rape perpetrated against her (e.g. the metaphorical description of the victim as advertising herself as rape-worthy or as 'mad' enough to ignore the risk of rape). In this way, the metaphorical frames mobilised do still function to maintain patriarchal gender power relations. In general, the metaphors underpinning linguistic descriptions of female and male rape appear to undermine entitlements to sympathy for female compared to male victims and to maintain a victim-blaming orientation, particularly towards female victims and male victims positioned as gay (as we saw in chapters 4 and 5). The use of metaphors subtly camouflages and signals various messages (Adams *et al.*, 1995) here of inequitable treatment of female and male rape victims in terms of accountability and blame. Many of the metaphors associated with female rape, relative to male rape, were part of speech acts that communicated negative affect about women and their experience of violence.

Throughout the book, we have examined the cultural sense-making resources, arguments and linguistic devices that have the capacity to sustain victim-blaming positions in talk about cases of rape. In particular we have highlighted how neo-liberal discourse constructs 'good citizens' as self-reflexive – knowledgeable in relation to the 'hazard/risk' and self-responsible for one's own personal security and happiness and how this discourse intersects with hegemonic understandings of gender and heterosexuality, providing the building blocks for the social construction of accountability in relation to sexual violence and, ultimately, the maintenance of patriarchy. In this context, victims are found culpable for acts of rape perpetrated against them, blamed for failing to be 'good neo-liberal citizens' and/or 'good (feminine) women' or 'good (masculine) men'. The only category of victim for which any sympathy was extended was the heterosexual man, partly on the grounds that rape was argued to deviate from 'normal sexual practice' and partly on the grounds that a heterosexual man is not socialised to expect, and thus can't be expected to protect himself from, sexual attack. This position of sympathy was often tinged with pity, however, for a man not 'masculine enough' to physically protect himself from attack.

A key theme in our analyses then is the link between accountability and blame for rape, and the social construction of 'hazard/risk'. It would seem that if a person can be positioned as aware of the possibility of rape risk, then they can be constructed as culpable for the rape. Alleged awareness of the risk of rape can be conferred in several ways for different categories of victim: in the form of 'the unnamed fear' of sexual victimisation in the public sphere, which *all women* are socialised into and expected to respect, observe and which confers a responsibility to engage in rational practices of risk assessment and prevention; in the form of the stereotype of the young, gay casual sex-seeking individual; and in the form of the experience of repeat victimisation. In the conversations we analysed, hazards become reified, to be treated as objective facts. Yet, constructions of 'hazard/risk' are just that – constructions to be built and sustained during the course of the interactive sequence. Making subtle links between what counts as 'hazard/risk', risk-taking and responsibility in a culture in which notions of self-responsibility are already tied into notions of good citizenship is thus a powerful argumentative strategy, leading to victim blame and legitimation and/or normalisation of the perpetrator's behaviour, avoiding the need for more overt attributions of blame.

It is interesting to note that the participants who discussed the case of female rape were *not* guilty of accusing the victim of confusing her experience with sex (i.e. few people argued that the incident described was not *rape*). Furthermore, simplistic notions of victim provocation were more often than not contested in these conversations. This is perhaps not surprising given that the rape in the vignette was constructed as a paradigmatic stranger rape. However, issues of *accountability* nevertheless did very clearly focus on the actions and character of the victim (and not the perpetrator) and were constructed in terms of a lack of 'common sense' or a failure to manage 'risk'. It is also interesting how the participants frequently compared themselves to the victim, claiming that they would not be similarly 'caught out' because they would have taken appropriate precautions to avoid rape and to secure and control their own fates. Neo-liberal norms for subjectivity – that we should be autonomous, free individuals with individual responsibility for our health, safety and happiness – therefore thoroughly permeate the accounts for rape and also construct the identity of the research participants as they discuss the rape vignette.

The evidence presented here suggests that the participants have taken on board the 'common sense' that practices of rape prevention are a matter for potential victims, and the assumed culpability for rape victim-hood that goes along with it. The criminal culpability of the rapist is obscured. Rape as an act is chastised, yet the solutions offered are limited to the re-education and *re-responsibilisation* of victims and potential victims. A radical understanding of rape in its patriarchal context, embedded within and productive of gender norms and power relations, is notably missing from these accounts, as are solutions that have the potential to directly challenge rape culture and the institutions and/or the gender norms that contribute to it.

Women's responsibility and agency in heterosexual encounters is at the heart of the backlash against radical feminist analyses of rape. Gavey (2005) draws our attention to the themes of individual responsibility and risk management in the writings of Camille Paglia, Katie Roiphe and others. In Paglia's writings notions of 'freedom' and 'excitement' are frequently conflated with the 'risk' and 'danger' of sex/rape, whipped up into an argument that positions individual responsibility for rape victim-hood as an artefact of equality between the sexes – deftly leaving to one side a critique of the sexual norms that dismiss rape as 'just sex' and refusing to hold men to account for rape. As Gavey argues, in general the backlash accounts share:

> an uncritical investment in a particular kind of modern, liberal subject – as autonomous, rational and free actors. Roiphe in particular wants women to be determined and self-determining subjects, boldly going out and playing by their own rules . . . invulnerable to social pressure . . . fully responsible for any compromising situation she ends up in . . . However, she has had to adopt a head-in-sand approach to the limits on individual agency and choice . . . in Roiphe's world, gendered power is neutered by wishful thinking.
>
> (Gavey, 2005: 71)

This model of personhood, promoting freedom of choice, freedom to self-assess risks and benefits and the acceptance of responsibility is the subjectivity constructed in the discourse of neo-liberalism. The *acceptance* of risk is a central theme in neo-liberal versions of enterprise culture given a positive spin in constructions of the socially desirable enterprising self (Doherty, 2000). In terms of gender relations then, breaking away from the restrictions of passive femininity is constructed as an activity for the bold, individualistic enterprising woman – something 'risky' – but with the potential reward of pleasure and sexual autonomy. However, enterprising selves are also expected to accept the consequences of failure, blaming no one but *themselves* for injury sustained in the 'cut and thrust' of everyday life. Social theorist Anthony Rose argues that neo-liberal rule depends upon conceiving of social actors as subjects of responsibility, autonomy and choice and creating a distance between these actors and the decisions of formal institutions and other social actors (Rose, 1996).

In this book, we have argued that there are serious limitations to individualistic forms of theorising in psychological science and serious practical and political consequences to the neo-liberal reasoning that permeates the accounts for rape that we have analysed. The dominant model of the person in psychological science – as rational, unitary, agentic, autonomous, 'self-contained' and self-controlled – reflects the dominant Western, neo-liberal understanding of personhood (Henriques *et al.*, 1984; Johnson, 1985; Sampson, 1977). As we argued in chapter 2, this model reinforces the view that individuals can be studied in a relatively isolated way from culture and history and therefore does nothing to challenge the neo-liberal norms and subjectivities that we have clearly shown underpin victim-blaming and self-blame in cases of rape.

However, going beyond reductive, individualistic ways of understanding human behaviour allows us to see how

> culturally saturated our own conceptions of ourselves are and how culturally shared patterns of meaning and normative practices limit us through the installation of frameworks of meaning and practice that guide us on how to be normal members of our cultures.
>
> (Gavey, 2005: 7)

We have shown that accounts for rape are saturated with normative assumptions about desirable personhood, not just in terms of gender and sexuality, but also in terms of expectations that we are autonomous beings in control of our own fates and individually responsible for outcomes. These cultural patterns of meaning provide a repertoire of arguments in response to rape claims that can be utilised in the service of victim-blame (or sometimes fleetingly, sympathy): 'silly' women get raped because they are not sufficiently *aware;* rape isn't *that much* of a trauma for women and gay men because rape is 'basically the same as sex' for these categories of victims; rape *is* recognised as traumatic for straight men, but sympathy is limited because only 'weak' men get raped. We also showed that in a cultural context of possible sanctions for taking up a harsh victim-blaming position, a culture in which public critique of rape myths, for example in the media and women's magazines, is now more commonplace; social participants are very skilled at attending to their own identities as sympathetic, enlightened individuals, but with the good common sense to avoid rape. All of this victim-blaming and self-congratulation of course leaves the path clear for rapists to get away with rape.

Despite social and political moves in recent years to highlight rape-victim blame as a major public concern, many rape victims continue to be routinely blamed. This is borne out by a recent ICM poll, conducted on behalf of Amnesty International (referred to in chapter 1), which showed, startlingly, that a 'blame culture' continues to exist in the UK concerning clothing, drinking, perceived promiscuity and personal safety in relation to women. For example, 34% of people in the UK believe that a woman is partially or totally responsible for being raped if she behaved in a flirtatious manner; 26% of those polled believed that she is partially or totally responsible for being raped if she was wearing sexy or revealing clothing; 22% held the same view if a woman had had many sexual partners; and 30% said that a woman was partially or totally responsible for being raped if she was drunk. Amnesty International's Kate Allen said that 'It is shocking that so many people will lay the blame for being raped at the feet of women themselves and the government must launch a new drive to counteract this sexist "blame culture"'. Our analyses suggest that these survey findings are likely to be the tip of the iceberg and do not hint at subtle, culturally embedded discourses and practices that sustain a rape-supportive culture. And if rape-supportive discourse is part of the 'common sense', it is also likely to be difficult to overturn or disrupt. We saw in chapter 4 that the seeds of dissent are also present in the form of ideological dilemmas, but that in practice it is difficult to sustain arguments that support patriarchal gender power relations in the sphere of sexual violence.

Subverting or changing beliefs about rape has been the preoccupation of many feminist thinkers. Gavey (2005) focuses on this issue by suggesting several methods of destabilising the deeply ingrained, 'common sense' notions of rape production, perpetuation and support for rape. She discusses using 'narratives of resistance' – for example, by 'making room for stories about how potential rape was successfully fought' (2005: 320), the destabilisation of gender binaries where men are stereotypically seen as active actors whilst women are passive sexual subjects (see also the discussion above), and the 're-working of discourses of sex and gender, masculinity and femininity, sexuality and heterosexuality in ways that make possible radically different forms of male and female sexual embodiment' – that is, 'rape-able' men and 'rapeable' women. Our research shows that we also need to add 'rapeable' gay men to this list. Gavey argues that only when these sexual scripts are fragmented and destabilised will possibilities of equality between men and women, and with this, an end to a rape-supportive culture be possible.

So how might this be practically possible – are there any places to start? Some writers have talked about the re-codification of women's (and men's) bodies (Cahill, cited in Gavey, 2005). One route (also mentioned briefly above) may be for us to challenge sexual norms and to engage with various forms of sexuality education or sexual/sexualising experience, promoting the democratisation of desire (McNair, 2002) and constructing female agency, sexual desire and sexual pleasures as positive and normative entitlements. But there is a tension and a danger to be carefully negotiated here; as we discussed above, the promotion of female sexual autonomy can so easily be used in the service of victim-blaming if the basic model of heterosexuality remains unchallenged.

Another possible strategy might be to present findings from discursive psychological research, as outlined here in chapters 4–6, to different groups in different social settings. This is already done within the context of teaching critical social psychologies to undergraduates in higher education institutions (something that we have been engaged in for a number of years), and could in theory be expanded to other settings, such as employment settings (although how accepting or digestible these findings may be in settings outside of higher education institutions remains to be seen). It is always interesting to observe the palpably shocking and transformational effect that discursive psychological research can have on a student's world-view, not least the 'penny dropping' of seeing language as constructing *versions* of the world which support different interests and agendas. Dell and Anderson have written about this effect:

> The epistemological assumptions underpinning critical psychologies, which deconstruct and decentre the subject (both the individual – academics and students alike – and the discipline of psychology) and make visible the humaneering project of psychology . . . not unexpectedly also impact on the student experience. As part of the process of being encouraged 'to participate in, even challenge, established intellectual authority' (Aronowitz, 2000: 143) and to 'interrogate the values implicit within psychology and to consider the values that *should* underlie theory, research and practice' (Prilleltensky and Nelson, 2002: 42 italics in original) students find both the subject matter and the pedagogical methods of critical psychology deeply unsettling, both intellectually and personally. Often in our experience, their long held beliefs and indeed everyday lives are decentered and deconstructed and in unexpected ways. We know that all education should come with a health warning. This is particularly true for students on critical psychology courses who find themselves questioning not only their intellectual antecedents (the nature of psychology) but also their everyday existence, the wider socio-economic systems that produce and sustain such existence, and their own relationship with activism.
>
> (Dell and Anderson, 2005: 29)

They go on:

> For example, it is clear that the aims of our courses achieve their goals, which are to encourage students to become critical thinkers and agentic in issues of social change, as evidenced by student feedback, assessment of students' work and our external examiners' comments. However, as teachers of critical psychology who are at the forefront of delivering these transformations, we are often less well prepared to deal with the difficulties that students' personal journeys often raise for them, and indeed the often strong emotional reactions that accompany such transformations and which can be played out (or acted up) in the classroom context. With regards to the emotive aspects of teaching critical psychology, how, for example, can we deal with students who come to question their previously deeply held beliefs – for example students who now view religion as just another discourse, with the emotional consequences that accompany such a loss of faith? Or, how do we deal with students who may have directly encountered some of the

issues such as racism, or sexism that are deconstructed on the course, and are angry, saddened, and even disempowered by such an analysis? And what about those who get disillusioned with psychology itself, not realising that critical approaches are asking *how* we should do psychology not *should* we do psychology?

(Dell and Anderson, 2005: 29)

Thus doing discursive research with students clearly has the potential to kick-start critical awareness and critical thinking and just maybe, the potential to transform world views and lived experience. This in turn may lead to a deeper awareness of the way they – we – use language and rhetoric in everyday interaction. This in turn may lead to more equitable, just and fair language use. And the very appreciation that gender and sexuality norms are just that, *norms*, offers potential for disruption and rebellion in our own discourse and practice.

Note

1. The concept of agency refers here to the notion of motivation (incentive and initiation of action) and intention (direction of that action).

REFERENCES

Abramson, L. and Martin, D. (1981). Depression and the causal inference process. In J. Harvey, W. Ickes and R. Kidd (Eds), *New Directions in Attribution Research*, Vol. 3. Hillsdale, NJ: Lawrence Erlbaum Associates.

Acock, A.C. and Ireland, N.K. (1983). Attribution of blame in rape cases: the impact of norm violation, gender and sex-role attitude. *Sex Roles*, 9, 179–192.

Adams, P., Towns, A. and Gavey, N. (1995). Dominance and entitlement: the rhetoric men use to discuss their violence towards women. *Discourse and Society*, 6 (3), 387–406.

Adler, Z. (2000). Male victims of sexual assault – legal issues and the causal inference process. In G. Mezey and M. King (Eds), *Male Victims of Sexual Assault*, 2nd edition. Oxford: Oxford University Press.

American Medical Association (1995). Sexual assault in America, at http://www.ama-assn.org

Amnesty International UK, *Sexual Assault Research Summary Report*, prepared by ICM, 12th October 2005 (http://www.amnesty.org.uk/new-details.asp?NewsID= 16618)

Anderson, I. (1996). Gender differences in attributional reasoning about rape. Unpublished doctoral dissertation, University of Sheffield.

Anderson, I. (1999). Characterological and behavioural blame in conversations about female and male rape. *Journal of Language and Social Psychology*, 18, 377–394.

Anderson, I. (2007). What is a typical rape? Effects of victim and participant gender in female and male rape perception. *British Journal of Social Psychology*, 46, 225–245.

Anderson, I. and Ahmed, B. (2003). Sexism in psychology and how to end it: feminist and critical debates in applied contexts. In R. Bayne and I. Horton (Eds), *Applied Psychology*. London: Sage.

Anderson, I. and Beattie, G. (2001). Depicted rapes: how similar are vignette and newspaper accounts of rape? *Semiotica*, 132, 1–21.

Anderson, I. and Doherty, K. (1996). Constructions of rape and consensual sex in conversation. Paper delivered to The British Psychological Society, London, December.

Anderson, I. and Doherty, K. (1997). Psychology, sexuality and power: constructing sex and violence. *Feminism and Psychology*, 7, 549–554.

REFERENCES

Anderson, I. and Lyons, A. (2005). The effects of perceived support, victim–perpetrator relationship and participant and victim gender on attributions of blame in female and male rape. *Journal of Applied Social Psychology*, 35, 1–19.

Anderson, I., Beattie, G. and Spencer, C. (2001). Can blaming victims of rape be logical? Attribution theory and discourse analytic perspectives. *Human Relations*, 54, 453–475.

Andrews, B. and Brewin, C. (1990). Attributions of blame for marital violence: a study of antecedents and consequences. *Journal of Marriage and Family*, 52, 757–767.

Antaki, C. (1984). Core concepts in attribution theory. In J. Nicholson and H. Beloff (Eds), *Psychology Survey 5*. Leicester: British Psychological Society.

Antaki, C. (1994). *Explaining and Arguing: The Social Organization of Accounts*. London: Sage.

Antaki, C. and Widdicombe, S. (Eds) (1998a). *Identities in Talk*. London: Sage.

Antaki, C. and Widdicombe, S. (1998b). Identity as an achievement and as a tool. In C. Antaki and S. Widdicombe (Eds), *Identities in Talk*. London: Sage.

Aronowitz, S. (2000). *The knowledge factory: Dismantling the corporate university and creating true higher learning*. Boston: Beacon Press.

Beattie, G. and Doherty, K. (1995a). 'I saw what really happened': The discursive construction of victims and perpetrators in firsthand accounts of paramilitary violence in Northern Ireland. *Journal of Language and Social Psychology*, 4 (14), 408–433.

Beattie, G. and Doherty, K. (1995b). Living the Troubles: a discourse analytic approach to understanding the reaction to violence in North Belfast. *Proceedings of the British Psychological Society*, 3 (1), 17.

Beck, U. (1992). *Risk Society: Toward a New Modernity*. London: Sage.

Bhavnani, K.-K. (1993). Tracing the contours: feminist research and feminist objectivity. *Women's Studies International Forum*, 16 (2), 95–104.

Billig, M. (1985). Prejudice, particularisation and categorisation: from a perceptual to a rhetorical approach. *European Journal of Social Psychology*, 15, 79–103.

Billig, M. (1987). *Arguing and Thinking: A Rhetorical Approach to Social Psychology*. Cambridge: Cambridge University Press.

Billig, M. (1988a). Methodology and scholarship in understanding ideological explanation. In C. Antaki (Ed.), *Analysing Everyday Explanation: A Casebook of Methods* (pp. 199–215). London: Sage.

Billig, M. (1988b). Common-places of the British Royal Family: a rhetorical analysis of plain and argumentative sense. *Text*, 8 (3), 191–217.

Billig, M., Condor, S., Edwards, D., Gane, M., Middleton, D. and Radley, A. (1988). *Ideological Dilemmas*. London: Sage.

Blackstone's Criminal Practice (1992). Oxford: Oxford University Press.

Bohner, G. (2001). Writing about rape: user of the passive voice and other distancing text features as an expression of perceived responsibility of the victim. *British Journal of Social Psychology*, 40, 515–529.

Borgida, E. and White, P. (1978). Social perception of rape victims: the impact of legal reform. *Law and Human Behaviour*, 2, 339–350.

Bowers, J. (1990). All hail the great abstraction: star wars and the politics of cognitive psychology. In I. Parker and J. Shotter (Eds), *Deconstructing Social Psychology*. London: Sage.

137

Brekke, N. and Borgida, E. (1988). Expert psychological testimony in rape trials: a social-cognitive analysis. *Journal of Personality and Social Psychology*, 55, 372–386.

Brewer, M.B. (1977). An information-processing approach to attribution of responsibility. *Journal of Experimental Social Psychology*, 13, 58–69.

Brewin, C. (1985). Depression and causal attributions: what is their relation? *Psychological Bulletin*, 98, 297–309.

Brewin, C. and Antaki, C. (1987). An analysis of ordinary explanations in clinical attribution research. *Journal of Social and Clinical Psychology*, 5, 79–98.

Bronfenbrenner, U. (1979). *The Ecology of Human Development: Experiments by Nature and Design*. Cambridge, MA: Harvard University Press.

Brown, J.M. and King, J. (1998). Gender differences in police officers' attitudes towards rape: results of an exploratory study. *Psychology Crime and Law*, 4, 265–279.

Brown, P. and Levinson, S.C. (1987). *Politeness: Studies in Interactional Sociolinguistics*. Cambridge: Cambridge University Press.

Brownmiller, S. (1975). *Against Our Will: Men, Women and Rape*. New York: Simon & Schuster.

Burgess, A. and Holmstrom, L. (1974). Rape trauma syndrome. *American Journal of Psychiatry*, 131.

Burman, E. and Parker, I. (1993). Introduction – discourse analysis: the turn to the text. In E. Burman and I. Parker (Eds), *Discourse Analytic Research: Repertoires and Readings of Texts in Action* (pp. 1–13). London: Routledge.

Burt, D. and DeMello, L. (2002). Attribution of rape blame as a function of victim gender and sexuality, and perceived similarity to the victim. *Journal of Homosexuality*, 43, 39–58.

Burt, M. (1980). Cultural myths and support for rape. *Journal of Personality and Social Psychology*, 38, 217–230.

Burt, M. and Estep, R. (1981). Who is victim? Definitional problems in sexual victimisation. *Victimology*, 6, 15–28.

Cahoon, D. and Edmonds, E. (1989). Male–female estimates of opposite sex first impressions concerning females' clothing styles. *Bulletin of the Psychonomic Society*, 27, 280–281.

Calhoun, L.G., Selby, J. and Warring, L. (1976). Social perception of the victim's causal role in rape: an exploratory study of four factors. *Human Relations*, 29, 517–526.

Calhoun, L., Selby, J., Cann, A. and Keller, G. (1978). The effects of victim physical attractiveness and sex of respondent on social reactions to victims of rape. *British Journal of Social and Clinical Psychology*, 17, 191–192.

Calhoun, L.G., Cann, A., Selby, J.W. and Magee, D.L. (1981). Victim emotional response: effects on social reactions to victims of rape. *British Journal of Social Psychology*, 20, 17–21.

Cameron, C. and Stritzke, W. (2003). Alcohol and acquaintance rape in Australia: testing the presupposition model of attributions about responsibility and blame. *Journal of Applied Social Psychology*, 33, 983–1008.

Campbell, R. and Johnson, C.R. (1997). Police officers' perceptions of rape: is there consistency between state law and individual beliefs? *Journal of Interpersonal Violence*, 12 (2), 255–274.

Cann, A., Calhoun, L. and Selby, J. (1979). Attributing responsibility to the victim of rape: influence of information regarding past sexual experience. *Human Relations*, 32, 57–67.

Castel, R. (1991). From dangerousness to risk. In G. Burchell, C. Gordon and P. Miller (Eds), *The Foucault Effect: Studies in Governmentality*. Chicago: University of Chicago Press.

Check, J.V.P. and Malamuth, N.M. (1983). Sex role stereotyping and reactions to depictions of stranger versus acquaintance rape. *Journal of Personality and Social Psychology*, 45, 344–356.

Check, J. and Malamuth, N.M. (1984). Can there be positive effects of participation in pornography experiments? *Journal of Sex Research*, 20, 14–31.

Check, J. and Malamuth, N. (1985). An empirical assessment of some feminist hypotheses about rape. *International Journal of Women's Studies*, 8, 414–423.

Cheng, P. and Novick, L. (1990). A probabilistic model of causal induction. *Journal of Personality and Social Psychology*, 58, 545–567.

Cheng, P. and Novick, L. (1991). Causes versus enabling conditions. *Cognition*, 40, 83–120.

Cheng, P. and Novick, L. (1992). Covariation in natural causal induction. *Psychological Review*, 99, 365–382.

Cherry, F. (1995). *The Stubborn Particulars of Social Psychology*. London: Routledge.

Childs, M. and Ellison, L. (Eds) (2000). *Feminist Perspectives on Evidence*. London: Cavendish Publishing.

Coller, S.A. and Resick, P.A. (1987) Women's attributions of responsibility for date rape: the influence of empathy and sex role stereotyping. *Violence and Victims*, 2, 115–125.

Condor, S. (1988). 'Race stereotypes' and racist discourse. *Text*, 8 (1–2), 69–89.

Connell, R.W. (1995). *Masculinities*. Cambridge: Polity Press.

Corner, J. and Harvey, S. (1991a). Introduction: Great Britain Limited. In J. Corner and S. Harvery (Eds), *Enterprise and Heritage: Crosscurrents of National Culture* (pp. 1–20). London: Routledge.

Corner, J. and Harvey, S. (1991b). Mediating tradition and modernity: the heritage/enterprise couplet. In J. Corner and S. Harvey (Eds), *Enterprise and Heritage: Crosscurrents of National Culture* (pp. 45–75). London: Routledge.

Costin, F. (1985). Beliefs about rape and women's social roles. *Archives of Sexual Behaviour*, 14, 319–325.

Costin, F. and Schwartz, N. (1987). Beliefs about rape and women's social roles: a four nation study. *Journal of Interpersonal Violence*, 2, 46–56.

Coxell, A., King, M., Mezey, G. and Gordon, D. (1999). Lifetime prevalence, characteristics, and associated problems of non-consensual sex in men: cross sectional survey. *British Medical Journal*, 318, 846–850.

Crawford, M. (1995). *Talking Difference: On Gender and Language*. London: Sage.

Critchlow, B. (1983). Blaming the booze: the attribution of responsibility for drunken behaviour. *Personality and Social Psychology Bulletin*, 9, 451–473.

Critchlow, B. (1985). The blame in the bottle: attributions about drunken behaviour. *Personality and Social Psychology Bulletin*, 11, 258–274.

Crotty, M. (1996). *Phenomenology and Nursing Research*. Melbourne: Churchill Livingstone.

Crotty, M. (1998). *The Foundations of Social Research: Meaning and Perspective in the Research Process*. London: Sage.

Damrosch, S.P. (1985). How perceived carelessness and time of attack affect nursing students' attributions about rape victims. *Psychological Reports*, 56, 531–536.

Damrosch, S., Gallo, B., Kulak, D. and Whitaker, C. (1987). Nurses' attributions about rape victims. *Research in Nursing and Health*, 10, 245–251.

Davies, M. (2000). Male rape: the invisible victims. *The Lesbian and Gay Psychology Review*, 1 (1), 11–15.

Davies, M. and McCartney, S. (2003). Effects of gender and sexuality on judgements of victim blame and rape myth acceptance in a depicted male rape. *Journal of Community and Applied Social Psychology*, 13, 391–398.

Davis, G. and Breslau, N. (1994). Post-traumatic stress disorder in victims of civilian trauma and criminal violence. *Psychiatric Clinics of North America*, 17, 289–299.

Deitz, S., Blackwell, K., Daley, P. and Bentley, B. (1982) Measurement of empathy toward rape victims and rapists. *Journal of Personality and Social Psychology*, 43, 372–384.

Deitz, S.R., Littman, M. and Bentley, B.J. (1984). Attribution of responsibility for rape: the influence of observer empathy, victim resistance and victim attractiveness. *Sex Roles*, 10, 261–280.

Dell, P. and Anderson, I. (2005). Practising critical psychology: politics, power and psychology departments. *International Journal of Critical Psychology*, 13, 14–31.

Devalle, M.N. and Norman, P. (1992). Causal attributions, health locus of control beliefs and life-style changes among preoperative coronary patients. *Psychology and Health*, 7 (3), 201–211.

Doherty, K. (1995). Subjectivity, reflexivity and the analysis of discourse. *Proceedings of the British Psychological Society*, 3 (1), 17.

Doherty, K. (2000). 'Going it alone': the discursive construction of identity and enterprise culture. Unpublished doctoral thesis, University of Sheffield.

Doherty, K. and Anderson, I. (1998). Talking about rape: perpetuating rape supportive culture. *The Psychologist*, 11 (12), 583–587.

Doherty, K. and Anderson, I. (2004). Making sense of male rape: constructions of gender, sexuality and experience of rape victims. *Journal of Community and Applied Social Psychology*, 14 (2), 85–103.

Doherty, K. and Malson, H. (1996). Variety and strategy in qualitative health research: issues and implications. *Proceedings of the British Psychological Society*, 4 (2), 109.

Donaldson, S. (1990). Rape of males. In W.R. Dynes (Ed.), *The Encyclopaedia of Homosexuality*. New York: Garland Publications.

Dougals, M. (1992). *Risk and Blame: Essays in Cultural Theory*. London: Routledge.

Dryden, C. (1999). *Being Married, Doing Gender: A Critical Analysis of Gender Relationships in Marriage*. London: Routledge.

Du Bois, B. (1983). Passionate scholarship: notes of values, knowing and method in feminist social science. In G. Bowles and R. Duelli Klein (Eds), *Theories of Women's Studies*. London: Routledge

Edley, N. (2000). Analysing masculinity: interpretative repertoires, ideological dilemmas and subject positions. In M. Wetherell, S. Taylor and S.J. Yates (Eds),

Discourse as Data: A Guide for Analysis. Milton Keynes: The Open University Press.

Edmonds, E.M. and Cahoon, D.D. (1986). Attitudes concerning crimes related to clothing worn by female victims. *Bulletin of the Psychonomic Society*, 24, 444–446.

Edwards, A. (1987). Male violence in feminist theory: an analysis of the changing conceptions of sex/gender violence and male dominance. In J. Hanmer and M. Maynard (Eds), *Women, Violence and Social Control*. London: Macmillan Press.

Edwards, D. (1991). Categories are for talking: on the cognitive and discursive bases of categorisation. *Theory and Psychology*, 1 (4), 515–542.

Edwards, D. (1997). *Discourse and Cognition*. London: Sage.

Edwards, D. (1998). The relevant thing about her: social identity categories in use. In C. Antaki and S. Widdicombe (Eds), *Identities in Talk*. London: Sage.

Edwards, D. and Potter, J. (1992). *Discursive Psychology*. London: Sage

Ericson, R., Barry, D. and Doyle, A. (2000). The moral hazards of neo-liberalism: lessons from the private insurance industry. *Economy and Society*, 29 (4), 352–558.

Feild, H. (1978a). Attitudes toward rape: a comparative analysis of police, rapists, crisis counsellors and citizens. *Journal of Personality and Social Psychology*, 36, 156–179.

Feild, H. (1978b). Juror background characteristics and attitudes toward rape. *Law and Human Behaviour*, 2, 73–93.

Feldman, P.J., Ullman, J. and Dunkel-Schetter, C. (1998). Women's reactions to rape victims: motivational processes associated with blame and social support. *Journal of Applied Social Psychology*, 28, 469–504.

Feldman-Summers, S. and Lindner, K. (1976). Perceptions of victims and defendants in criminal assault cases. *Criminal Justice and Behaviour*, 3, 135–150.

Feldman-Summers, S. and Palmer, G. (1980). Rape as viewed by judges, prosecutors and police officers. *Criminal Justice and Behaviour*, 7, 19–40.

Ferguson, P., Duthie, D. and Graf, R. (1987). Attribution of responsibility to rapist and victim: the influence of victim's attractiveness and rape related information. *Journal of Interpersonal Violence*, 2, 243–250.

Fincham, F. and Bradbury, T. (1987). The impact of attributions in marriage: a longitudinal analysis. *Journal of Personality and Social Psychology*, 53, 510–517.

Finney, A. (2006). Domestic violence, sexual assault and stalking: findings from the 2004/05 British Crime Survey. Home Office Online Report 12/06.

Fiske, S.T. and Taylor, S.E. (1991). *Social Cognition*, 2nd edition. New York: McGraw-Hill.

Försterling, F. (2001). *Attribution: An Introduction to Theories, Research and Applications*. East Sussex: Psychology Press.

Fox, N.J. (1999). Postmodern reflections: deconstructing 'risk', 'health' and 'work'. In N. Daykin and L. Doyal (Eds), *Health and Work: Critical Perspectives*. Basingstoke: Macmillan Press.

Frese, B., Moya, M. and Megats, J. (2004). Social perception of rape. *Journal of Interpersonal Violence*, 19, 143–161.

Frith, H. (1999). Reputations, relationships and refusing sex: the difficulty of saying 'no' and of being heard. *Psychology of Women Section Review*, 1 (2), 5–25.

Gagnon, J.H. and Simon, W. (1973). *Sexual Conduct: The Social Sources of Human Sexuality*. Chicago: Aldine Publishing Co.

Gale, A. (1997). The reconstruction of British psychology. *The Psychologist*, 10 (1), 11–15.

Garnets, L., Herek, G. and Levy, B. (1990). Violence and victimization of lesbians and gay men: mental health consequences. *Journal of Interpersonal Violence* 5 (3), 366–383.

Gavey, N. (1989). Feminist poststructuralism and discourse analysis. *Psychology of Women Quarterly*, 13, 459–475.

Gavey, N. (2005). *Just Sex? The Cultural Scaffolding of Rape*. East Sussex: Routledge.

Gerber, G., Cronin, J. and Steigman, H. (2004). Attributions of blame in sexual assault to perpetrators and victims of both genders. *Journal of Applied Social Psychology*, 34, 2149–2165.

Gerdes, E.P., Dammann, E.J. and Heilig, K.E. (1988). Perceptions of rape victims and assailants: effects of physical attractiveness, acquaintance and subject gender. *Sex Roles*, 19, 141–153.

Gergen, K. (1985). The social constructionist movement in modern psychology. *American Psychologist*, 40 (3), 266–275.

Giacopassi, D. and Dull, R. (1986). Gender and racial differences in the acceptance of rape myths within a college population. *Sex Roles*, 15, 63–75.

Gibbs, R. and Franks, H. (2002). Embodied metaphor in women's narratives about their experiences with cancer. *Health Communication*, 14 (2), 139–165.

Gill, R. (1995). Relativism, reflexivity and politics: interrogating discourse analysis from a feminist perspective. In S. Wilkinson and C. Kitzinger (Eds), *Feminism and Discourse: Psychological Perspectives* (pp. 165–186). London: Sage.

Gilmartin-Zena, P. (1983). Attribution theory and rape victim responsibility. *Deviant Behaviour*, 4, 357–374.

Goffman, E. (1967). On facework: an analysis of ritual elements in social interaction. In E. Goffman (Ed.), *Interaction Ritual* (pp. 5–46). New York: Pantheon Books.

Gordon, M. and Riger, S. (1981). *The Female Fear: The Social Cost of Rape*. Urbana: University of Illinois Press.

Goyer, P. and Eddleman, H. (1984). Same sex rape of nonincarcerated men. *American Journal of Psychiatry*, 141 (4), 576–579.

Gregory, J. and Lees, S. (1999). *Policing Sexual Assault*. London: Routledge.

Griffin, C. (1989). 'I'm not a women's libber, but . . .' Feminism, consciousness and identity. In S. Skevington and D. Baker (Eds), *The Social Identity of Women*. London: Sage.

Griffin, C. (1995). Feminism, social psychology and qualitative research. *The Psychologist*, 266–468.

Griffin, C. and Phoenix, A. (1994). The relationship between qualitative and quantitative research: lessons from feminist psychology. *Journal of Community and Applied Social Psychology*, 4 (4), 287–299.

Griffin, S. (1971). 'Rape: the all-American crime'. *Ramparts*, 10, 26–35.

Groth, N. and Burgess, A. (1980). Male rape: offenders and victims. *American Journal of Psychiatry*, 137 (7), 806–809.

Hall, S. and Jacques, M. (1983). Introduction. In S. Hall and M. Jacques (Eds), *The*

Politics of Thatcherism (pp. 9–16). London: Lawrence & Wishart in association with Marxism Today.

Harding, S. (1991). *Whose Science? Whose Knowledge?* New York: Cornell University Press.

Heider, F. (1958). *The Psychology of Interpersonal Relations.* New York: Wiley.

Henriques, J., Hollway, W., Urwin, C., Venn, C. and Walkerdine, V. (1984). *Changing the Subject: Psychology, Social Regulation and Subjectivity.* London: Methuen.

Heritage, J. (1984). *Garfinkel and Ethnomethodology.* Cambridge: Polity Press.

Hewitt, J.P. and Stokes, R. (1975). Disclaimers. *American Sociological Review*, 40, 1–11.

Hickson, F., Davies, P., Hunt, A., Weatherburn, P., McManus, T. and Coxon, P. (1994). Gay men as victims of nonconsensual sex. *Archives of Sexual Behaviour*, 23 (3), 281–294.

Hillman, R., O'Mara, N., Taylor-Robinson, D. and Harris, J. (1990). Medical and social aspects of sexual assault of males: a survey of 100 victims. *British Journal of General Practice*, 40, 502–504.

Hilton, D.J. (1988). Logic and causal attribution. In D.J. Hilton (Ed.), *Contemporary Science and Natural Explanation: Commonsense Conceptions of Causality.* Brighton: Harvester Press.

Hilton, D.J. (1990). Conversational processes and causal explanation. *Psychological Bulletin*, 107, 65–81.

Hollway, W. (1989). *Subjectivity and Method in Psychology: Gender, Meaning and Science.* London: Sage.

Holmstrom, L. and Burgess, A. (1978). *The Victim of Rape: Institutional Reactions.* New York: Wiley.

Houston, D., McKee, K. and Wilson, J. (2000). Attributional style, efficacy and the enhancement of well-being among housebound older people. *Basic and Applied Social Psychology*, 22 (4), 309–317.

Hutton, W. (1997). *The State to Come.* London: Vintage.

Isely, P. (1998). Sexual assault of men: American research supports studies from the UK. *Medicine, Science and the Law*, 38 (1), 74–80.

Isely, P. and Gehrenbeck-Shim, D. (1997). Sexual assault of men in the community. *Journal of Community Psychology*, 25 (2), 159–166.

Jackson, M. (1987). Facts of life or the eroticisation of women's oppression? Sexology and the social construction of heterosexuality. In P. Caplan (Ed.), *The Cultural Construction of Sexuality.* London: Routledge.

Jacobson, M. (1981). Effects of victim's and defendant's physical attractiveness on subjects' judgements in a rape case. *Sex Roles*, 7, 247–255.

Jacobson, M. and Popovich, P. (1983). Victim attractiveness and perceptions of responsibility in an ambiguous rape case. *Psychology of Women Quarterly*, 8, 100–104.

Jayusi, L. (1984). *Categorisation and the Moral Order.* London: Routledge & Kegan Paul.

Jenkins, M. and Dambrot, F. (1987). The attribution of date rape: observers' attitudes and sexual experiences and the dating situation. *Journal of Applied Social Psychology*, 17, 875–895.

Jennings, D.F. (1994). *Multiple Perspectives of Entrepreneurship: Text, Readings and Cases*. Cincinnati: South-Western Publishing Company.

Johnson, F. (1985). The Western concept of self. In A.J. Marsella, G. Devos and F.L.K. Hsu (Eds), *Culture and the Self: Asian and Western Perspectives*. New York: Tavistock.

Johnson, J.D. and Jackson, L.A. (1988). Assessing the effects of factors that might underlie the differential perception of acquaintance and stranger rape. *Sex Roles*, 19, 37–44.

Johnson, J.D., Jackson, L.A. and Smith, G.J. (1989). The role of ambiguity and gender in mediating the effects of salient cognitions. *Personality and Social Psychology Bulletin*, 15, 52–60.

Jones, C. and Aronson, E. (1973). Attribution of fault to a rape victim as a function of respectability of the victim. *Journal of Personality and Social Psychology*, 26, 415–419.

Jones, C. and Davis, K. (1965). From acts to dispositions: the attribution process in person perception. In L. Berkowitz (Ed.), *Advances in Experimental Social Psychology*, Vol. 2. New York: Academic Press.

Jones, C., Kanouse, D., Kelley, H., Nisbett, R., Valins, S. and Weiner, B. (1972). *Attribution: Perceiving the Causes of Behaviour*. Morristown, NJ: General Learning Press.

Kanekar, S. and Kolsawalla, M. (1977). Responsibility in relation to respectability. *The Journal of Social Psychology*, 102, 183–188.

Kanekar, S. and Kolsowalla, M. (1980). Responsibility of a rape victim in relation to her respectability, attractiveness and provocativeness. *Journal of Social Psychology*, 112, 153–154.

Kanekar, S. and Nazareth, A. (1988). Attributed rape victim's fault as a function of her attractiveness, physical hurt and emotional disturbance. *Social Behaviour*, 3, 37–40.

Kanekar, S. and Vaz, L. (1988). Attribution of causal and moral responsibility to a victim of rape. *Applied Psychology: An International Review*, 37, 35–49.

Kanekar, S., Pinto, N. and Mazumdar, D. (1985). Causal and moral responsibility of victims of rape and robbery. *Journal of Applied Social Psychology*, 15, 622–637.

Kassing, L. and Prieto, L. (2003). The rape myth and blame-based beliefs of counsellors in training toward male victims of rape. *Journal of Counseling and Development*, 81, 455–461.

Kaufman, A., DiVasto, P., Jackson, R., Voorhees, D. and Christy, J. (1980). Male rape victims: noninstitutionalized assault. *American Journal of Psychiatry*, 137, 221–223.

Kelley, H. (1967). Attribution theory in social psychology. In D. Levine (Ed.), *Nebraska Symposium on Motivation*, Vol. 2 (pp. 192–238). Lincoln: University of Nebraska Press.

Kelley, H. (1973). The processes of causal attribution. *American Psychologist*, 28, 107–128.

Kelley, H. and Michela, J. (1980). Attribution theory and research. *Annual Review of Psychology*, 31, 457–501

Kelly, L. (1987). The continuum of sexual violence. In J. Hanmer and M. Maynard (Eds), *Women, Violence and Social Control*. London: Macmillan Press.

Kerr, N.L. and Kurtz, S.T. (1977). Effects of a victim's suffering and respectability on mock juror judgements: further evidence on the just world theory. *Representative Research in Social Psychology*, 8, 42–56.

King, M.B. and Woollett, E. (1997). Sexually assaulted males: 115 men consulting a counseling service. *Archives of Sexual Behaviour*, 26, 579–588.

Kirmayer, L. (1992). The body's insistence on meaning: metaphor as presentation and representation in illness experience. *Medical Anthropology Quarterly*, 6 (4), 323–346.

Kitzinger, C. (2000). Doing feminist conversation analysis. *Feminism and Psychology*, 10 (2), 163–193.

Kleinke, C.L. and Meyer, C. (1990). Evaluation of rape victim by men and women with high and low belief in a just world. *Psychology of Women Quarterly*, 14, 343–353.

Koss, M. and Harvey, M. (1991). *The Rape Victim: Clinical and Community Interventions*. Newbury Park: Sage.

Krahé, B. (1988). Victim and observer characteristics as determinants of responsibility attributions to victims of rape. *Journal of Applied Social Psychology*, 18, 50–58.

Krahé, B. (1991). Social psychological issues in the study of rape. In W. Stroebe and M. Hewstone (Eds), *European Review of Psychology*. Chichester: John Wiley & Sons.

Kristiansen, G.M. and Giulietti, R. (1990). Perceptions of wife abuse: effects of gender, attitudes toward women and just-world beliefs among college students. *Psychology of Women Quarterly*, 14, 177–189.

Krulewitz, J. and Nash, J. (1979). Effects of rape victim resistance, assault outcome and sex of observer on attributions about rape. *Journal of Personality*, 47, 557–574.

Kvale, S. (1992a). Introduction: from the archaeology of the psyche to the architecture of cultural landscapes. In S. Kvale (Ed.), *Psychology and Postmodernism* (pp. 1–16). London: Sage.

Kvale, S. (1992b). Postmodern psychology: a contradiction in terms? In S. Kvale (Ed.), *Psychology and Postmodernism* (pp. 31–57). London: Sage.

Lakoff, G. and Johnson, M. (1980). *Metaphors We Live By*. Chicago: University of Chicago Press.

Lalljee, M., Brown, L.M. and Ginsburg, G.P. (1984). Attitudes: disposition, behaviour or evaluation? *British Journal of Social Psychology*, 23, 233–244.

L'Armand, K. and Pepitone, A. (1982). Judgements of rape: a study of victim–rapist relationship and victim sexual history. *Personality and Social Psychology Bulletin*, 8, 134–139.

LeDoux, J. and Hazelwood, R. (1985). Police attitudes and beliefs toward rape. *Journal of Police Science and Administration*, 13, 211–220.

Lee, H. and Cheung, F. (1991). The attitudes toward rape victims scale: reliability and validity in a Chinese context. *Sex Roles*, 24, 599–603.

Lee, J. (1984). Innocent victims and evil-doers. *Women's Studies International Forum*, 7 (1), 69–73.

Lees, S. (1993). Judicial rape. *Women's Studies International Forum*, 16 (1), 11–36.

Lees, S. (1997). *Ruling Passions: Sexual Violence, Reputation and the Law*. Buckingham: Open University Press.

Lerner, M. and Matthews, G. (1967). Reactions to suffering of others under conditions of indirect responsibility. *Journal of Personality and Social Psychology*, 5, 319–325.

Lonsway, K.A. and Fitzgerald, L.F. (1994). Rape myths: in review. *Psychology of Women Quarterly*, 18, 133–164.

Luginbuhl, J. and Mullin, C. (1981). Rape and responsibility: how and how much is the victim blamed? *Sex Roles*, 7, 547–558.

Malamuth, N.M. and Check, J.V.P. (1980a). Sexual arousal to rape and consenting depictions: the importance of the woman's arousal. *Journal of Abnormal Psychology*, 89, 763–766.

Malamuth, N.M. and Check, J.V.P. (1980b). Penile tumescence and perceptual responses to rape as a function of victim's perceived reactions. *Journal of Applied Social Psychology*, 10, 528–547.

Mason, G., Riger, S. and Foley, L. (2004). The impact of past sexual experiences on attributions of responsibility for rape. *Journal of Interpersonal Violence*, 19, 1157–1171.

Masters, W.H. and Johnson, V.E. (1966). *Human Sexual Response*. London: Churchill.

Mayerson, S. and Taylor, D. (1987). The effects of rape myth pornography on women's attitudes and the mediating role of sex-role stereotyping. *Sex Roles*, 17, 321–338.

McCaul, K., Veltum, L., Boyechko, V. and Crawford, J. (1990). Understanding attributions of victim blame for rape: sex, violence and foreseeability. *Journal of Applied Social Psychology*, 20, 1–26.

McMullen, R.J. (1990). *Male Rape: Breaking the Silence of the Last Taboo*. London: Gay Men's Press.

McNair, B. (2002). *Striptease Culture: Sex, the Media and the Democratisation of Desire*. London: Routledge.

Mill, J.S. (1973). A system of logic (8th edition). In J.M. Robson (Ed.), *Collected Works of John Stuart Mill* (Vols. 7 and 8). Toronto: University of Toronto Press.

Mitchell, D., Hirschman, R. and Nagayama Hall, G. (1999). Attributions of victim responsibility, pleasure and trauma in male rape. *Journal of Sex Research*, 36, 369–373.

Moir, J. (1993). Occupational career choice: accounts and contradictions. In E. Burman and I. Parker (Eds), *Discourse Analytic Research: Repertoires and Readings of Texts in Action* (pp. 17–34). London: Routledge.

Muelenhard, C. and Linton, M. (1987). Date rape and sexual aggression in dating situations: incidence and risk factors. *Journal of Counselling Psychology*, 34, 180–196.

Muller, R.T., Caldwell, R.A. and Hunter, J.E. (1994). Factors predicting the blaming of victims of physical child abuse or rape. *Canadian Journal of Behavioural Science*, 26, 259–279.

Muram, D., Hellman, R. and Cassinello, B. (1995). Prevalence of negative attitudes among police officers toward rape victims. *Adolescent and Pediatric Gynecology*, 8 (2), 89–91.

Myers, M. (1989). Men sexually assaulted as adults and sexually abused as boys. *Archives of Sexual Behaviour*, 18 (3), 203–215.

REFERENCES

Myers, M., Templer, D. and Brown, R. (1984). Coping ability of women who become victims of rape. *Journal of Consulting and Clinical Psychology*, 52, 73–78.

Ngaire, N. (1992). Windows on the legal mind: the evocation of rape in legal writing. *Melbourne University Law Review*, 18, 741–767.

Nicolson, P. (1994). Anatomy and destiny: sexuality and the female body. In P. Choi and P. Nicolson (Eds), *Female Sexuality: Psychology, Biology and Social Context*. London: Harvester Wheatsheaf.

Oakley, A. (1974). *The Sociology of Housework*. London: Martin Robertson.

Oakley, A. (1981). Interviewing women: a contradiction in terms. In H. Roberts (Ed.), *Doing Feminist Research*. London: Routledge.

Ong, A. and Ward, C. (1999). The effects of sex and power schemas, attitudes toward women, and victim resistance on rape attributions. *Journal of Applied Social Psychology*, 29, 362–376.

Pallack, S. and Davies, J. (1982). Finding fault versus attributing responsibility: using facts differently. *Personality and Social Psychology Bulletin*, 8, 454–459.

Parker, I. (1992). *Discourse Dynamics: Critical Analysis for Social and Individual Psychology*. London: Routledge.

Parker, I. (1994). Reflexive research and the grounding of analysis: social psychology and the psy-complex. *Journal of Community and Applied Social Psychology*, 4 (4) 239–252.

Parker, I. (1997). Discursive psychology. In D. Fox and I. Prilleltensky (Eds), *Critical Psychology: An Introduction* (pp. 284–298). London: Sage.

Paulsen, K. (1979). Attribution of fault to a victim of rape as a function of locus of control. *Journal of Social Psychology*, 107, 131–132.

Penelope, J. (1990). *Speaking Freely*. New York: Pergamon.

Perrott, S. and Webber, N. (1996). Attitudes toward male and female victims of sexual assault: implications for services to the male victim. *Journal of Psychology & Human Sexuality*, 8, 19–38.

Petersen, A.R. (1996). Risk and the regulated self: the discourse of health promotion as politics of uncertainty. *Australian and New Zealand Journal of Sociology*, 32 (1), 44–57.

Pfaff, K., Gibbs, R. and Johnson, M. (1997). Metaphor in using and understanding euphemism and dysphemism. *Applied Psycholinguistics*, 18, 59–83.

Pino, N. and Meier, R. (1999). Gender differences in rape reporting. *Sex Roles*, 40, 979–990.

Polkinghorne, D.E. (1992). Postmodern epistemology of practise. In S. Kvale (Ed.), *Psychology and Postmodernism* (pp. 146–165). London: Sage.

Pollard, P. (1992). Judgements about victims and attackers in depicted rapes: a review. *British Journal of Social Psychology*, 31, 307–326.

Potter, J. (1988a). Cutting cakes: a study of psychologists' social categorisations. *Philosophical Psychology*, 1 (1), 17–33.

Potter, J. (1988b). What is reflexive about discourse analysis? The case of reading readings. In S. Woolgar (Ed.), *Knowledge and Reflexivity: New Frontiers in the Sociology of Knowledge* (pp. 37–52). London: Sage.

Potter, J. (1996). *Representing Reality: Discourse, Rhetoric and Social Construction*. London: Sage.

Potter, J. and Halliday, Q. (1990). Community leaders as a device for warranting versions of crowd events. *Journal of Pragmatics*, 14, 81–90.

Potter, J. and Reicher, S. (1987). Discourses of community and conflict: the organisation of social categories in accounts of a riot. *British Journal of Social Psychology*, 26, 25–40.

Potter, J. and Wetherell, M. (1987). *Discourse and Social Psychology: Beyond Attitudes and Behaviour*. London: Sage.

Potter, J. and Wetherell, M. (1988). Accomplishing attitudes: fact and evaluation in racist discourse. *Text*, 8 (1–2), 51–68.

Potter, J. and Wetherell, M. (1995). Discourse analysis. In J. Smith, R. Harre and L. Van Langenhove (Eds), *Rethinking Methods in Psychology* (pp. 80–92). London: Sage.

Potter, J., Wetherell, M., Gill, R. and Edwards, D. (1990). Discourse: noun, verb or social practice? *Philosophical Psychology*, 3 (2), 205–217.

Potter, J., Edwards, D. and Wetherell, M. (1993). A model of discourse in action. *American Behavioural Scientist*, 36 (3), 383–401.

Prillentensky, I. and Nelson, G. (2002). *Doing Psychology: Critically making a difference in diverse settings*. Basingstoke: Palgrave Macmillan.

Protecting the Public: Strengthening protection against sex offenders and reforming the laws on sexual offences, HMSO, November 2002.

Raitt, F. and Zeedyk, S. (2000). *The Implicit Relation of Psychology and Law: Women and Syndrome Evidence*. London: Routledge.

Regan, L. and Kelly, L. (2003). *Rape: Still a Forgotten Issue*. London: Child and Women Abuse Studies Unit, London Metropolitan University.

Reicher, S. (1994). Commentary: particular methods and general assumptions. *Journal of Community and Applied Social Psychology*, 4 (4), Special Issue: 'Qualitative Social Psychology', 299–303.

Rempala, D. and Bernieri, F. (2005). The consideration of rape: the effect of target information disparity on judgements of guilt. *Journal of Applied Social Psychology*, 35, 536–550.

Renner, K., Whackett, C. and Ganderton, S. (1988). The 'social' nature of sexual assault. *Canadian Psychology*, 29, 163–173.

Richardson, D. and Campbell, J.L. (1982). Alcohol and rape: the effect of alcohol on attributions of blame for rape. *Personality and Social Psychology Bulletin*, 8, 468–476.

Richardson, F.C. and Fowers, B.J. (1997). Critical theory, postmodernism and hermeneutics: insights for critical psychology. In D. Fox and I. Prilleltensky (Eds), *Critical Psychology: An Introduction* (pp. 265–283). London: Sage.

Riger, S. (1992). Epistemological debates, feminist voices: science, social values and the study of women. *American Psychologist*, 47 (6), 730–740.

Riger, S. and Gordon, M.T. (1981). The structure of rape prevention beliefs. *Personality and Social Psychology Bulletin*, 5, 186–190.

Rochman, S. (1991). Silent victims: bring male rape out of the closet. *The Advocate*, 30, 38–43.

Rogers, P. (1997). Post traumatic stress disorder following male rape. *Journal of Mental Health*, 6 (1), 5–9.

Rose, N. (1996). *Inventing Our Selves: Psychology, Power, and Personhood*. Cambridge: Cambridge University Press.

Rozee, P.D. and Koss, M.P. (2001). Rape: a century of resistance. *Psychology of Women Quarterly*, 25, 295–311.

Russell, D.E. (1982). *Rape in Marriage*. New York: Macmillan.

Sacks, H. (1972). An initial investigation into the usability of conversational data for doing sociology. In D. Sudnow (Ed.), *Studies in Social Interaction* (pp. 31–74). London: Free Press.

Sacks, H. (1974). On the analysability of stories by children. In R. Turner (Ed.), *Ethnomethodology* (pp. 216–232). Harmondsworth: Penguin.

Sampson, E.E. (1977). Psychology and the American ideal. *Personality and Social Psychology*, 35 (11), 767–782.

Sampson, E.E. (1981). Cognitive psychology as ideology. *American Psychologist*, 36 (7), 730–743.

Saunders, D.G. and Size, P.B. (1986). Attitudes about woman abuse among police officers, victims and victim advocates. *Journal of Interpersonal Violence*, 1, 25–42.

Scarce, M. (1997). *Male on Male Rape: The Hidden Toll of Stigma and Shame*. New York: Plenum Press.

Schegloff, E.A. (1997). Whose text? Whose context? *Discourse and Society*, 8 (2), 165–187.

Schneider, L., Soh-Chiew Ee, J. and Aronson, H. (1994). Effects of victim gender and physical vs. psychological trauma on observers' perceptions of sexual assault and its after-effects. *Sex Roles*, 30 (11–12), 793–808.

Schultz, D. and Schneider, L. (1991). The role of sexual provocativeness, rape history and observer gender in perceptions of blame in sexual assault. *Journal of Interpersonal Violence*, 6, 94–101.

Schwarz, N. and Brand, J. (1983). Effects of salience of rape on sex-role attitudes, trust and self-esteem in non-raped women. *European Journal of Social Psychology*, 13, 71–76.

Schwartz, M. and DeKeseredy, W. (1997). *Sexual Assault on the College Campus: The Role of Male Peer Support*. Thousand Oaks: Sage.

Scott, M.B. and Lyman, S.M. (1968). Accounts. *American Sociological Review*, 33, 46–62.

Scully, D. (1990). *Understanding Sexual Violence: A Study of Convicted Rapists*. London: HarperCollins.

Scully, D. and Marolla, J. (1984). Convicted rapists' vocabulary of motive: excuses and justifications. *Social Problems*, 31 (5), 530–544.

Selby, J., Calhoun, L. and Brock, T. (1977). Sex differences in the social perception of rape victims. *Personality and Social Psychology Bulletin*, 3, 412–415.

Seligman, C., Brickman, J. and Koulack, D. (1977). Rape and physical attractiveness: assigning responsibility to victims. *Journal of Personality*, 45, 412–415.

Shaver, K.G. (1970). Defensive attribution: effects of severity and relevance on the responsibility assigned for an accident. *Journal of Personality and Social Psychology*, 14, 101–113.

Shaver, K. (1981). Back to basics: the role of the theory in the attribution of causality. In J. Harvey, W. Ickes and R. Kidd (Eds), *New Directions in Attribution Research*, Vol. 3. Hillsdale: Lawrence Erlbaum Associates.

Shaver, K. (1985). *The Attribution of Blame: Causality, Responsibility and Blameworthiness*. New York: Springer-Verlag.

Shaver, K. and Drown, D. (1986). On causality, responsibility and self-blame: a theoretical note. *Journal of Personality and Social Psychology*, 50, 697–702.

Sherif, C. (1987). Bias in psychology. In S. Harding (Ed.), *Feminism and Methodology*. Milton Keynes: Open University Press.

Shotland, R. and Goodstein, L. (1983). Just because she doesn't want to doesn't mean it's rape: an experimentally based causal model of the perception of rape in a dating situation. *Social Psychology Quarterly*, 46, 220–232.

Shotter, J. (1993). *Conversational Realities: Constructing Life through Language*. London: Sage.

Shotter, J. (1995). In conversation: joint action, shared intentionality and ethics. *Discourse and Society*, 5 (1), 49–73.

Smith, R., Pine, C. and Hawley, M. (1988). Social cognitions about adult male victims of female sexual assault. *Journal of Sex Research*, 24, 101–112.

Smith, R.E., Keating, J.P., Hester, R.K. and Mitchell, H.E. (1976). Role and justice considerations in the attribution of responsibility to a rape victim. *Journal of Research in Personality*, 10, 346–357.

Spence, J., Helmreich, R. and Stapp, J. (1973). A short version of the Attitudes Toward Women Scale (AWS). *Bulletin of the Psychonomic Society*, 2, 219–220.

Stanley, J. (1977). Paradigmatic woman: the prostitute. In D.L. Shores and C.P. Hines (Eds), *Papers in Language Variation* (pp. 303–321). Alabama: The University of Alabama Press.

Stormo, K., Lang, A. and Stritzke, W. (1997). Attributions about acquaintance rape: the role of alcohol and individual differences. *Journal of Applied Social Psychology*, 27, 279–305.

Strong, S. (1970). Causal attribution in counselling and psychotherapy. *Journal of Counselling Psychology*, 17, 388–399.

Struckman-Johnson, C. and Struckman-Johnson, D. (1992). Acceptance of male rape myths among college men and women. *Sex Roles*, 27 (3–4), 85–100.

Struckman-Johnson, C. and Struckman-Johnson, D. (1994). Men pressured and forced into sexual experience. *Archives of Sexual Behaviour*, 23 (1), 93–114.

Temkin, J. (1996). Doctors, rape and criminal justice. *The Howard Journal of Criminal Justice*, 35 (1), 1–20.

Temkin, J. (1999). Reporting rape in London: a qualitative study. *The Howard Journal of Criminal Justice*, 38 (1), 17–41.

Tewksbury, R. and Adkins, M. (1992). Rape myths and emergency room personnel. *Response*, 14 (4), 10–15.

Thornton, B. (1977). Effect of rape victim's attractiveness in a jury simulation. *Personality and Social Psychology Bulletin*, 3, 666–669.

Thornton, B. and Ryckman, R. (1983). The influence of a rape victim's physical attractiveness on observers' attributions of responsibility. *Human Relations*, 36, 549–562.

Tieger, T. (1981). Self-rated likelihood of raping and the social perception of rape. *Journal of Research in Personality*, 15, 147–158.

Turner, S. (2000). Surviving sexual assault and sexual torture. In G. Mezey and M. King (Eds), *Male Victims of Sexual Assault*, 2nd edition. Oxford: Oxford University Press.

Tyson, G. (2003). Adolescent attributions of responsibility and blame for date rape. *Australian Journal of Psychology*, 55, 218–223.

Ullman, S. (1996). Social reactions, coping strategies, and self-blame attributions in adjustment to sexual assault. *Psychology of Women Quarterly*, 20, 505–526.

Ussher, J. (1989). *The Psychology of the Female Body*. London: Routledge.

Ussher, J. (1997). *Fantasies of Femininity: Reframing the Boundaries of Sex*. London: Penguin.

van Dijk, T.A. (1987). *Communicating Racism: Ethnic Prejudice in Thought and Talk*. London: Sage.

Van Langenhove, L. (1995). The theoretical foundations of experimental psychology and its alternatives. In J. Smith, R. Harre and L. Van Langenhove (Eds), *Rethinking Psychology* (pp. 10–23). London: Sage.

VanWie, V. and Gross, A. (1995). Females' perception of date rape: an examination of two contextual variables. *Violence against Women*, 1, 351–366.

Verberg, N., Desmarais, S., Wood, E. and Senn, C. (2000). Gender differences in survey respondents' written definitions of date rape. *Canadian Journal of Human Sexuality*, 9, 181–191.

Viki, G.T. and Abrams, D. (2002) But she was unfaithful: benevolent sexism and reactions to rape victims who violate traditional gender role expectations. *Sex Roles*, 47, 289–293.

Wakelin, A. and Long, K. (2003). Effects of victim gender and sexuality on attributions of blame to rape victims. *Sex Roles*, 49, 477–487.

Walby, S. (1990). *Theorising Patriarchy*. Oxford: Blackwell.

Walster, E. (1966). Assignment of responsibility for an accident. *Journal of Personality and Social Psychology*, 3, 73–79.

Ward, C. (1988). The Attitudes Towards Rape Victims scale: construction, validation and cross-cultural applicability. *Psychology of Women Quarterly*, 12, 127–146.

Ward, C. (1995). *Attitudes toward Rape: Feminist and Social Psychological Perspectives*. London: Sage.

Watson, D.R. (1978). Categorization, authorization and blame-negotiation in conversation. *Sociology*, 12, 105–113.

Watson, D.R. (1983). The presentation of victim and motive in discourse: the case of police interrogations and interviews. *Victimology: An International Journal*, 8 (1–2), 31–52.

Watson, R. and Weinberg, T. (1982). Interviews and the interactional construction of accounts of homosexual identity. *Social Analysis*, 11, 56–78.

Weatherall, A. and Walton, M. (1999). The metaphorical construction of sexual experience in a speech community of New Zealand university students. *British Journal of Social Psychology*, 4 (38), 479–498.

Weeks, J. (1986). *Sexuality*. London: Routledge.

Weeks, J. (2003). *Sexuality*, 2nd edition. London: Routledge.

Weinberg, M.S. (1976). *Sex Research: Studies from the Kinsey Institute*. Oxford: Oxford University Press.

Weiner, B., Frieze, I., Kukla, A., Reed, L., Rest, S. and Rosenbaum, R. (1972). Perceiving the causes of success and failure. In E. Jones, D. Kanouse, H. Kelley, R. Nisbett, S. Valins and B. Weiner (Eds), *Attribution: Perceiving the Causes of Behaviour*. Morristown: General Learning Press.

West, M. (2000). Homophobia: covert and overt. In G. Mezey and M. King (Eds), *Male Victims of Sexual Assault*, 2nd edition. Oxford: Oxford University Press.

Wetherell, M. (1998). Positioning and interpretative repertoires: conversation analysis and post-structuralism in dialogue. *Discourse and Society*, 9 (3), 387–412.

Wetherell, M. and Potter, J. (1988). Discourse analysis and the identification of interpretative repertoires. In C. Antaki (Ed.), *Analysing Everyday Explanation. A Casebook of Methods* (pp. 168–183). London: Sage.

Wetherell, M. and Potter, J. (1989). Narrative characters and accounting for violence. In J. Shotter and K. Gergen (Eds), *Texts of Identity* (pp. 206–219). London: Sage.

Wetherell, M. and Potter, J. (1992). *Mapping the Language of Racism: Discourse and the Legitimation of Exploitation*. Hemel Hempstead: Harvester Wheatsheaf.

Whatley, M. and Riggio, R. (1993). Gender differences in attributions of blame for male rape victims. *Journal of Interpersonal Violence*, 8, 502–511.

Widdicombe, S. (1995). Identity, politics and talk: a case for the mundane and the everyday. In S. Wilkinson and C. Kitzinger (Eds), *Feminism and Discourse: Psychological Perspectives*. London: Sage.

Widdicombe, S. (1998). Identity as an analysts' and a participants' resource. In C. Antaki and S. Widdicombe (Eds), *Identities in Talk*. London: Sage.

Widdicombe, S. and Woofitt, R. (1990). 'Being' versus 'doing' punk: on achieving authenticity as a member. *Journal of Language and Social Psychology*, 9, 257–277.

Wilkinson, I. (2001). Social theories of risk perception. *Current Sociology*, 49 (1), 1–22.

Wilkinson, S. (1988). The role of reflexivity in feminist psychology. *Women's Studies International Forum*, 11 (5), 493–502.

Wilkinson, S. (1997). Feminist psychology. In D. Fox and I. Prilleltensky (Eds), *Critical Psychology: An Introduction*. London: Sage.

Wilkinson, S. and Kitzinger, C. (1995). *Discourse and Feminism*. London: Sage.

Williams, J.E. (1984). Secondary victimisation: confronting public attitudes about rape. *Victimology: An International Journal*, 9, 66–81.

Willig, C. (2001). Introducing Qualitative Research in Psychology: Adventures in Theory and Method. Buckingham: Open University Press.

Wood, G. (2000). The Achilles hole: gender boundary maintenance and the anus. *Psychology of Women Section Review*, 2 (2), 26–40.

Wood, L. and Rennie, H. (1994). Formulating rape: the discursive construction of victims and villains. *Discourse and Society*, 5, 125–148.

Woofitt, R. (1992). *Telling Tales of the Unexpected: The Organisation of Factual Discourse*. London: Harvester Wheasheaf.

Workman, J.E. and Freeburg, E.W. (1999). An examination of date rape, victim dress, and perceiver variables within the context of attribution theory. *Sex Roles*, 41, 261–278.

Wowk, M. (1984). Blame allocation, sex and gender in a murder interrogation. *Women's Studies International Forum*, 7 (1), 75–82.

Yamawaki, N. and Tschanz, B. (2005). Rape perception differences between Japanese and American college students: on the mediating influence of gender role traditionality. *Sex Roles*, 52, 379–392.

Yescavage, K. (1999). Teaching women a lesson: sexually aggressive and sexually nonaggressive men's perceptions of acquaintance and date rape. *Violence against Women*, 5, 796–812.

INDEX

Note: page numbers in *italics* refer to information contained in table: